The UFO Phenomenon

The UFO Phenomenon

The UFO Phenomenon

By the Editors of Time-Life Books

TIME-LIFE BOOKS, ALEXANDRIA, VIRGINIA

CONTENTS

CHAPTER 1
The Elusive Visitors
8

Essay   Fear and Hope on Film
28

CHAPTER 2
Into the Saucer Era
36

Essay   Kidnappers from Space
57

CHAPTER 3
A Time of Close Encounters
64

Essay   Project Blue Book
87

CHAPTER 4
A Deepening Controversy
98

CHAPTER 5
The Enduring Enigma
120

Essay   A Universe of Possibilities
145

Acknowledgments
152

Picture Credits
152

Bibliography
153

Index
155

The Elusive Visitors

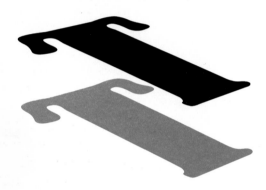

he December night was chilly and damp, and the two middle-aged women turned up the car heater as they drove along the deserted Texas road. It was soon after Christmas, 1980. The women and the small boy with them had traveled to a town about fifteen miles from Houston for dinner; now, as they made their way home, the child noticed something strange in the sky. A blazing light was gliding toward them over the pines.

As it approached, the light resolved itself into a brilliant, diamond-shaped object. Flames shot out from its underside. In her fifty-one years, Betty Cash, the driver, had never seen anything like it. Nor had Vickie Landrum, age fifty-seven, who pulled her seven-year-old grandson, Colby, close to her as the object slowed and then hovered over the roadway as if preparing to land.

Betty Cash stopped the car, and the three of them watched, dumb struck. The bizarre craft continued to hover about sixty-five yards away, emitting a beeping noise. Curiosity overcoming their fear, they stepped out of the car for a better view, although the terrified boy soon persuaded his grandmother to return to the vehicle. Intense heat pulsed from the object, forcing Betty Cash, as she came back to the car, to wrap her hand in her coat before grasping the searing metal of the door handle.

Eventually the craft began moving up and away. As it did so, an even stranger thing happened. A squadron of helicopters—more than twenty in all, many of them big, double-rotor machines like those used for carrying military cargo— appeared and attempted, in a welter of noise, to surround it. When the object sped away, accompanied by the swarming helicopters, the three tried to follow in the car. From a different angle, the phantom ship became cigar-shaped, a bright, oblong cylinder of light. Then it vanished, along with the helicopters, in the distance.

Betty Cash dropped her passengers off at their home and returned to hers. By this time she was feeling ill. Over the next few hours, all three witnesses developed sunburnlike blisters, nausea, and diarrhea. Betty Cash's symptoms were the worst, presumably because she had exposed herself the longest to the object's radiant heat. Sick and frightened, she sought medical treatment and was hospitalized for two weeks as a burn victim. But several days passed before the doctors heard, from Colby, about the incident that preceded the group's injuries.

Investigators studied the case for several years without coming close to identifying the fiery craft or even tracking down the more mundane helicopters. Although other witnesses in the area reported that they too had seen a dazzling light and double-rotor helicopters that night—identifying the larger choppers from photographs as CH-47 Chinooks—local military bases all denied having had such aircraft in the region on that December night. The U.S. government disclaimed ownership of the glowing apparition. Betty Cash, Vickie Landrum, and her grandson were left with only their lingering injuries and an unfinished story.

In its elusiveness, the so-called Cash-Landrum incident—just one of many such events recorded each year—is typical of reports of mysterious objects flashing across the sky and, sometimes, touching down on the surface of the earth. Indeed, the very term used to describe such phenomena, unidentified flying objects, or UFOs—coined by a U.S. Air Force officer in 1951—shows how little is known about these sightings. David Jacobs, an American expert in the field, defines a UFO as "the report of an extraordinary airborne or landed object, or related experience, that remains anomalous after proper scientific analysis." The term is clearly not equivalent to the popular "flying saucer," although it can, in theory, include spaceships piloted by alien

creatures. Using this definition, which encompasses any number of disparate sightings, few people would dispute the existence of UFOs.

Disputes do arise, however, when investigators seek to determine exactly what a given UFO was. On those rare occasions when physical evidence is at hand—when the object has been retrieved, for instance, and shown to be part of a disintegrating satellite—the mystery can be considered solved. But most sightings of unidentified flying objects yield no tangible clues, only eyewitness accounts.

In these cases, two complicating factors come into play. The first is witness reliability. Even when those claiming to have seen UFOs are regarded as credible, it may be difficult or impossible to reconstruct exactly what it was that they saw. The objective, physical act of seeing can be vastly different from the subjective act of interpreting what is seen. The viewer forms judgments even in the act of observation; these judgments then become further altered over time as they pass through the distorting filter of memory. The second complication in UFO cases is the bias of the investigator. Hard-core skeptics and ardent believers will inevitably reach different conclusions about an ambiguous case—and, indeed, many UFO cases are ambiguous. Even so, an astonishingly high number of Americans believe in UFOs. And, if pressed, many will admit to having seen them. (Fear of ridicule seems to prevent most witnesses from rushing out to report their sightings.) A 1987 Gallup poll showed

An intense, burning light pours from the UFO that appeared over a lonely Texas highway

in December of 1980. Witness Vickie Landrum described the craft as "a diamond of fire."

that 49 percent of Americans aware of UFOs were convinced of their existence, 30 percent thought they were imaginary, and 21 percent were unsure. An earlier survey indicated that as many as one adult American in eleven—a projected thirteen million people—had actually seen a UFO.

Skeptics frequently seek to portray UFO believers as fringe personalities and occultists who are unable to accept modern society. But surveys show that believers are, in fact, no more interested in the occult and no less satisfied with life than anyone else is. The one characteristic that UFO witnesses have in common, according to one study, is that they are more inclined to accept the notion of extraterrestrial life.

A sizable number of people today envision UFOs exactly as the vehicles are portrayed in most science-fiction films and books—as spacecraft carrying extraterrestrial beings from technologically advanced worlds. This is, of course, a relatively recent conception that has been stimulated, perhaps, by our expanding knowledge of outer space as well as by the pervasive images of fiction and motion pictures. But strange sights appeared in the skies long before space flight—or manned flight of any kind—was possible. And in each century these visions took on identities that tell much about the world view of those who saw them. In antiquity, for example, people discerned angelic messengers; in the nineteenth century, they saw dirigibles. Today, awed observers look skyward and see glowing envoys from other worlds.

nd yet, a common theme seems to link such sightings from earliest history through today. Gravity-bound humans, gazing at the endless sky, seem always to have felt that there is more to existence than can be seen on the earth's surface, that life might come in more shapes than those we know, that we are not alone among the myriad stars sparkling in the boundless cosmos. The record of mysterious aerial sightings reaches back to the dawn of written history. Seen in the light of modern knowledge and theories, however, accounts of such incidents are far from conclusive. Clearly, if the modern and presumably scientific world has

been unable to establish the nature of recent reports of unidentified flying objects, then conjectures that are based on ancient records can hardly be more conclusive. Even so, ancient and medieval chronicles of UFO-like sightings are fascinating and suggestive, and they often sound surprisingly like today's descriptions.

The oldest accounts, say UFO researchers—or ufologists, as they are often called—come to us as legends. For instance, a venerable Chinese tale speaks of a far-off "land of flying carts" inhabited by one-armed, three-eyed people riding winged chariots with gilded wheels. The *Drona Parva,* a Sanskrit text, describes aerial dogfights among gods piloting flying machines called *vimanas.* During the battles, according to one translation, a "blazing missile possessed of the radiance of smokeless fire was discharged." Such reports are not confined to Eastern lore, however. Some students of UFO history, such as it is, claim that the most impressive UFO stories are found in the Bible—called by one writer "the greatest flying saucer book of them all."

The Old Testament prophet Elijah, for example, ascended into the sky on a "chariot of fire" caught in a whirlwind. Jacob's vision, recorded in Genesis, of angels climbing a ladder into heaven has also been interpreted as a UFO event. The Book of Exodus also provides intriguing possibilities for UFOs. The account of Moses leading the Israelites out of Egypt and across Sinai to the Promised Land states: "The Lord went before them by day in a pillar of cloud to lead them along the way, and by night in a pillar of fire to give them light, that they might travel by day and by night." According to biblical scholar and Presbyterian minister Barry H. Downing, the so-called pillars of cloud and fire could have been a UFO, whose exhaust may also have parted the Red Sea. Downing's other spacecraft candidates include angels carrying messages from God and the cloud on which Christ ascended into heaven.

The most vivid and elaborate of the Bible's possible UFO sightings comes from the prophet Ezekiel, a priest in one of Babylon's captive Jewish settlements. When he was thirty years old, in about 593 B.C., he had an extraordinary vision: "As I looked, behold, a stormy wind came out of the north,

Testimony of the Ancients

An early Colombian artifact resembles a delta-winged aircraft.

"The past teemed with unknown gods who visited the primeval earth in manned spaceships." Or so says author Erich von Däniken in his 1968 book on the existence of extraterrestrials titled *Chariots of the Gods?* This best seller popularized the irrepressible writer's belief that visitors from space mated with human ancestors to create a race with superior intelligence.

To support his ancient-astronaut theory, von Däniken and others subscribing to his views examined the monuments, art, and artifacts of various cultures. Basing his conclusion on research that was admittedly spotty and sometimes misinterpreted, von Däniken subsequently claimed that some of these artifacts represented spaceships and cosmic travelers who descended to earth in primitive times. The writer also decided that

such colossal works as the stone statues on Easter Island and the pyramids of Egypt could not have been crafted without the aid of technologically advanced visitors from the stars. Scientists have thoroughly debunked these notions, but still intriguing are those examples of early art whose meanings have remained undeciphered over the years. Von Däniken and his followers consider these objects not only proof of his theories but a legacy from humankind's alien forebears. Three samples are shown here.

Perhaps an alien whose helmet carries a cosmic message, this figure appears in rock paintings of the Australian aborigines.

This clay sculpture, traced to a pre-Japanese culture, has been described as a space voyager.

and a great cloud, with brightness round about it, and fire flashing forth continually, and in the midst of the fire, as it were gleaming bronze. And from the midst of it came the likeness of four living creatures. And this was their appearance: they had the form of men, but each had four faces, and each of them had four wings."

Ezekiel's description, which appears at the opening of the Old Testament book that bears his name, continues at some length. The living creatures moved about together, and from their center came "something that looked like burning coals of fire, like torches moving to and fro." The creatures themselves, it seems, were part of a larger structure comprising four sets of sparkling rings, each set a wheel within a wheel. Above the figures, Ezekiel saw a kind of burning godhead, "like glowing metal, as if full of fire," cloaked in a brilliant light.

Ezekiel interpreted this sight as "the likeness of the glory of the Lord." But some UFO enthusiasts have seized on the vision as describing the arrival of an extraterrestrial spaceship. When the controversial Swiss author Erich von Däniken—who has been accused of everything from slipshod research to outright fraud—proposed this idea in his book *Chariots of the Gods?*, published in 1968, he aroused at least one reader to action.

Josef F. Blumrich, an engineer with the National Aeronautics and Space Administration, scoffed at von Däniken's idea of spaceship design. A native Austrian involved in the design of aircraft and rockets since 1934, Blumrich had played a role in building NASA's huge *Saturn V* rocket, which took astronauts to the moon. If anybody knew about spacecraft design, he did.

Blumrich was convinced that Ezekiel's wheel would fall apart under a rocket engineer's rigorous examination. But to his utter surprise, he found that the description could be adapted into a practical design for a landing module launched from a mother spaceship (in the prophet's vision, the glowing metal godhead). Blumrich worked out the design in detail and published an account of it in a 1973 book titled *The Spaceships of Ezekiel.* "Seldom," he wrote, "has a total defeat been so rewarding, so fascinating, and so delightful!" According to Blumrich, the four "living creatures" could have been four sets of landing gear, each with a wheel for maneuvering over

This engraving shows the prophet Ezekiel's UFO-like vision: four winged creatures and their four-wheeled vehicle.

the ground. The "wings" would have been helicopter blades used for final positioning prior to touchdown, while a rocket engine in the craft's conical body supplied main propulsion.

The notion that Ezekiel saw a spacecraft was by no means universally accepted, of course. Harvard University astronomer Donald H. Menzel countered that Ezekiel was taken in by an optical illusion. Menzel argued that the prophet has given us "singularly accurate descriptions, albeit in symbolic and picturesque language," of a rare and complex meteorological phenomenon known as a parhelion. Formed by sunlight refracting through ice crystals, a full parhelion may consist of two concentric rings surrounding the sun and crossed with spokelike vertical and horizontal streaks of light. Two or even four of these sun dogs or mock suns may also appear on either side of and above and below the real sun. Finally, an inverted arc of light may sit on top of the outer ring. According to Menzel, with a little imagination the effect is that of a huge, shimmering chariot moving with the sun.

Menzel also offered natural explanations for other alleged biblical sightings of UFOs. Jacob perhaps saw not a ladder but the aurora borealis—a display of gases glowing in the upper atmosphere. And the sea that parted for Moses might have been a vast mirage, a mirrorlike layer of hot air above the desert floor. Such a mirage, said Menzel, will seem to part, then close back on itself as a person moves through it.

Those who reject legends or the Bible as valid UFO sources can still find possibilities in historical records. Chroniclers of Alexander the Great, for instance, report that his army was harassed by a pair of flying objects in 329 B.C. And according to some imaginative ufologists, the French cleric Agobard, Archbishop of Lyons, was writing of possible spaceship visitations when he observed in the ninth century that members of his flock maintained their region was plagued by "aerial sailors" who arrived on ships in the clouds and depredated orchards and wheat fields. Agobard dismissed believers in such tales as "folk blinded by deep stupidity" but related an incident illustrating just how strongly the belief was held. Once, he wrote, he saw four people—three men and a woman—displayed in chains; they had been accused of being passengers who had fallen from the intrusive aerial vessels. So angered were the assembled citizens of Lyons that they stoned the four to death as punishment for their supposed misdeeds. Apparently, though, the accusers later recanted their charges. A somewhat similar tale has it that in the thirteenth century an aerial craft snagged its anchor on a pile of stones in an English city; a crewman who slid down the rope to free the anchor was surrounded by a crowd of curious earthlings and asphyxiated.

Other alleged sightings in the distant past include a spectacular event over the German city of Nuremberg in April 1561, when spheres and disks appeared in the sky and engaged in an aerial ballet. Residents of Basel, Switzerland, witnessed a similar display five years later. According to contemporary accounts, the sky was suddenly dotted with large black spheres that were zooming toward the sun or maneuvering about each other. Then, as quickly and mysteriously as

they had appeared, they turned a fiery red and vanished. The great British astronomer Edmond Halley of comet fame also spied a series of unexplained aerial objects in March of the year 1716. One of them lit up the sky for more than two hours and was so brilliant that Halley could read a printed text by its light. As described by the astronomer, the glow finally began to wane and then suddenly flared up again "as if new fuel [had] been cast on a fire."

These early accounts are suggestive at best; whether they describe true UFOs is a matter of

Josef F. Blumrich (right) set out in 1968 to debunk the notion that Ezekiel's wheel was an alien spaceship. But the NASA engineer designed a viable craft (below) from the prophet's description.

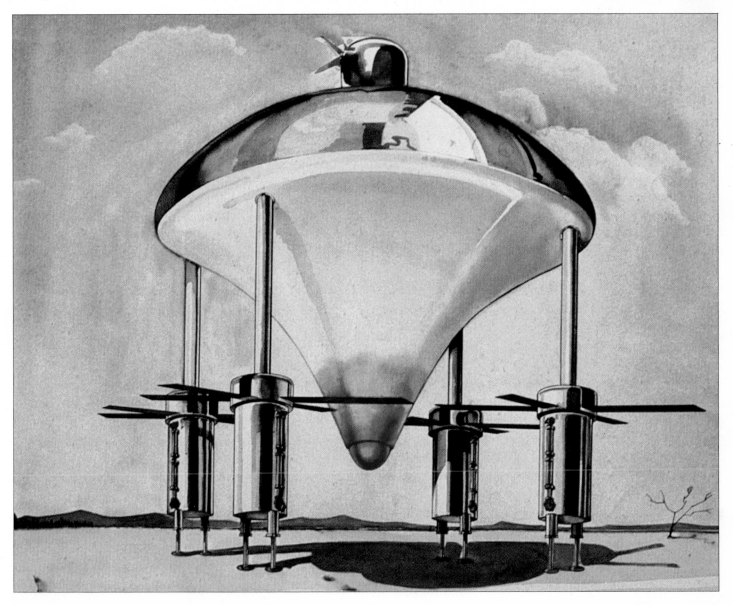

interpretation. Researchers have a hard enough time simply verifying the authenticity of documents containing such tales. Inevitably, this has led some enterprising enthusiasts to manufacture their own "ancient" texts. The false story then spreads when one writer accepts it as genuine and uses it in a book, which becomes a source for others.

n a U.S. government study of unidentified flying objects published in 1969, author Samuel Rosenberg examines three such spurious cases. The first is a purported ancient Indian chronicle from the so-called *Book of Dyzan,* containing a remarkable account of what sounds like a failed attempt by extraterrestrials to colonize the earth. According to the story, alien colonists arrived in a metal craft that circled the earth several times before landing to establish a settlement. Dissension in the group eventually led to civil war, with one side launching "a great shining lance that rode on a beam of light" and exploded in a huge fireball on the enemy's city. The Dyzan tale, which has been quoted at length in a number of pro-UFO books, would be an outstanding candidate for a UFO landing. Unfortunately, when Rosenberg traced the story to its source, he found that it stemmed wholly from the imagination of the nineteenth-century occultist Madame Helena Petrovna Blavatsky, who included it in her monumental tome *The Secret Doctrine,* which was published in 1886.

Rosenberg's second case involves an account that was supposedly translated from a crumbling papyrus among the Vatican's Egyptian holdings. The tale, said to have come from the collection of a certain Professor Tulli and to have been translated by a Prince de Rachelwitz, tells of a fleet of unidentified flying objects that descended on Egypt 3,500 years ago during the reign of Pharaoh Thutmose III. However, Rosenberg's attempts to trace this papyrus in 1968 proved fruitless. The Vatican said it had no record of it; Tulli was dead and his papers were dispersed. Further, the Vatican reported that neither Tulli nor Rachelwitz was an expert; the Vatican's current Egyptologist suggested that Tulli had been deceived by a bogus papyrus. Rosenberg asserts that a close reading of

the UFO account shows that it almost certainly dates from recent times and is derived from the biblical story of Ezekiel.

Rosenberg had similar results when he traced the origins of an alleged sighting at Byland Abbey in Yorkshire, England. The story, which is presented in at least six books about UFOs, describes the extraordinary appearance, in the year A.D. 1290, of a UFO that coasted over the abbey as the monks were sitting down to dinner. Supposedly, a medieval chronicler noted that "when Henry the Abbot was about to say grace, John, one of the brethren, came in and said there was a great portent outside. Then they all went out and LO! *a large round silver thing like a disk flew slowly over them,* and excited the greatest terror." Again, the incident is a wonderfully vivid account that does not stand up to examination. Rosenberg's sleuthing uncovered the story's much more recent origins: It was concocted in the early 1950s by a pair of high-school pranksters who fobbed it off on the public in a letter published in the London *Times.*

Rosenberg does not dismiss the possibility of UFOs visiting earth in times long past but offers the Dyzan, Tulli, and Byland Abbey accounts as cautionary. "My conclusion: all accounts of 'UFO-like sightings handed down through the ages' are doubtful—until verified."

To be sure, well-attested reports of strange aerial objects continued into the scientific and industrial age. By the 1800s such sightings had become increasingly well documented in newspapers and the scientific press. The English *Journal of Natural History and Philosophy and Chemistry,* for example, published the experience of an observer at Hatton Garden, London, in 1809. The gentleman in question was astonished by the sight of "many meteors" darting around a black cloud during a thunderstorm. "They were like dazzling specks of light, dancing and traipsing thro' the clouds. One increased in size till it became of the brilliancy and magnitude of Venus, on a clear evening. But I could see no body in the light. It moved with great rapidity." Astronomers peering through telescopes frequently noted mysterious shapes passing in front of the sun and moon. Ocean sightings were also common. In May 1879, a passenger aboard a ship in the

Hovering in the background of this Renaissance painting of the Madonna and Child is an object radiating beams of light. To some, the mysterious item represents a UFO.

The Search for Clues in Biblical Art

For some UFO investigators, the momentous events set out in the Bible hold meanings beyond the scope of any religion that has yet been organized. These researchers view the biblical chronicles as a unique written history spanning a millennium that was fraught with paranormal activity, including UFO appearances.

Examined from this point of view, the Bible yields dozens of examples of

This detail from a fourteenth-century fresco depicting the Crucifixion shows a man—possibly a prophet heeding God's call to heaven—traversing the sky in an egg-shaped vehicle.

unidentified flying objects. Almost any unusual vision in the heavens can be seen as an alien visitation. Some ufologists, for example, believe the star of Bethlehem—which led the three wise men to the infant Jesus—was a flying saucer. And one New York minister concluded that God could have been an alien endeavoring to guide humans on earth during crises.

Artistic interpretations of such events have appeared throughout the centuries. As if to support the biblical ufologists' claims, some include strange, unidentifiable objects in the skies. Three examples of these works are shown here.

In this scene from a medieval tapestry portraying the life of the Virgin Mary, one mysterious element has captured the attention of some UFO investigators: the black domed object hovering above the skyline.

Persian Gulf watched in amazement as two giant, luminous wheels spun slowly toward the ocean; a similar phenomenon was reported to have taken place in the same area about a year later. In June 1881, two sons of the Prince of Wales—one of them the future King George V—were steaming off the coast of Australia when they and others aboard saw something like an airborne, fully illuminated ship. Some accounts have it that the mystery vessel was the ghostly *Flying Dutchman;* others maintain that it was a UFO.

Perhaps the most remarkable observations occurred in the United States toward the end of the nineteenth century. Between November 1896 and April 1897, the country reeled under an extraordinary series of sightings that started in the state of California and spread eastward. The wavelike nature of the phenomenon—beginning with a few observations, swelling to a peak, and then eventually subsiding—was to become a regular characteristic of modern UFO sightings.

It all began on the stormy afternoon of November 17, 1896, in Sacramento, the California capital, some fifty miles northeast of San Francisco. A trolleyman named Charles Lusk was standing outside his house and looking up at the roiling sky when to his immense surprise he saw a bright light cruising perhaps 1,000 feet overhead. A faint shape seemed to be moving along right behind it. Others, at the nearby capitol building, glimpsed the "wandering apparition," as one newspaper called it, and climbed up to the top of the rotunda for a better view. Another resident claimed to have seen not only the object—which was de-

A contemporary painting records dramatic haloes seen over Stockholm, Sweden, in April 1535—possibly caused by light refracting through ice crystals.

scribed as cigar-shaped, with an underslung gondola and a pair of side wheels like an old riverboat—but also two men aboard it, peddling furiously on something like a bicycle frame; one of them was overheard saying to the other, "We will get to San Francisco about half past twelve." Later that evening, in fact, a similar apparition was seen gliding majestically over San Francisco, flashing a searchlight on the city and sending the local seals scurrying off their rocks into the protective waters of the Golden Gate.

Over the next two weeks, West Coast newspapers played the story of the mysterious flying machine for all it was worth. Where it might pop up next was anyone's guess. On November 24, witnesses reported it over San Jose as well as 750 miles north at Tacoma, Washington. The next day it was spied over Oakland and Los Angeles, 400 miles to the south. The press was inclined to be skeptical, however. A headline in William Randolph Hearst's San Francisco *Examiner* dismissed the sightings as "probably due to liquor," while the rival *Chronicle* suggested caustically that what people were actually seeing was the ghost of Diogenes, the figure from Greek legend who wandered the world with lamp in hand, seeking an honest man.

Most people, however, seemed to accept the reality of the enigmatic vehicle and believed it to be an airship launched by an anonymous inventor. And considering the temper of the times, this seemed a reasonable enough assumption. The United States was experiencing the first bloom of a great technological era, when anything seemed possible. The electric light, the telephone, phonograph, and other recent inventions were transforming American life.

Although it would be another seven years before the Wright brothers' flight at Kitty Hawk, the inevitability of passenger-carrying airships was widely accepted. A dirigible-like balloon (with a rigid steel frame and driven by an engine) had flown over Paris as early as 1852. American inventor Solomon Andrews went aloft in a similar craft near New York City in 1865, and four years later in San Francisco an expatriate Englishman named Fred Marriot piloted a cigar-shaped balloon with two wings and steam-driven propellers. By the 1890s, Americans and Europeans were conducting well-publicized experiments with manned gliders, and the U.S. Patent Office was flooded with designs for flying machines of both the dirigible and the heavier-than-air types.

Technology's shining promise was also reflected in the new literary genre of science fiction, whose master, the Frenchman Jules Verne, enjoyed an enormous following in America. Verne's *Robur the Conqueror,* published in the United States in 1887, concerned a globe-girdling airship called the *Albatross.* A popular and prolific American writer named Luis Philip Senareus (his total output has been estimated at 40 million words) produced three stories in the 1880s built around airships. America's first full-time science-fiction writer was an alcoholic Californian named Robert Duncan Milne; his stories, which often featured airships, were frequently published in San Francisco papers in the years before the 1896-97 wave. Other ideas taking root in the public imagination included antigravity machines and the possible habitation of Mars by an advanced civilization—a proposal made by none other than Percival Lowell, the country's leading astronomer. In short, by 1896 the American imagination could comfortably accommodate not only airships but even *space*ships crossing the interplanetary void.

In this climate of invention and creativity, the airship theory that unfolded in that winter of 1896 did not seem too farfetched. As the sightings accumulated, a lawyer known forever after as Airship Collins announced that he represent-

ed a wealthy but unnamed inventor who had assembled the craft in the hills north of Sacramento. A rival attorney soon stepped up to claim that *he* was the agent for the unknown inventor, who had actually built two airships—one in California, the other in New Jersey. The Spanish-American War was brewing, and the rival lawyer asserted that his client planned to use the marvelous flying machine to bomb Havana.

After a month as front-page news, the airship story began to subside on the West Coast. The wave was far from spent, however. In February the craft surfaced again, this time in the Midwest. The first sightings came out of Nebraska near the towns of Hastings and Invale, where witnesses described the vessel as having "a conical shape, perhaps thirty to forty feet in length," with a bright headlight and six smaller running lights, wings, and a large fan-shaped rudder. Skeptics had laughed off the first accounts as the inebriated visions of saloon patrons. The Omaha *Bee,* however, took the story seriously and stressed that later sightings came from upstanding church folk.

Over the next two months, the phantom ship appeared over other towns and cities in Nebraska, and in Iowa, Kansas, Arkansas, Texas, and Tennessee as well. This epidemic of reports included several cases of reputed face-to-face meetings with a vessel's occupants. A Chattanooga resident told of finding an airship on the spur of a mountain outside the city; a certain Professor Charles Davidson and his crew were making repairs to the craft and told of having sailed east from Sacramento aboard it a month before. A citizen of Harrisburg, Arkansas, also met the crew, which was made up of a woman, two young men, and a patriarchal inventor-captain with piercing black eyes and whiskers down to his belly. The old man, he said, had discovered the secret of antigravity and planned to display the machine in public after flying it to Mars.

In Missouri, one man swore he had met a "short two-legged creature" who used hypnosis to hold him prisoner aboard the aircraft for three weeks. The St. Louis *Post-Dispatch* titillated its readers with the tale of Mr. W. H.

A comet streaking across the nighttime sky can be mistaken for a UFO. The comet West (below) was photographed passing over New Hampshire in 1976.

An aurora visible in the night skies over Hawaii (left) resulted when the 1962 detonation of the high-altitude nuclear bomb Starfish released charged particles into the atmosphere.

This formation of lenticular, or lens-shaped, clouds (below) resembled a fleet of flying saucers as it drifted over Santos, Brazil. Rarely seen, these clouds sometimes generate UFO reports.

A Range of Natural Deceptions

Excited witnesses of unidentified flying objects have often found—sometimes to their dismay—that they were fooled by Mother Nature. Celestial bodies such as comets, meteors, and planets are easily misidentified, and the earth's constantly changing atmosphere can produce many strange distortions of those objects. For example, stars or planets may become magnified, change color, or seem to reappear from below the horizon. These and other natural occurrences, such as rare cloud formations and mysterious types of lightning, have all been mistaken at one time or another for UFOs. Several examples of the deceptive phenomena are shown here.

High-altitude objects cast a shadow—a Brocken specter—on clouds.

Ball lightning—luminous, electrically charged spheres that pulsate through the air—can accompany violent atmospheric activity.

Sun pillars, dense columns of light-reflecting ice crystals, appear as streaks above or below a low sun.

Light-refracting ice crystals can project a mock sun, or sun dog (above, right), at the same height as the original.

Mysterious airships, reported over the United States in late 1896 and early 1897, prompted the country's first major wave of UFO sightings. Newspapers avidly followed the story, publishing illustrations of the cigar-shaped objects drifting over (from left) Sacramento, Oakland, and San Francisco, California, and a Chicago suburb.

Hopkins, who came upon a gleaming metal craft and its Olympian crew: a bearded man "of noble proportions and majestic countenance" and a beautiful naked woman ("dressed in nature's garb," as the paper discreetly put it) with golden hair flowing to her waist.

Reports continued to pour in. In April, a newspaper vendor in the Chicago suburb of Rogers Park took what may have been history's first UFO photograph, which one newspaper used as the basis for a pen-and-ink sketch. Alas, the photograph itself—which rival papers examined and pronounced a fake—soon disappeared forever.

In the wake of the mystery airship, people began to find letters reputedly dropped by its crew. One was discovered tied to a reed near Astoria, Illinois, and addressed to none other than inventor Thomas A. Edison. The Wizard of Menlo Park dismissed the message, written to him in code and signed "C. L. Harris, electrician Airship N.3," as "a pure fake" without bothering to decipher it. He went on to declare that although airships might be possible some day, they would

never be more than toys. Another letter was found attached to an iron rod stuck in the ground at a Wisconsin farm, datelined "Aboard the airship Pegasus." The missive claimed that "application for the patents for a parallel plane airship will be filed simultaneously at Washington and the European capitals. It is propelled by steam and is lighted by electricity, and has a carrying power of 1,000 pounds."

Sightings petered out toward the end of April. As one of the oddest episodes in American history came to an end, people were just as mystified about its true nature as they had been at the beginning. For some, however, the airship stories were clearly more enjoyable as fiction than as fact.

Despite their growing technological sophistication, turn-of-the-century Americans remained a simple people in many ways. The United States was, to a considerable extent, still a rural society, close to its frontier roots and possessing a knee-slapping sense of humor as broad as the prairie sky. The tall tale—told with an absolutely straight face—was a staple in American humor, and preposterous stories had long proliferated, not only around the cracker barrels of country stores but also in the columns of both small-town and big-city newspapers. As early as 1844, for example, poet and free-lance journalist Edgar Allan Poe had penned for the

Baltimore *Sun* a so-called factual account of a transatlantic balloon flight—a feat not really accomplished until 1978.

So if a few people caught up in the airship craziness felt like stretching the truth, they were just part of a venerable tradition. Apparently nobody practiced this time-honored art better than did one Alexander Hamilton, a farmer who told a reporter of a colossal 300-foot-long airship descending on his spread near the town of Yates Center, Kansas, on April 23, 1897. When Hamilton and two others rushed to investigate, he said, they noticed inside the craft's glass compartment "six of the strangest beings I ever saw. They were jabbering together but we could not understand a word they said." Then the ship took off, carrying with it one of Hamilton's heifers. It hovered over the farm for a time before disappearing into the sky. The next day, a farmer some distance away recovered the hide, legs, and head of the purloined cow. Hamilton's amazing tale concludes:

"After identifying the hide by my brand, I went home. But every time I would drop to sleep I would see the cursed thing, with its big lights and hideous people. I don't know whether they are devils or angels or what; but we all saw them, and my whole family saw the ship, and I don't want any more to do with them."

It was a sensational story, even by the standards of airship accounts. Moreover, Hamilton was a rock-solid citizen and former state senator whose tale was accompanied by an affidavit, signed by twelve community leaders, attesting to his reputation for veracity. More than sixty years later, some ufologists would rediscover the story and tout it as testimony that could not easily be explained away. Subsequent detective work by UFO researcher Jerome Clark, however, deflated these fantastic events. Clark's investigation showed conclusively that the entire episode was a tongue-in-cheek hoax perpetrated by Hamilton and the signers of the affidavit—all members of the local liars club.

Tall tales and hoaxes could hardly explain the extraordinary event that occurred in Russia about a decade later. On the morning of June 30, 1908, something huge and terrifying hurtled out of the sky and exploded over a region called Tunguska in remote Siberia. One witness reported that the sky was split in two by the tremendous blast. Another saw an elongated flaming object trailing dust. The cataclysm shattered windowpanes, shook the ground, and propelled a searing wind across the desolate landscape, felling trees as if they were matchsticks and igniting 1,200 square miles of forest.

Scientists would later estimate the power of the blast to have been equivalent to that of a twenty-megaton nuclear bomb.

The Tunguska explosion has remained a mystery, fueling a number of competing explanations. Among the more imaginative are the antimatter and the black hole collision theories: If antimatter—which is made up of particles with abnormally reversed electrical charges—was to leak from an alternate universe into ours, it would explode spectacularly upon contact with normal matter. Similarly, even the tiniest black hole (an invisible, ultra-dense celestial phenomenon) would wreak havoc if it collided with the earth. The existence of miniature black holes has not been proven, however. All black holes known to astronomers are so massive that they would most assuredly destroy the earth.

Not surprisingly, some students of the explosion suggest that it resulted from a UFO disintegrating in the atmosphere. Several Soviet scientists claim to have found unusually high radioactivity in the Tunguska soil and assert that it came from the spaceship's nuclear engine. Their calculations of the object's trajectory also led them to believe that the visitor decelerated upon entering the atmosphere. Some ufologists are convinced therefore that the occupants of a crashing spaceship deliberately changed course to avoid hitting an inhabited area.

Other scientists have found no evidence for either the radioactivity or changed trajectory, however. The weight of evidence now points to a collision between the earth and a comet, or perhaps an asteroid, as the explanation for the

Flattened and scorched trees in Siberia mark the scene of the 1908 explosion of a fiery object from space—probably a comet.

Tunguska blast. Calculations show the object, whatever it might have been, was probably 100 yards across, weighed a million tons, and plunged at a speed of 70,000 miles per hour to a flaming death by atmospheric friction.

One year after the Tunguska incident, the world experienced its second major wave of UFO sightings. This time the scope of the phenomenon was international, as reports came in from Europe, North America, South Africa, Japan, New Zealand, and other parts of the globe between the years 1909 and 1913. It began in southwestern England as witnesses told of seeing a large oblong object with a powerful light cruising high above them at night.

Included among the testimony was at least one encounter with the occupants of a mystery craft. An elderly Welshman hiking one day in the mountains said he came upon a huge cigar-shaped machine on the ground next to two crewmen. Dressed in fur caps and coats, the men "jabbered furiously to each other in a strange lingo," according to the startled witness, then took off in their noisy machine at his approach. Speculation centered on possible secret test flights of the new zeppelins, a type of large dirigible the Germans were known to be developing. Similar sightings occurred again in England in early 1913 and were also attributed to the Germans, who just eighteen months later would be at war with Great Britain. However, no documentation has ever been found to prove the zeppelin hypothesis.

On the other side of the Atlantic, meanwhile, Americans had their own UFO experiences to ponder. In December 1909, a Worcester, Massachusetts, policeman walking his predawn beat was puzzled by a fiery light moving overhead. During the next several days, the same light—or something very much like it—was seen by residents of two other towns, and on December 23 it made an appearance over Boston. Some sharp-eyed New Englanders swore that a dark shape, like that of an airship, accompanied the light. To the delight of children who assumed that the craft must be Santa Claus, the UFO visited Boston again on Christmas Eve, and then reappeared the next day more than a hundred miles to the southwest over New Haven, Connecticut.

Suspicion focused on a Worcester manufacturer of heating equipment named Wallace E. Tillinghast. Early in December, Tillinghast had proclaimed to the press that he had built a new type of airplane and had test-flown it on at least twenty occasions, all at night. Fear of someone stealing his idea, he said, prevented him from showing his marvelous machine to the public. If his claims were true, such an invention would be the logical candidate for New England's mysterious visitor. However, the inscrutable Tillinghast kept coy about any responsibility he may have had for the bizarre events. Later investigations indicated he may actually have built a flying machine, but if so it almost certainly never left the ground. The entire episode remains another of the many enigmas in the history of UFO sightings.

If the 1909 reports seem like a replay of the California airship flap, the next series of sightings appears to be a vision of a jet-powered future. In February 1913, citizens of both Canada and the United States witnessed a squadron of moving lights arcing through the night sky from Saskatchewan, across Minnesota, Michigan, New York, and New England, and out over the Atlantic Ocean. A sound like that of distant thunder accompanied the lights, which seemed to fly in precise formation. Scientists who looked into the sightings hypothesized that the observers had seen a group of meteors plummeting through the earth's atmosphere. Later, however, UFO enthusiasts would maintain that the baffling lights could have been interstellar spacecraft; meteors, they observed, do not usually fly in formation. The case remains unresolved.

One other event from this era took place before what may have been the largest crowd ever to witness a UFO—if indeed it was a UFO. In 1917, on the rainy afternoon of October 13, a crowd of 50,000 people in Fatima, Portugal, watched in amazement as the clouds parted to reveal a huge silver disk spinning like a windmill and dancing about the sky. The object gave off heat, and some of the witnesses would later state that their rain-soaked clothes had dried in minutes from exposure to it. After plunging toward the earth, the disk

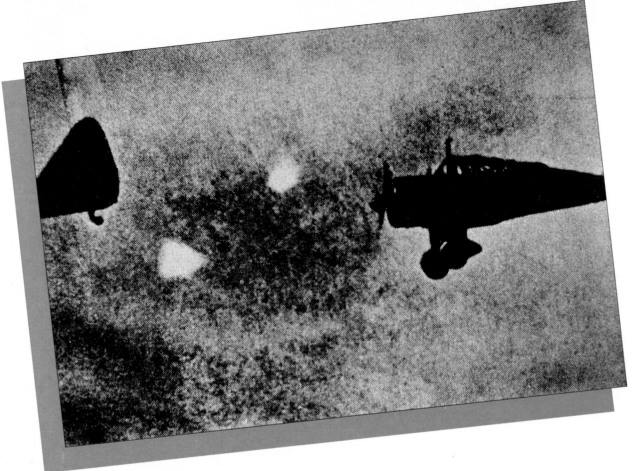

Unexplained fireballs, dubbed "foo fighters," buzzed both Allied and Axis aircraft late in World War II.

climbed back into the sky and disappeared into the sun.

This extraordinary spectacle fulfilled the prophecy of three young peasant girls who claimed to have spoken to the Virgin Mary. She told them, they said, that on October 13 she would reveal herself, "so that everyone would have to believe." The Catholic Church declared it a miracle, but ufologists point to the striking similarities between this event and many reports of alleged UFOs.

Such reports were sporadic for the quarter century following the occurrence at Fatima. By the 1940s, Europe, Asia, and North America were caught up in World War II, a conflict that, more than any previous war, fueled the engine of technological advancement. Out of World War II came radar, jet airplanes, supersonic rockets, and the apocalyptic might of the atomic bomb. All were developed in secret. It is not surprising, then, that whenever something strange was seen in the sky, the witnesses' first impulse was to attribute it to some new weapon in the enemy's arsenal.

This was exactly the response American commanders had to bewildering reports flooding in from air force pilots in the autumn of 1944. The sightings began over the Rhine River; eerie, luminous balls, the pilots said, were appearing

out of nowhere and chasing their planes. The fiery disks, some red, some orange or white, seemed to be toying with the aircraft, diving and darting through the sky in madcap maneuvers, occasionally blinking on and off like Christmas-tree lights. As many as ten might track a plane. The airmen called them "foo fighters," a name derived from a nonsense line in the popular "Smokey Stover" comic strip: "Where there's foo, there's fire." (The cartoonist apparently took the word from the French *feu,* meaning fire.) The Germans were down to their last, desperate defense by this time, and the bizarre foo fighters—or "kraut balls," as they were also known—seemed right in character with the presumed cleverness of German technology. But the notion that these fireballs might be secret weapons soon faded, since none had ever harmed an Allied plane. Also, as Americans learned after the war, German pilots saw them, too—and assumed they were Allied secret weapons.

Bomber crews over the Pacific and pilots who were flying in the Korean and Vietnam wars would also report having seen foo-like phenomena, leading some ufologists to suggest that the glowing objects were extraterrestrials who had come to spy on earthly military operations. Skeptics, on the other hand, provided more down-to-earth explanations, such as static electricity, ball lightning, or reflections from ice crystals that had formed in cockpit-window imperfections. The mystery has yet to be solved.

By 1946 the world war had ended but the cold war was just beginning. Contributing to the mounting suspicion between the United States and the Soviet Union was a wave of mysterious sightings over the Baltic Sea and Scandinavia. The peculiar activity started in late May, when residents of northern Sweden began to see strange rocketlike shapes careening overhead. These curious reports came from remote areas and were largely ignored until a few weeks later on June 9, when the citizens of Helsinki, Finland, were flabbergasted by an object that cut across the pale night sky, trailing smoke and leaving a phantom afterglow in its wake.

As additional sightings came in from other parts of northern Europe, reports of the ''ghost rockets'' and ''spook bombs'' dominated the newspapers. Accounts of the unidentified objects' shape and behavior varied. While most witnesses described what they had seen as missiles, others believed they saw gray spheres or fireballs or even pinwheel-like affairs spraying out sparks. To some they looked like cigars or footballs, and one witness described them as ''seagulls without heads.'' They flew straight, some said; no, claimed others—they climbed, dived, even rolled and reversed direction. Some flashed across the sky like meteors. Others hardly moved.

Eventually, well over 1,000 sightings would be reported over seven months in Sweden alone; similar reports flowed in

This object, photographed in 1946, was just one of more than 1,000 ''ghost rockets'' seen in Scandinavian skies that year.

from as far afield as Portugal, North Africa, Italy, Greece, and India. In northern Europe, suspicions turned immediately to the Soviets, who just a year before had captured the German V-2 rocket base at Peenemünde on the Baltic Sea. The V-2, which terrorized London and other Allied cities in the closing year of the war, was an awesome supersonic weapon—essentially the first ballistic missile. Was it possible that the Russians had developed something similar and were test-firing it over the Baltic? The Kremlin denied this was the case, but the possibility made officials in Sweden, Norway, and Denmark skittish enough to impose a news blackout on all UFO sightings. Swedish military forces went on the alert, and the United States sent the retired air force general Jimmy Doolittle to assist them in their investigation. Ultimately, the Swedish Defense Ministry would determine that 80 percent of the sightings could be explained as conventional aircraft or such natural events as meteors, stars, planets, and clouds. Nevertheless, at least 200 of the reported sightings, the Swedes said, ''cannot be the phenomena of nature or products of the imagination.''

It would not be the last time that investigators would reach a ''tantalizing inconclusiveness''—the felicitous phrase used in a United States government study twenty years later—as they probed the mystery of unidentified flying objects. At the same time, the scientific leaps resulting from World War II made the notion of extraterrestrial visitors, once the fancy of science-fiction writers, seem more realistic. As investigators would soon find out, foo fighters and ghost rockets were just the beginning.

Fear and Hope on Film

Unidentified flying objects, with their connotation of alien visitors, strike some resonant chords in the human psyche—resonant and essentially contradictory. We welcome the notion of meeting with other intelligent beings. We picture them as benign, helpful, even messianic, and trust that their coming heralds the beginning of a great adventure. At the same time, however, we sometimes fear them. The unknown is intrinsically frightening, after all, and the idea of alien intruders can evoke xenophobia in its purest form. What if they are not so friendly? Instead of promising a beginning, they might bode an end.

Popular culture reflects such ambivalence. Consider the movies. In the science-fiction classic *War of the Worlds,* for instance, humans cower while Martians in crescent-shaped ships rigged with cobra-like death rays deal destruction. But in *Close Encounters of the Third Kind,* the killer craft give way to a great, spangled carousel bearing beneficent little beings who commune musically with the onlookers and hint at wondrous adventures in store. The charming E.T., with his affectionate nature, is juxtaposed against the meanness of some humans, calling into question just who the real aliens are. In *It Came from Outer Space,* the visitors are both good and bad. They land and begin usurping human bodies, although it turns out that they are harmless space voyagers stranded on earth for repairs.

We do not yet know the truth about UFOs. But their portrayal may reveal truths about ourselves.

Stars Barbara Rush and Richard Carlson (foreground)
join fellow earthlings cringing in irrational fear of benign aliens in the
1953 film It Came from Outer Space.

In whirling splendor, a mammoth alien mother ship settles earthward at the climax of Close Encounters of the Third Kind. Below, child actor Cary Guffey is bathed in light from the extraterrestrial craft hovering outside his house. In this metaphorical Close Encounters sequence, the boy's terrified mother scrambles madly to secure her home against the aliens, while the innocent child opens the door to welcome them in pristine delight. The visitors take him aboard their ship for a time before returning him safely to his mother.

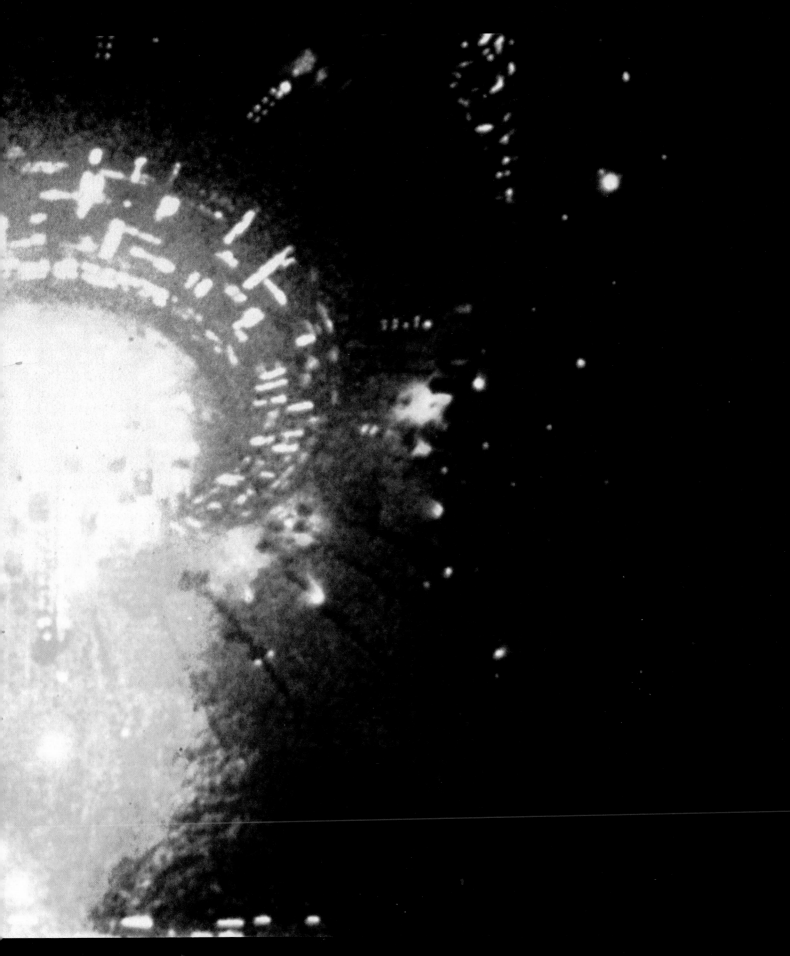

About to head home, E.T. lays a fond finger on the forehead of his friend Elliott (Henry Thomas), promising that the two of them will always be close in spirit. In this film, children save the little alien from the predations of grown-ups. In both E.T. and Close Encounters of the Third Kind, director Steven Spielberg seems to urge adults toward a childlike capacity for awe and wonder at all life, wherever it comes from.

CHAPTER 2

Into the Saucer Era

n June 24, 1947, Kenneth Arnold, a thirty-two-year-old Boise, Idaho, businessman, was flying his single-engine plane at 9,200 feet over the Cascade Mountains of Washington. It was a fine, sunny afternoon, and Arnold was admiring the glorious view when suddenly a blue-white flash broke his reverie. "Explosion!" he thought instantly. It seemed close. The clock on his instrument panel read a few minutes before 3:00.

His heart pounded as he waited for the sound and shock wave of the blast. Seconds passed. Nothing. Arnold scanned the sky in all directions. "The only actual plane I saw," he later recalled, "was a DC-4 far to my left and rear, apparently on its San Francisco-Seattle run." He began to breathe easier—and then another brilliant blue-white flash lit the cockpit.

This time, he saw that the light came from the north, ahead of his plane. In the far distance, he made out a formation of dazzling objects skimming the mountaintops at incredible speed. Arnold decided that they must be a squadron of the new air force jet fighters that were just coming into service. Distance was hard to gauge, but he thought they might be twenty miles away, nine of them flying in a tight echelon. Every few seconds two or three would dip or bank slightly and reflect a blaze of sunlight from their mirrorlike surfaces. Arnold judged their wingspan to be forty-five to fifty feet, and he made up his mind to measure their speed. When the first object shot past Mount Rainier, his panel clock read exactly one minute to 3:00. When the last one zipped past the crest of Mount Adams, the elapsed time was one minute, forty-two seconds. Arnold checked his map; the peaks were forty-seven miles apart. He worked out the mathematics. The speed was 1,656 miles per hour, nearly three times faster than any jet he had ever heard of.

Arnold landed at Yakima at about 4:00 P.M. and raced to tell his friend Al Baxter, manager of Central Aircraft. Baxter called in several of his pilots to listen to the amazing tale. One of the flyers thought the objects might be a salvo of guided missiles from a nearby test range. But why the banking and turning? Such abilities did not fit any rockets they knew.

A little later Arnold took off for Pendleton, Oregon. The news of his experience had preceded him, and a gaggle of reporters surrounded his plane at the airport. When Arnold told his story, he was barraged with questions, many of them sharp and doubtful. But he stuck to his account, and eventually even the skeptics were impressed. Arnold seemed the solidest of citizens, a successful salesman of fire-fighting equipment and an experienced search and rescue pilot. He had logged more than 4,000 hours in the air and had flown the Cascades many times.

When he was asked to describe the mysterious objects, he struggled for the right words. He thought they looked like speedboats in rough water, or maybe the tail of a Chinese kite blowing in the wind. Then he said, "They flew like a saucer would if you skipped it across the water."

Some reporters persisted in questioning Arnold's calculations, wondering about the accuracy of his timing. He had not used a stopwatch or any sort of sighting device but had simply done it by eye. Even so, the lowest estimate of speed was 1,350 miles per hour. The objects could not have been jets, and they did not fly like missiles. Most of those who listened to Ken Arnold that day were convinced that he had seen something extremely unusual, something perhaps not of this world. The thought was eerie—and a little alarming.

The Cascades incident provoked considerable debate and comment—some of it scoffing—among scientists. Arnold himself was too credible to be dismissed as a crank, and he did not act like a prankster or publicity seeker. The critics focused on the likelihood of honest error or illusion. One scientist pointed out that the human

eye does not have the resolving power to distinguish objects forty-five to fifty feet across at twenty miles. Arnold must have misjudged the distance; the objects he saw had to have been much closer. They were probably a flight of military jets flying at subsonic speed, which would have appeared fantastically fast at near range. Another argued that because Arnold had established distance using the mountains as fixed reference points, his estimate of size had to be wrong; the objects were much bigger than he judged—bombers most likely. The air force would not say whether it did or did not have any planes aloft near the Cascades at that time; the military men merely put it down as an optical illusion, a mirage in which the tips of the mountains appeared to float above the earth as a consequence of a layer of warm air.

Whatever Kenneth Arnold did or did not see, his report marked the beginning of what came to be known as the modern flying saucer era. Within a few days of June 24, at least twenty other people in widely scattered parts of the country told of seeing similar objects in the sky. Some of the sightings reportedly occurred on the very day of Arnold's encounter. Some had preceded it. A few came a day or so later. In any case, a historian of the period wrote, "the floodgates were now open for the rush of reports that was soon to follow. But it had taken a man of Arnold's character and forthright conviction to open them."

What followed was a phenomenon in its own right. In the next five years or so, thousands upon thousands of sightings of unidentified flying objects would be claimed in North America. The sightings would come in waves, periods of relative quiet ending with floods that would engender hundreds of reports in a single month. UFOs would become a staple of the press—and of comedians and cartoonists. As UFOs came to fill the public consciousness, millions of words would be written about them, and scientists would engage in long, sometimes acrimonious debate. Could UFOs possibly be real? If so, what might be the intelligence behind them? And what did this intelligence want? Was it hostile? Friendly? Merely curious? Where did these things come from? Did they originate on earth? Or were they machines and creatures from somewhere out there, somewhere out among those mysteriously winking stars in the black vastness of space?

True believers found meaning in virtually every report, while total skeptics refused to credit even their own eyes. The United States Air Force, guardian of the nation's skies, agonized for years over the phenomenon, publicly downplaying the UFOs yet at the same time scrutinizing the accounts of them, most particularly those of its own highly trained aircrews. Investigations were started, stopped, and started again under various security classifications. Sometimes the air force cooperated with private researchers; sometimes it refused to divulge any information about UFOs. Underlying all was the nagging fear that perhaps some of these inexplicable objects were Soviet secret weapons.

s time went on, official Washington almost seemed to conclude that the unrelenting furor over UFOs was itself a greater danger to public calm and safety than the UFOs themselves. Increasingly, the air force and other government agencies labored to deny, ridicule, explain away, or otherwise lay to rest the UFO phenomenon. The campaign was marked by confusion, contradiction, and at times, outright falsehood. And it failed dismally to achieve its purpose. The unfathomable UFOs continued to intrigue the American public with a succession of ever more fascinating and disturbing visitations.

Kenneth Arnold might have wondered what he had wrought that day he flew over the Cascades. On his heels came a surge of sightings that reached 100 a day during the week of July 5. So many people reported they were seeing so many things that even sensation-seeking newspapers were surfeited, and a note of ridicule began to creep into the stories. Soon the press was automatically labeling every claim a hoax or the work of a crackpot. This scornful incredulity was reinforced by air force statements confidently branding every report a mistake. Indeed, only a few weeks after the Arnold sighting, the air force announced it was no longer looking into UFOs; a press release from headquarters in Washington stated that a preliminary study had "not produced enough fact to warrant further investigation." But the air force was nowhere near as sure as it wanted people to think.

The elaborate show of unconcern was merely a cover for a classified project designed to pin down the facts about UFOs. The very same day that Washington reported no interest, the Air Materiel Command at Wright Field, Ohio, announced that it was investigating further to determine whether the objects were meteorological phenomena. Then a cloak of secrecy was thrown over the project for fear that the UFOs might somehow be the work of the Russians.

For the next six months, air force researchers sifted through the reports and found 156 worthy of further study. So interesting were the results that the investigators requested a more complete probe. And at the end of 1947, the commanding officer at Wright Field sent a message to the Pentagon stating flatly that "the phenomenon reported is something real and not visionary or fictitious." Washington was impressed enough to establish a project, code named Sign, at Wright Field with orders to collect and evaluate "all information concerning sightings and phenomena in the atmosphere which can be construed to be of concern to the national security."

One startling occurrence that helped galvanize the air force into action had taken place in the southwestern desert several weeks after the Arnold sighting over the mountains of Washington state. It was the first report of a crashed UFO.

The incident was marked by confusion and conflicting accounts in the press and by the air force, whose officers at first confirmed the story, then denied it.

Everyone agreed, however, that something odd had happened on July 2 at Roswell, New Mexico. It began with descriptions of a large glowing object flying at high speed at about 9:50 P.M. Later that night, Mac Brazel, a sheep rancher northwest of Roswell, heard a tremendous explosion in the atmosphere that was much louder than the thunderstorm then sweeping the area. In the morning Brazel reputedly found fragments of a foil-like substance, very thin and pliable but extremely tough, scattered over a quarter-mile of ground. By another account, Brazel also found a disk-shaped object that he turned over to the intelligence officer at Roswell Army Air Field. Speculation was intense until July 8, when the *Roswell Daily Record* quoted Lieutenant Warren Haught, a public relations officer at the base: "The many rumors regarding the flying disk became a reality yesterday when the intelligence office of the 509th Bomb Group of the Eighth Air Force, Roswell Army Air Field, was fortunate enough to gain possession of a disk through the cooperation of one of the local ranchers and the sheriff's office of Chaves County."

Although there were few other details, the mere confirmation that some sort of UFO had been recovered caused a sensation. Telephone lines to the base were tied up for days, but the air force said nothing more. The strange disk fragments were taken to Eighth Air Force Headquarters in Fort Worth, Texas, where Brigadier General Roger Ramey went on the radio to call it all a mistake. What Mac Brazel had found, said the general, was the wreckage of a weather device.

Air force officers exhibit debris from the 1947 crash of a flying object in Roswell, New Mexico.

That was, in fact, what a number of skeptics had thought from the first. But the air force would not elaborate beyond holding a press conference at which General Ramey permitted photographers to take a few shots of some twisted wreckage. When the photographers complained that they had not been allowed close enough, a second press conference was held. This time, however, the cameramen claimed that the wreckage was not the same; the fragments had been switched. And there the story rested, in a sort of limbo, with public and press guessing what might have happened. For years afterward, UFO enthusiasts would insist that the air force was engaging in a cover-up of the real story, and in 1987 documents would surface allegedly showing that the space-craft and the bodies of four crewmen had in fact been re-covered and kept from public view.

In the wake of the Roswell incident, UFO reports surged again. That very week, some of the first photos purporting to show UFOs in flight were snapped in Phoenix, Arizona. The photographer was William A. Rhodes, who described himself as a scientific consultant. At dusk on July 7, reported Rhodes, he was in his house when he heard a loud roaring noise outside. For some reason, he said, he thought it might be a flying saucer and rushed out with his camera just in time to snap two shots of an object flashing away to the south-west. Rhodes said that it was shaped something like a man's shoe heel—which corresponded closely to the description

Ken Arnold had given of the objects over the Cascades.

The pictures ran in the Arizona *Republic* on July 9. Rhodes later related that, during the following week, he was visited by an FBI agent and an air force intelligence officer, both of whom questioned him closely. They asked Rhodes to lend them the negatives for evaluation, and he complied. The following month, said Rhodes, he asked for his negatives back but was informed by letter that they could not be returned. Early in 1948, said Rhodes, two officers from Project Sign came out to interview him. But that was the last of it; Rhodes never heard from the air force again—and never reported another UFO. As for the air force, in its files the Phoenix sighting is labeled a "possible hoax," although some intelligence officers reportedly regarded the pictures as authentic. In any case, there was never a satisfactory explanation of why the air force judged it to be a hoax or why, for that matter, some officers disagreed with the official verdict. Like so much about UFOs, the story drifted into obscurity as newer, more dramatic incidents claimed the headlines.

The public perception of UFOs had been that they were fascinating but harmless. But at this time, a grim element entered the picture: A young fighter pilot was killed while chasing one. Even skeptics conceded that the reports were no longer quite the laughing matter they had once been, and believers found new fuel for their fears: The strange objects might be not only extraterrestrial but perhaps deadly as well.

The incident began like many of the others. Shortly after noon on January 7, 1948, a number of people in western Kentucky reportedly saw a strange object racing through the sky at high speed. It was huge, between 250 and 300 feet in diameter, and it looked, said one observer, a little like "an ice cream cone topped with red." There were plenty of creditable witnesses, including the tower operators and the base commander at Godman Air Force Base, near Fort Knox, where the thing swooped overhead sometime later. As it happened, four Air National Guard F-51 Mustang fighters were coming in to land and were radioed to peel off and have a closer look.

One plane was low on fuel and continued in, but the pilots of the other three prop-driven Mustangs, led by Captain

Thomas Mantell, rammed home their throttles and climbed swiftly toward the object. One flyer said it seemed metallic and confirmed that it was "of tremendous size." His wingman described it as "round like a teardrop, and at times almost fluid."At this point, two of the F-51s broke off the chase, but flight leader Mantell radioed that he would try for an even closer inspection. By now it was 3:15, and Mantell radioed the tower: "I'm going to 20,000 feet and if I'm no closer then, I'll abandon chase." That was the last anyone heard from him. A few hours later, Mantell's body was found in the wreckage of his F-51 Mustang near Fort Knox.

An air force investigation concluded that Mantell had blacked out around 20,000 feet from lack of oxygen and had simply spun to earth; none of the fighters had been carrying oxygen on the training mission, said the air force, and Mantell had foolishly flown too high. The air force suggested that the strange object that had lured him to his death was nothing more than the planet Venus shining in the midafternoon sky.

he air force explanations sounded odd to some people. Private calculations of the planet's elevation and azimuth in relation to Mantell's course when last seen indicated that this was impossible. The incident contributed to scary rumors that Mantell had been shot from the sky by an alien spacecraft. Later, investigators suggested an explanation that the air force had not been aware of at the time. The U.S. Navy was engaged in high-altitude research under a program called Project Skyhook. Mantell, said the researchers, could have been chasing one of the project's stratospheric balloons.

In any case, the incident convinced the Pentagon that it needed stronger scientific help to evaluate the reports coming in to Project Sign. The scholar chosen was J. Allen Hynek, a professor of astronomy at Ohio State University, near Wright Field. Hynek later said the air force seemed as impressed by his strong skepticism about UFOs as by his credentials. It was as though the air force just wished UFOs would go away and was relieved at Hynek's disbelief.

Once or twice per month, Hynek would drive the sixty

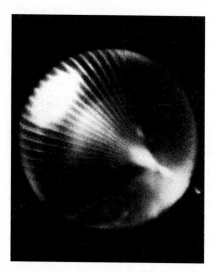

Several UFO sightings during the 1940s and 1950s were attributed by the air force to the misidentification of military aircraft. For instance, some witnesses might actually have seen research balloons (left) made of a translucent plastic that glistened or changed colors in sunlight. Others may have been misled by two wingless, saucer-shaped test planes, developed by the navy (below) and the army and air force (opposite). β.5.

miles from Ohio State to Wright Field and go through a stack of UFO reports, saying, "Well, this is obviously a meteor," or "This is not a meteor, but I'll bet you it's a balloon." Hynek later confessed that he always started from the assumption that there was a natural explanation for everything. It was a reasonable enough attitude; the problem was that the evidence did not always support such an explanation.

One episode that severely strained Hynek's hypothesis occurred a few months later, on July 23, 1948. For the first time, two obviously competent and dispassionate observers got a closeup look at a UFO—and unlike the unfortunate Captain Mantell, returned to tell about it. They were Captain C. S. Chiles and his copilot, J. B. Whitted, flying an Eastern Airlines DC-3 transport from Houston to Boston. At 2:45 A.M., they were at 5,000 feet a few miles south of Montgomery, Alabama, when Chiles saw a dull red glow in the sky ahead, approaching them from a little above and to the right. Chiles remarked casually to Whitted that it was a new military jet.

The night was clear, with a few broken clouds and a bright moon. Both pilots could see the object racing in their direction. The DC-3's red and green warning lights were functioning perfectly. The pilots assumed that the jet would spot them and veer off. Chiles and Whitted could feel the sweat start on their brows as they watched the thing continue straight for them, growing larger by the second. In the horrifying moments before collision, they racked the cumbersome DC-3 into a rivet-popping bank to the left. At that instant, the object changed course slightly to

pass less than 100 feet off their right wing. It was flying at about 700 miles per hour, they thought, and as they watched, it pulled into a steep climb with a burst of orange flame from the rear and disappeared into the clouds. Both the pilot and copilot had seen the thing clearly; indeed, the image was burned into their memories. Chiles and Whitted described the aircraft as wingless and cigar-shaped, with rows of windows along the fuselage that glowed as brightly as magnesium flares. Professor Hynek interpreted the sighting as a meteor. Another astronomer shrugged and put it down to a pair of super-heated imaginations. But the Chiles-Whitted sighting had a profound impact at Project Sign—to the point where a number of staff members joined in writing an unofficial estimate of the situation, saying that at least some of the UFOs being reported might be extraterrestrial.

The report went through channels to General Hoyt S. Vandenberg, Air Force Chief of Staff, who rejected it for lack of evidence. The report had been classified top secret on its way up the chain of command, and after its rejection all copies were burned. The authors of the extraterrestrial hypothesis were regarded as having lost credibility on Project Sign.

Whatever dampening effect the Vandenberg verdict might have had on the Sign

researchers, though, it did nothing to diminish the number of UFO reports that the air force had to deal with. The sightings continued to flood in, and within a few months, Project Sign members were puzzling over yet another amazing incident.

Once more the report came from a trained and presumably sober-minded professional, a fighter pilot who, on October 1, had chased a UFO through the night skies over North Dakota. The episode began as Lieutenant George Gorman was about to land at Fargo after a routine patrol flight in his F-51 Mustang. When he commenced his approach, he noticed what appeared to be the taillight of another aircraft 1,000 yards away. Gorman queried the control tower about it and was advised that no other plane was in the vicinity except for a Piper Cub, which he could plainly see below him. Gorman slid his Mustang in for a closer look at the strange light. "It was about six to eight inches in diameter," he recalled, "clear, white, and completely round, with a sort of fuzz at the edges. It was blinking on and off." As Gorman approached the light, it suddenly veered away in a sharp left turn and dove for the ground. Gorman threw his fighter into a 400 mile-per-hour dive but could not gain on the intruder, which all at once reversed course and started ascending steeply.

Fighter pilot that he was, Gorman went after the thing. "Suddenly, it made a sharp right turn," he said, "and we headed straight at each other. Just when we were about to collide, I guess I got scared." Gorman slammed his Mustang into a dive and saw the object pass about 500 feet over him.

The chase continued. Again Gorman swung up and cut toward it. Again it turned and headed straight for him. This time, the intruder broke off just short of a collision and went into a vertical climb. Gorman followed it, but at 14,000 feet he lost airspeed; his Mustang shuddered and fell into a stall. At that, the object turned on a north by northwest heading and shot out of sight.

The interception had lasted for a gut-wrenching twenty-seven minutes. Gorman, who had served as an instructor pilot during World War II, later concluded that the unknown object was "controlled by thought." The maneuvers were just too sharp and too swift to have been performed otherwise.

Early in 1949, the air force appeared to embark on a new approach to UFOs. The security of Project Sign had been compromised by numerous stories in the press; it was therefore canceled. The staff's final report recommended that future activity be carried on "at a minimum level" and that its special project status be terminated as soon as it became clear that UFO sightings posed no threat to U.S. security. What investigation there was would henceforth be code named Project Grudge; it was a curious code name, with a dictionary meaning of "deep-seated resentment or ill will," and it drew comment when it became known. But the air force denied any special significance. The project would, however, proceed in secrecy.

Again, the air force seemed to be saying two things at once by minimizing the importance of UFOs while declining to release information about them. Critics suggested that the air force did not want too many people looking too closely into UFOs, that it wanted to control whatever research there would be. By classifying the reports, particularly the so-called good sightings, it prevented independent scientists from conducting studies, thereby forestalling any conclusions about UFOs that it might not approve. Project Grudge's mandate, it seemed to the critics, was to deny or explain away all sightings. They complained that it shifted the focus from the phenomena to the people who reported them.

That spring, with the air force's cooperation, a writer named Sydney Shalett attacked the whole notion of UFOs with a scathing two-part article in the *Saturday Evening Post*. Shalett dismissed all UFO reports as mistakes, hoaxes, or illusions and advised that if a UFO should happen to crash, witnesses should "by all means secure the pieces—if they seem harmless." But, he added, "at the same time, maybe you'd better buttress yourself with an affidavit from your clergyman, doctor, or banker."

The sarcasm was lost on many readers. Shortly after the article appeared, the number of UFO sightings hit an all-time high. Wondering if perhaps the article itself had triggered the

A Wild Goose Chase

which were designed to revolve in opposite directions and had short rotor blades jutting from their rims—were separated by the pilot's cockpit, located near the motor mount.

Although the investigators had found their evidence, the inventor's whereabouts were unknown. A former carpenter, Caldwell had taught himself aeronautics from books before forming his manufacturing company. He was even less educated, however, about the business world and had blithely issued stock whenever he needed more money to finance his venture. By 1940, Maryland's attorney general began conducting hearings on Caldwell's affairs. Caldwell soon vanished, leaving his prototype machines behind.

Investigators were able, however, to interview a man who claimed to have piloted the disk-shaped helicopter in a Washington, D.C., test flight ten years

In May 1949 the air force task unit assigned to investigate UFO reports received a tantalizing letter. The writer, a man living in the state of Maryland, explained that years earlier he had purchased stock in a small local company formed to manufacture aircraft. He had recently become concerned, however, that descriptions of the firm's proposed aircraft closely resembled those of the flying saucers he had read about. He felt compelled to pass this information to the authorities studying UFO sightings.

Acting on this tip—and hoping it would solve some still unexplained UFO reports—a team of air force investigators launched an inquiry into the dealings of the aeronautics firm, which was known as the Gray Goose Corporation and had been founded by Jonathan E. Caldwell. The search led the team and Maryland state police to a farm in Glen Burnie, Maryland, a suburb eleven miles south of Baltimore.

There, stored in an unused tobacco shed, were the weather-beaten remains of two of the Gray Goose Corporation's experimental flying machines, which were noticeably saucerlike in design. One of the devices, discovered lying in pieces in the shed *(above and right),* was a small helicopter with a conventional fuselage. But mounted over the cockpit was a tripod supporting a disk fourteen feet in diameter, from which blades projected.

The other, far less conventional craft was a spool-like structure consisting of two circular plywood and steel-reinforced frames, resembling huge cheese boxes. The two sections—

earlier. On the basis of the date of the flight and the pilot's report that the craft stayed aloft only a few minutes at an altitude of about forty feet, the investigators concluded that it could not have been the subject of a UFO sighting. Hence, the suspicions of Caldwell's stockholder yielded nothing, and local saucer reports remained, for the time being, a mystery.

surge, the air force hastily issued a press release stating that all the sightings were products of a sort of mass hysteria and misidentifications of natural phenomena. Clearly, the campaign to put the quietus on UFOs was not working.

roject Grudge lasted only six months and was then largely disbanded. Its final report dealt with 244 sightings and earnestly attempted to explain them all in terms of natural events. In the end, however, fifty-six of the sightings, or 23 percent, defied easy explanation. The report concluded, without offering any evidence, that these unexplained occurrences were the result of psychological aberrations on the part of the observers. The report recommended that the study of UFOs be cut back because its very existence might encourage people to believe that there was some substance to them.

In late December 1949, the Project Grudge records were placed in storage, and most of its personnel were transferred to other jobs. Only a few researchers remained to collect sighting reports and file them away. Nevertheless, the air force was still curious enough about certain of the reports to launch a new and secret study known as Project Twinkle.

More aptly named than Grudge, Twinkle was to make a detailed study of green fireballs that reliable observers had seen between 1947 and 1949 in northern New Mexico. The things resembled meteors—except for their bright green color and the fact that they moved slowly on a flat trajectory. The air force set up an observation post 105 miles southeast of the Los Alamos nuclear test site. It was an area where numerous fireballs had been observed in the past. The researchers were armed with cameras, telescopes, theodolites, and other optical equipment. They waited . . . and they waited. For six months they manned the post and saw nothing.

Meanwhile, a rash of fireball sightings had occurred at Holloman Air Force Base, 150 miles to the south. The Twinkle crew packed up their gear and moved to Holloman—where they waited with growing frustration for another six months and saw nothing. Some staff members found it significant that the fireballs ceased when the air force went looking for them. At any rate, the air force decided to shrug off the fireballs and terminated Project Twinkle.

Inevitably, tales of the air force's frustration, confusion, and deep-lying concern got out, and this only served to increase belief among those so inclined. An early and prominent champion of UFOs was one Donald E. Keyhoe. Born in 1897, Keyhoe was a U.S. Naval Academy graduate and a retired Marine Corps major. He had served as an aircraft and balloon pilot in World War II before becoming a free-lance journalist and had a reputation as a somewhat cynical aviation writer with high-level military contacts.

Late in 1949, *True,* a mass circulation men's adventure magazine, commissioned Keyhoe to write a comprehensive, independently researched article on flying saucers. Keyhoe may not have been a believer when he started. But he most certainly was when he finished.

In January 1950, *True* published under Keyhoe's byline an article entitled "The Flying Saucers Are Real." It caused an instant sensation, becoming one of the most widely read and discussed articles in recent publishing history. Keyhoe offered no conclusive evidence of his own that UFOs were real. Rather, he built his case around the apparent disarray the air force found itself in. He claimed that none of his high-level sources would talk about UFOs, which he took as powerful evidence that there was truth to the reports. He argued that the air force would not talk because it was hiding something tremendously important—and what else could it be if not that UFOs were real and came from outer space? Keyhoe thought that the authorities were covering up vital facts because they feared a nationwide panic. And once he had come to believe his theory, he took every denial or explanation as further proof that the public was being kept in the dark about a matter of utmost national importance. In the article, Keyhoe hinted that he did have some positive evidence for his belief; he suggested that certain unnamed sources had confirmed to him the existence of UFOs.

Two months later, *True* published another flying-saucers-are-real story. It, too, caused a furor. The author this time was Commander Robert B. McLaughlin, a naval officer and guided-missile expert on active duty at the White Sands Proving Grounds in New Mexico. McLaughlin wrote that on April 24, 1949, he and a group of other engineers had been preparing to launch a Project Skyhook high-altitude research balloon. As a preliminary, they had released a small weather balloon to establish wind patterns aloft. And when the theodolite operator swung his instrument to track the balloon, a strange object had crossed its path.

McLaughlin reported that the object was elliptical and close to 105 feet in diameter. It was flying at the extremely high altitude of about fifty-six miles, and the engineers calculated that it was moving through space at five miles per second—18,000 miles per hour. At the end of its trajectory across the horizon, it soared higher at 9,000 miles per hour until it was lost from view. The object, said McLaughlin, was visible for one minute, and all the observers agreed that it was flat white in color. McLaughlin wrote that he was convinced the object "was a flying saucer, and further that these disks are spaceships from another planet."

The White Sands sighting carried weight. Here was an experienced naval officer backed by a crew of engineers and a technician with a theodolite. What is more, McLaughlin largely eliminated any possible "balloon" explanation by stating that they had released a second weather balloon fif-

teen minutes later; it did not behave in any way like the unidentified object, he said firmly. Even the severest critic had to think about this report. And the sighting grew in importance when it came out that the navy had cleared McLaughlin's article for publication, even though it sharply contradicted the findings of Project Grudge.

The sighting itself was not the only point of debate in the article. McLaughlin was one of the first to note a pattern of UFO incidents around military bases and atomic facilities in the southwest. He calculated that the planet Mars had been in an excellent position to observe doings on Earth on July 16, 1945, the day the first atomic bomb was exploded in New Mexico; the flash might have been bright enough to be visible from that planet, and thus have prompted a visit by curious Martians. Critics responded that more sightings should be expected at closely guarded facilities because more people there are on watch. True enough, but it could then be said about the sightings themselves that the quality of the observers lent credence to the reports.

Still, one thing that had been missing through it all was any reasonable photograph of a UFO. But that changed dramatically on May 11, 1950, when Paul Trent, a farmer in McMinnville, Oregon, took two clear photographs of what looked very much like a hovering saucer.

In 1950, Donald E. Keyhoe created a sensation by claiming the government was hiding UFO evidence.

An eager crowd searches the sky over Mexico City for UFOs in 1950. Sightings had been occurring in waves throughout the world.

Trent's wife had been out back feeding her rabbits at about 7:30 in the evening when she saw a metallic, disk-shaped object gliding slowly overhead. She screamed to her husband and got her camera; Paul Trent rushed out and managed to snap two pictures before the thing disappeared. The Trents did not exploit their pictures. They showed them to a few friends, and eventually word reached the local newspaper, which printed them a month later.

The McMinnville pictures were subjected to intense scrutiny *(pages 138-139)* by both flying saucer advocates and skeptics, and later by air force investigators working for the so-called Condon committee, a government-sponsored UFO study launched in the mid-1960s. The committee's report, published in 1969, dismissed all other purported UFO photographs as either hoaxes or shots of natural phenomena—but not these pictures. Said the report: "All factors investigated, geometric, psychological and physical, appear to be consistent with the assertion that an extraordinary flying ob-

ject, silvery, metallic, disk-shaped, tens of meters in diameter and evidently artificial, flew within sight of two witnesses." The report did not positively rule out a hoax but noted that "there are some physical factors, such as the accuracy of certain photometric measures of the original negatives, which argue against a fabrication." Or to translate from the officialese, the pictures looked genuine.

That report was nineteen years in coming. In the meantime the most creditable case for UFOs continued to be made by professionals, most often military aviators. But considering the prevailing Washington mood about unidentified flying objects, many officers were reluctant to go public with their sightings for fear of ridicule or damage to their careers. Some fliers only spoke up publicly years later. A striking example appeared in the June 1973 issue of *Naval Aviation News,* an official fleet publication. The story was called "Unidentified Flying Object—A Provocative Tale." Related by an anonymous pilot who signed himself "B," it told of an event that had taken place more than twenty years before.

On February 10, 1951, according to B, he had been flying a four-engine cargo plane west across the North Atlantic on a course for Newfoundland. The plane was three and a half hours out of Iceland, at 10,000 feet, and making 200 knots ground speed (230 miles per hour). A weather ship off the coast of Greenland reported normal conditions on the route.

Just before dawn, B noticed a yellow glow in the western sky; it seemed to be thirty or thirty-five miles away. "My impression," he recalled, "was that there was a small city ahead." Both B and "K," his copilot, thought they had drifted toward Greenland. But the navigator checked and reported the plane exactly on course. When the plane was about fifteen miles from the glow, the apparition began to look like a circular pattern of lights. B then thought that it might be coming from two ships moored together. At a range of about five miles, the lights, by that point brilliant white, suddenly went out. A yellow halo appeared on the water where they had been; the halo turned orange and then a fiery red. B related that the halo "started moving towards us at a fantastic speed. It looked as though we were going to be engulfed."

B desperately maneuvered to avoid the onrushing object—which then swung around and joined a loose formation with the plane, 200 to 300 feet ahead and 100 feet below. "It appeared to be from 200 to 300 feet in diameter, translucent or metallic, shaped like a saucer," according to B. Then the object reversed course and streaked away at a speed that B estimated to be in excess of 1,500 miles per hour.

A shaken crewman radioed the field at Gander, Newfoundland, to report the sighting and learn if the object was visible on radar. When the plane landed, said B, he and his crew were debriefed by intelligence officers, and they were required to make a full report when they arrived in the United States. B concluded by stating that sometime later he learned that Gander radar had tracked an object moving through the sky at a speed greater than 1,800 miles per hour.

Matters were coming to a head for the air force. Later that year, on September 10, an air force pilot over Fort Monmouth, New Jersey, spotted a round, silver, flattish object with a diameter of thirty to fifty feet. He radioed in the report, and a nearby radar station managed to track the object. By then, almost two years had passed since the air force had more or less shelved its Project Grudge, and the UFO phenomenon was no closer to dying out than before. In fact, there was an increasing body of evidence that suggested a need for further study, serious study.

Late in September, on orders from the Air Force Chief of Intelligence, Project Grudge was reactivated, and Captain Edward J. Ruppelt was appointed its boss. A coolheaded World War II bombardier, Ruppelt was the right man for the job: He was convinced that UFOs were worth investigating, but he was determined to be absolutely evenhanded about it, neither an advocate nor a debunker.

Ruppelt understood the reluctance of many military pilots to report UFO sightings. He made up standardized forms, sent them to all commands, and got a directive from the Pentagon instructing every air force unit anywhere in the world to report UFO sightings promptly. In addition, he retained J. Allen Hynek as his chief scientific consultant; for all Hynek's tendency to see UFOs as natural and earthly in origin, he remained a top-flight scientist with an invaluable fund of knowledge about earlier UFO sightings. Moreover, Ruppelt began a new system of cooperation with the press by issuing regular releases about sightings and investigations.

erhaps the more open policy was a factor, but 1952 became a boom year for UFOs, with a stunning 1,501 reports. That spring, when it became apparent that a UFO wave was building, the air force decided to upgrade Grudge to a separate organization called Project Blue Book. For starters, Ruppelt briefed top officers of the Air Defense Command on the project and enlisted their help in using the command's radarscope cameras to help detect UFOs.

One series of sightings that captured Ruppelt's interest came to be known as the Lubbock lights. Over a two-week period in August and September 1951, hundreds of people had seen strange nighttime objects in the skies over Lubbock, Texas. The sequence began at 9:00 P.M. on August 25, when a man and his wife were startled by what appeared to be a huge, wing-shaped UFO with blue lights on its trailing edge passing over the outskirts of Albuquerque, New Mexico, at an altitude of some 1,000 feet. About twenty minutes later in Lubbock, three college professors taking their ease on a porch saw a semicircular formation of lights sweep overhead at high speed. But the lights came and went so swiftly that no one got a good look. The professors were annoyed and vowed to be more alert if the lights returned. Just over an hour later, the lights were back, and this time the professors determined that they were softly glowing bluish objects flying in a loose formation.

The next day, a nearby Air Defense Command radar station reported that its equipment had registered an unidentified target at 13,000 feet. It was traveling at 900 miles per hour, half again as fast as any jet fighter then in service. Dozens of people in and around Lubbock said that they had seen the lights, and one woman drew a picture of a wing-shaped object remarkably like the one in Albuquerque.

The lights returned to Lubbock five days later, and this time, Carl Hart, Jr., a freshman at Texas Technical College, managed to get five photographs with his 35-mm Kodak camera. The photos showed a V formation of lights. The images did not coincide with the lights seen by the three professors; these lights were in an irregular pattern. The air force ana-

lyzed the negatives and found no evidence that they had been faked. But that did not jibe with the assessment of at least one eminent scientist: Donald H. Menzel, a professor of astrophysics at Harvard University, who had emerged as a powerful critic of UFOs.

Menzel did not mince words. He stated frankly that he did not believe even in the possibility of UFOs' being extraterrestrial visitors; he either offered a scientific explanation for every sighting or dismissed it as a fraud. Menzel viewed his role as that of defending the bastions of learning against the forces of ignorance—and greed. Said an editor who knew him: "Menzel was convinced of his own infallibility, and he thought anyone who was interested in UFOs was a charlatan, or such a person wouldn't be interested."

Menzel was scornful of the Lubbock lights, observing that if the lights were traveling as fast as the Lubbock professors said, then no one could have photographed them with a relatively unsophisticated camera, such as Hart's Kodak.

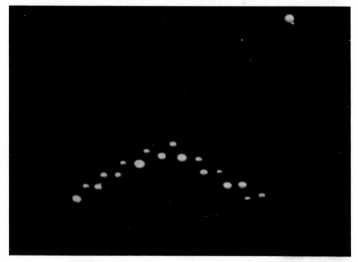

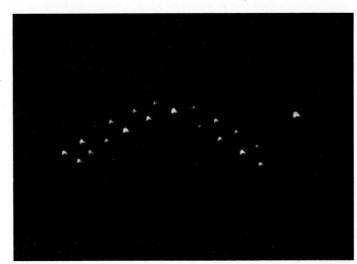

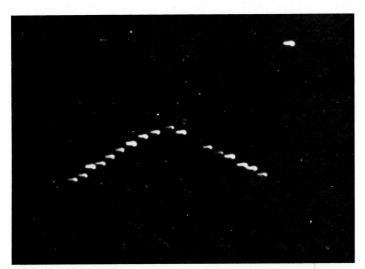

Menzel decreed that the Lubbock lights were merely the reflections of streetlights, automobile headlights, or house lights against a rippling layer of fine haze "probably just over the heads of the observers." In a two-part article for *Look* magazine in June 1952, he described a historical sighting dating back to 1893 that sounded similar to the Lubbock lights. Menzel also published a photograph of a formation of UFOs that he had faked in his laboratory. Menzel's point, apparently, was that since the photos could have been faked, they probably were. It is not known how Captain Ruppelt and

the Blue Book investigators felt about Menzel's faked photographs. But they did eventually conclude that the Lubbock lights were natural phenomena.

Nevertheless, many people found the explanations unconvincing, and in early 1952, *Life* magazine gave a team of writers and researchers an assignment to produce a definitive article on UFOs. The *Life* team got full cooperation from Captain Ruppelt and his staff members, who opened their files and declassified sighting reports on request.

When the *Life* story was published in April, it caused an uproar that made the reaction to Donald Keyhoe's *True* article pale by comparison. Said *Life:* "These objects cannot be explained by present science as natural phenomena—but solely as artificial devices created and operated by a high intelligence." The article gave details of ten previously unpublished reports, which the writers argued could not be explained by the usual references to balloons, mirages, inversions, or mental aberrations. And one noted scientist,

Donald H. Menzel shows how ground lights might create UFO-like images under certain atmospheric conditions.

Walter Reidel, former director of the German wartime rocket base at Peenemünde, was quoted as saying that he believed in the extraterrestrial origin of UFOs. When the air force was questioned about the article, it responded: "The article is factual, but *Life's* conclusions are its own."

Following the *Life* story, the monthly level of UFO sightings went from the normal 10 or 20 to 99 in April and 149 in June. They came from every part of the country, and the number kept rising. In July there were 536, three times the June figure; on July 28 alone, there were 50 reports. The wave began to subside in August, with 326, and then the sightings tailed off to about 50 a month for the rest of the year.

Ruppelt and his Blue Book staff were overwhelmed. They could barely screen, classify, and file the reports. There was no time to investigate more than a handful of them. Indeed, the *New York Times* reported that so many inquiries about UFOs were coming to all intelligence agencies of the government that "regular intelligence work had been affected."

During the wave of 1952, Blue Book's Captain Ruppelt counted no fewer than 16,000 newspaper items about UFOs in one six-month period. Just as it appeared that things might be calming down, some sensational new report would capture the headlines all over again. One of the year's most fascinating sightings occurred at about 8:10 P.M. on July 14

near Norfolk, Virginia. The evening was clear and visibility was unlimited. The pilot and copilot of a Pan American DC-4, flying at 8,000 feet on the New York-Miami run, saw a glow in the sky that soon resolved itself into six fiery red objects, each of them about 100 feet in diameter. "Their shape was clearly outlined and evidently circular," said Captain William B. Nash. "The edges were well-defined, not phosphorescent or fuzzy in the least."

As Nash and copilot William Fortenberry watched in amazement, the six disks in a narrow echelon formation were joined by two more, all flying at about 2,000 feet over the waters of the Chesapeake Bay. When the disks were almost under the airliner, they dimmed slightly and flipped on edge in unison. The edges seemed to be about fifteen feet thick, and the top surfaces appeared flat. Nash and Fortenberry radioed a report to be forwarded to the air force, and at 7:00 the next morning they were asked to come in for questioning. After more than two hours of interrogation, first separately, then together, Nash and Fortenberry were told that the disks had been observed by seven other groups in the area.

Project Blue Book checked the positions of all known military and civilian aircraft in the vicinity at the time but found nothing to account for the sighting—which went into the files as officially "unexplained." Harvard's

The Orgone Bandits

Wilhelm Reich, a noted Austrian psychoanalyst, claimed to have seen unidentified flying objects several times. The alien occupants of these ships from other worlds were hostile, he believed, and were intent on robbing the earth of what Reich described as a precious substance called orgone—a cosmic life energy allegedly present in air, water, and all organic matter. He said that the saucers were propelled by orgone and that orgone's blue color accounted for the bluish lights that are often described by witnesses to UFO incidents.

In place of orgone, Reich suggested, the spaceships were releasing a negative energy he called "deadly orgone," which caused sickness in humans and left the land a parched desert.

Professor Menzel carried on a lengthy correspondence with Captain Nash, once suggesting that the pilot had been fooled by fireflies trapped between the double panes in the cockpit window. Later, despite weather reports to the contrary, Menzel concluded that the sighting was caused by lights on the ground distorted by haze and a temperature inversion.

By then, UFOs were generating such excitement around the country—and raising so many unanswered questions—that two private research groups were formed to collect and examine UFO information independently of the air force. The most active, the Aerial Phenomena Research Organization, known by the acronym APRO, was founded by Coral and Jim Lorenzen, private UFO researchers in Sturgeon Bay, Wisconsin; APRO had so much to talk about that it published a bimonthly newsletter.

Just four days after the Nash-Fortenberry incident over the Chesapeake Bay, a fantastic series of sightings nearby set everyone's UFO antennae twanging. This time the drama began at Washington's National Airport, a few miles from the White House. The first occurred at 11:40 on the night of July 19, when air controllers at National picked up seven slow-moving objects on two radarscopes. According to the senior controller, Harry G. Barnes, the radar showed the objects to be about fifteen miles from the airport and traveling between 100 and 130 miles per hour.

Barnes called the airport tower and learned that the local radar operator was picking up the same images. Fifteen miles away, across the Potomac River in Maryland, controllers at Andrews Air Force Base were seeing the identical blips on their radar. At 3:00 A.M., Barnes officially notified the U.S. Air Force Air Defense Command. It took the air force half an hour to respond, but finally a pair of radar-equipped F-94 night fighters roared in, made a few noisy passes over the field, scanned the nearby skies—and found nothing. As soon as the jets departed, the blips magically reappeared on the radar screens and remained there, moving slowly until daybreak. The air force said nothing, but the news leaked out and the story broke like a thunderclap in the morning papers. The tight-lipped air force refused to admit to clamoring reporters that it had actually scrambled jets to intercept the UFOs.

Professor Menzel once again called the incident a case of temperature inversion. He correctly pointed out that in such cases ghostly blips have been known to appear on radarscopes, something that most people did not know. But controller Barnes did not accept the explanation. "Inversion blips are always recognized by experts," he declared. "We are familiar with what weather conditions, flying birds, and such things can cause on radar." There was no rebuttal from Menzel.

The UFOs returned to

The Evidence of the Radar Screen

If skeptics of the phenomenon of unidentified flying objects had a motto, it would probably be "show me proof." Proof exists, say many UFO investigators in reply to this charge, pointing to visual sightings that are backed up by the presumably objective eye of radar.

Radar, an acronym for radio detect-

side lobes can project a weak return from an object detected by the main beam; the two blips of light moving across the radarscope will appear as a small target chasing a larger one. Abnormal atmospheric conditions may also cause reflected waves to move or to portray targets outside the normal

field of the beam and distort their size, speed, or altitude.

Phantom images have appeared on both ground-based and aircraft radar, and experienced operators know how to interpret them. But more than a few observers have been baffled by some returns that have crossed their screens, and a number of radar-tracked UFO episodes remain unexplained—at least to the satisfaction of those who tracked them.

Although radar may add some credibility to UFO sightings, cautious researchers—such as the British ufologist Jenny Randles—recognize the limitations of the science. "Radar evidence is not, unfortunately, a talisman for the ufologist," she explains, "but is as complex and ambiguous in its interpretation as any other kind of report."

A radar operator on an air force jet that was flying near Bermuda in 1954 detected seven unidentified objects moving in unison across his radarscope. Although a radio check indicated no naval activity in the area, the incident was later attributed to ship movement.

ing and ranging, works by directing electromagnetic waves at an object. The waves reflect from the target back to a receiving device that determines the object's distance, direction, and rate of speed. This information is translated into video signals and displayed on a screen.

Unfortunately, radar is not foolproof. Frequently, radar reflections—or returns, as they are called—appear on the screen where no target is present. Some phantom returns are easily recognized as waves bouncing off ground objects. Others, however, are more difficult to identify.

Radio waves diffracted from the main beam, called side lobes, may transmit a return that seems to come from an object in the path of the main beam. If the target is moving, the misplaced return moves too. In addition,

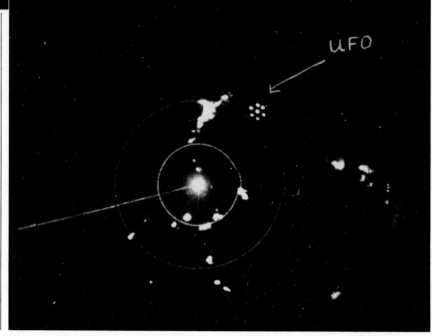

*Air traffic controller Harry G. Barnes
tracked some of the UFOs that were reported
over Washington, D.C., in 1952. The air
force blamed the sightings on temperature inversions.*

Washington a week later, on July 26. At 10:30 that evening, the air traffic radar at National Airport again picked up blips. There were five or six objects, which seemed to be moving south. Once more, Harry Barnes checked with the Andrews tower in Maryland; the controllers there also had unknown targets showing on their scopes. And the pilots of departing and arriving airliners radioed reports of strange sightings near the airport.

At 11:00 P.M., Barnes called the Pentagon, which responded with no more alacrity than before. At 11:25, a pair of F-94s came howling over Washington. Again, the UFOs instantly disappeared from the radar screens. After ten minutes of fruitless search, the interceptors headed home. Back came the UFOs. At 3:20 A.M., with the UFOs constantly on radar, the air force sent in another pair of F-94s. But now the UFOs remained visible on the screens, and one of the jet fighters reported a visual sighting of four lights. At one point, the pilot radioed that the lights were surrounding his plane. What should he do? he asked the ground controllers. Before the controllers could respond, the lights sped away.

Next morning, the Pentagon was inundated with queries. Even President Harry Truman asked an aide to find out what in the world—or out of it—was going on. Finally, on July 29, Major General John A. Samford, director of air force intelligence, held a press conference. He told reporters he was convinced that all the sightings over Washington in the past two weeks had been caused by temperature inversions. The general said that outside scientists would be asked to examine the reports more closely—but there is no evidence that such a panel was ever assembled.

The news media by and large accepted the air force's explanation or dismissed the incidents as a sort of mass hallucination. If the latter was true, the masses remained highly hallucinatory, for the UFO reports continued. Early in 1953 the air force and the Central Intelligence Agency were worried that the reports could prove dangerous to national security. The CIA was concerned that the Soviets might use a wave of UFO reports as a cover for an aerial attack on the U.S. or deliberately confuse the U.S. into thinking that flights of bombers were merely more of those funny little men from Mars. At the very least, argued the CIA, the UFO craze could undermine public confidence in the U.S. military. Thus it became high-level policy to convince the country that UFOs simply did not exist.

With the air force's blessing, the CIA formed a panel of five noted scientists otherwise not involved with UFOs. Chaired by H. P. Robertson, a physics and weapons expert at the prestigious California Institute of Technology, the group included Nobel laureate Luis Alvarez, who had played a major role in developing the atomic bomb, and Samuel Goudsmit, an associate of Albert Einstein with numerous theoretical advances to his own credit.

The Robertson panel assembled in Washington on January 14, 1953. Over a three-day period, it was given seventy-five UFO reports. The scientists studied eight in close detail, took a general look at fifteen, and viewed two color film clips that showed maneuvering lights in the sky. All told, the panel spent twelve hours considering UFO phenomena. To some, that did not seem like a great deal of time, yet it was enough for the panel to firmly conclude that UFOs posed no physical risk to national security, but "continued emphasis on the reporting of these phenomena does result in a threat."

The scientists recommended that Project Blue Book spend more time allaying public anxiety over UFOs than collecting and assessing data. They suggested that private UFO research groups be placed under surveillance because they might be used for "subversive purposes." The panel also recommended a campaign by national security agencies to "strip the UFO phenomenon of its special status and eliminate their aura of mystery," and it outlined a program of public education for "training and debunking."

The Robertson report enabled the air force to say for the next fifteen years that an impartial scientific body had examined the UFO data and had found absolutely no evidence of anything unusual in the atmosphere. Its issuance, in fact, marked the beginning of the most concentrated campaign to date against UFOs.

The air force, which had begun by skeptically investigating the phenomena and had swung between openness and secrecy in its dealings with the public, now came down hard on the side of secrecy. Beginning in August 1953, all UFO reports were squelched whenever possible, all information was classified. And in December, the Joint Chiefs of Staff moved to plug any leaks by making the unauthorized release of information a crime under the Espionage Act, punishable by a $10,000 fine or up to ten years in prison. Contrary to the Robertson panel's recommendation, however, Project Blue Book was not accorded an educational role but was downgraded to a virtual nonentity. The cooperative Captain Ruppelt had left the project and the air force in August; by then, only he and two assistants remained of what had once been a ten-person staff. Blue Book became a mere repository of records and was assigned to Airman First Class Max Futch.

But the government's decision to forcibly deflate the UFO phenomenon was only partially successful. Although the dictum had its desired effect on government agencies, it did nothing to prevent people from seeing things in the sky or writing about them. In the years since Kenneth Arnold's eerie encounter over the Cascades, flying saucers had become an apparently ineradicable part of the American scene, both feared and laughed about, the subject of Hollywood horror films as well as scholarly books. In October 1953, that ardent champion Donald E. Keyhoe published his best-selling *Flying Saucers from Outer Space.* Hard on his heels followed the equally avid debunker, Donald H. Menzel, with *Flying Saucers,* a studious denial published by Harvard University Press. And so it went.

In October, *Look* magazine bought excerpts from Keyhoe's book. Fearing the *Look* article would inflame more UFO reports, the air force got the magazine to include a disclaimer and allow air force scientists to dispute various points. But the more the air force tried to explain, the more Keyhoe asserted it was covering up what amounted to an invasion from outer space. He insisted that UFOs were extraterrestrial. Likewise, nothing would change the mind of Menzel, whose book mocked and attacked anyone who claimed to have seen a UFO, explaining everything as a natural phenomenon, optical illusion, or hoax.

Between these two jousters stood the wondering American public. Much about UFOs beggared belief, of course. Yet there was still that element of uncertainty, that possibility. Over the years, a number of mysterious incidents had defied rational explanation, and such incidents would continue to occur. And some of them would go far beyond being mere sightings of strange objects in flight.

"The eye is easily tricked," according to illusionist John Mulholland, shown here making china saucers fly. In a 1952 Popular Science article, the magician attributed UFO sightings to overworked imaginations.

Kidnappers from Space

Since the early 1960s, more and more people have reported not only seeing UFOs but being taken aboard spacecraft against their will. While details differ, many of the incidents seem to follow a similar pattern. Most intriguing, perhaps, is the common claim that after the victims observe a UFO, they are surprised to find an hour or two has passed of which they have no recollection. In the days and months that follow, they may experience nightmares, flashbacks, or extreme anxiety. Eventually they begin to recall—on their own or through hypnosis—that during the "missing time" they were abducted by aliens.

Skeptics view these reports, which often include tales of probing physical examinations and even impregnation by extraterrestrials, as complete fabrications or perhaps hallucinations. Some imaginative UFO researchers, on the other hand, theorize that if the abduction stories are true, aliens may be conducting long-term studies of humans and performing genetic experiments in hopes of creating a human-alien hybrid.

Whatever the merits of this theory, psychiatrists who have examined alleged abduction victims find signs that they have undergone a severe trauma. Some of the details of their ordeals—how the abduction took place, what the aliens looked like, what the victims felt and saw—are recounted on the following pages.

An Interrupted Journey

"**W**e were driving along on a tarred road and all of a sudden, without any warning or rhyme or reason or anything, Barney stopped suddenly and made this sharp turn off the highway." Thus did Betty Hill, speaking under hypnosis, describe the first in a series of bizarre events that began on a September night in 1961 as she and her husband were driving through the New Hampshire countryside.

While some people report encountering aliens in their homes, most are driving at night on dark, desolate roads. They think they see a lit object flying over the car or hovering in the distance, or feel they are being watched. As they continue on their journey, the steering wheel seems to be wrenched from the driver's control; the car is guided by an outside force until it ultimately veers sharply off the road.

Such was the recollection of Steven Kilburn, a student at the University of Maryland when he was supposedly abducted in 1973. Under hypnosis, he described "two lights in the sky, going over the highway, over the trees. I see a shadow of something. I'm coming down the hill, and I finally get to about the spot where I think it will be and I pull over. I don't really want to go over there, but the car went to the right—it was really violent, as if sucked by a giant magnet."

Just before a victim's car halts, the electrical system is said to fail mysteriously; the radio blares static and then the engine dies. The driver tries frantically to restart the engine, but to no avail. Some victims report staying within the car; others step outside. Despite their terror, most remain rooted to the spot, unable to obey their basic, self-protective impulses to run away or call for help.

In the Presence of the Unearthly

After Steven Kilburn's car lurched to a stop beside a deserted Maryland highway, he watched dumb struck as three figures approached from a nearby field. "They're really strange," he recalled under hypnosis. "They're small, below my shoulder. I see the faces and they're white, chalky, they look like they're made out of rubber. There's one, he's the boss. His eyes are really shiny, they look black. I don't see any pupils. His head is not round, it's like an inverted teardrop. There is a nose, like a tiny, little raised ridge and two little holes, like little pin holes."

Most people who tell of being abducted have described their alien kidnappers as short—three to five feet tall—but emphasize that the leader of the group is slightly taller. Some speak of alien beings with large domed heads set on small bodies, slits for eyes, and long, thin fingers and hands.

The victims all report having felt afraid as the strange-looking beings advanced. But they also tell of an almost tranquilizing numbness or paralysis that overtook them, perhaps imposed by the aliens. As Barney Hill recalled, "I started to get out of my car and put one foot on the ground. Two men were standing beside me helping me out. I felt very relaxed, yet very frightened."

Charles E. Hickson, a forty-five-year-old shipyard foreman, was fishing one evening in 1973 when he and a companion observed an elongated, oval object with flashing blue lights. The object hovered about two feet off the ground, he said, then "it seemed to open up, but really there wasn't a door there at all, and three creatures came floating out toward us. I was so scared, I couldn't believe it was happening." His friend fainted at the sight; Hickson remained standing, his limbs completely paralyzed. Then, he recalled, he was lifted by two of the aliens, and the group glided back into the spaceship.

At the Mercy of Aliens

Whitley Strieber could not explain exactly how he got inside a spacecraft on the night of December 26, 1985. One moment, he said, he was in a wooded area, the captive of two alien intruders; the next, he was whisked from the ground. "I saw branches moving past my face, then a sweep of treetops. Then a gray floor obscured my vision, slipping below my feet like an iris closing." He soon found himself on a table in "a small operating theater," surrounded by beings from another world.

Most people who report their abductions by aliens remember being led into a brightly lit room and subjected to a painful physical examination. Charles Hickson said his body was scanned by an instrument that looked like a big eye. Betty Hill recalled that flakes of skin from her arm and samples of hair, ear wax, and fingernail clippings were taken.

Both Betty Hill and Betty Andreasson, another alleged abductee, claimed they were examined with a machine from which long, needle-tipped wires protruded. A needle was inserted into each woman's navel for what Hill's abductor called a "pregnancy test." Some UFO researchers interpret this procedure as one in which ova may have been removed from their reproductive tracts.

Men have spoken of parallel experiences. Some describe forced sexual relations with alien females, and several recall being plied with a device to extract sperm samples.

But the most disconcerting cases involve young women who, during alleged encounters with aliens, are subjected to a type of artificial insemination. They become pregnant, yet discover later that they are no longer carrying a child. Under hypnosis, these women recall a second encounter with aliens and another gynecological procedure. This time, UFO abduction researchers believe, the hybrid fetus is removed.

CHAPTER 3

A Time of Close Encounters

illy Ray Taylor was thirsty. Night was falling, but the August heat lingered in the hills of southwestern Kentucky. The twenty-one-year-old Taylor was only looking for a cool drink when he ventured out of the house to visit the farm's well; what he apparently saw sent him dashing back to the farmhouse in a state of high excitement.

The eleven members of the Sutton family, who lived in the house and worked the farm, heard their visitor's story with disbelief. A flying saucer, he exclaimed—a craft with an exhaust all the colors of the rainbow—had just flown over his head and plunged into a gully a few hundred yards from the house. The Suttons laughed him off. But they began to take him a little more seriously half an hour later, when the family dog started barking and then dashed under the house with his tail between his legs.

As they told the story afterward, Taylor and another adult, Lucky Sutton, went to the door and looked out to see a glowing figure approaching the house. It came close enough for the two men to make out a forty-inch-tall creature with a round, oversized head; large, luminous yellow eyes; and talon-tipped arms that nearly dragged the ground. Sutton and Taylor did not bother with a neighborly welcome. They backed into the house and reached for a 20-gauge shotgun and a .22-caliber rifle.

When the small creature came within twenty feet of the door, Taylor and Sutton opened fire. The figure somersaulted and disappeared. The two men ventured outside and saw a similar creature on the roof. Sutton fired and the being tumbled. They spotted a third alien—if such it was—perched in a maple tree and again shot toward it. The creature merely floated to the ground and ran away with an awkward, lopsided gait. As another figure rounded a corner of the house, Sutton opened up with his shotgun at point-blank range; the pellets sounded as if they had struck a metal bucket, and the creature was unfazed, although it retreated.

After a while, the two men stopped shooting. They hunkered down in the house and tried to keep the younger Sutton children calm when the aliens peered into the windows. Finally, the terrified family sprinted to their cars and sped off to nearby Hopkinsville to fetch the police.

The official response was prompt and thorough. Local and state police and a photographer drove back to the Sutton farm with the family and scoured the area; they found, according to one report, only a luminescent patch on the ground where one of the small creatures had supposedly landed after being knocked from its perch. The investigators left the site at 2:15 A.M., and the household went to bed—but they were not there for long.

The aliens returned. Once again they persisted in gazing into the farmhouse windows, and once again the Kentucky countryside rang with the men's shotgun blasts, which succeeded in blowing many holes through the window screens but failed to draw blood from the otherworldly intruders. At 5:15, just before dawn, according to the Suttons, the creatures vanished, never to reappear.

The ordeal had not ended, however. For days, the farm was swarming with reporters from all over the state and those surrounding it. Sightseers poured in, tramping through the acreage looking for signs of the aliens and barging into the house asking to photograph the exasperated farmers. UFO investigators were also there, combing the site.

No physical evidence —other than the supposed glowing patch that remained on the earth—was found to support the story told by Taylor and the Suttons. Investigators did conclude, however, that these people were sincere and sane and that they had no interest in exploiting the case for publicity. And there the matter would rest.

The Kelly-Hopkinsville event, as it has come to be known for the farm's location between the towns of Hopkinsville and Kelly, took place on August 21 and 22, 1955. It is considered a classic example of what would later be termed a close encounter of the third kind: a close-range sighting of a UFO and animated creatures. To be sure, such encounters had been reported before; the mystery airships of 1897 had supposedly disgorged some mysterious occupants *(pages 18-22)*. But the 1950s and early 1960s marked the beginning of a remarkable wave of alien-sighting claims, ranging from distant glimpses of humanoids to more frightening stories of abduction and experimentation.

Many ufologists separate so-called contactees—those individuals who claim to have been assigned some special mission by benevolent aliens—from other UFO reporters. Contactees, many of whom first announced themselves in the 1950s, do not fit the pattern exhibited by other close-encounter witnesses: They usually recount a long series of meetings or even voyages with quasi-angelic space beings who have chosen the contactees as their envoys on earth.

Also in a separate category are abductees, who say they have been kidnapped and taken aboard alien spacecraft against their will. Most of the abductees report having been subjected to bizarre experiments; almost all claim to have communicated telepathically with extraterrestrial beings. The full memory of such experiences often seems to have been blocked from the person's recall until it is unlocked by hypnosis *(pages 57-63)*.

Such stories of direct contact with aliens may have made up the most startling part of the growing body of UFO lore, but the majority of reports continued to involve unexplained aerial events. Despite the efforts of the air force to downplay them, sightings of unidentified flying objects were recorded in increasing numbers into the late 1960s. Some of the reports did, in fact, turn out to be transparent hoaxes and were quickly exposed. However, an impressive number of them came from such witnesses as air force combat pilots and reputable police officers. Their stories seem as baffling now as they were then.

One such event was the high-speed aerial chase that took place between an air force jet and a UFO over the American heartland in the summer of 1957. Ufologists consider the incident a prime example of a radar/visual sighting.

During the early morning hours of July 17, a Boeing RB-47 out of Forbes Air Force Base in Topeka, Kansas, flew over the Gulf of Mexico on a navigation exercise. It carried six officers and was loaded with electronic gear. There were few clouds and no thunderstorms in the sky as the jet reconnaissance bomber cruised at an altitude of 34,000 feet. All was calm until the RB-47 turned for home and crossed the coastline near Gulfport, Mississippi. Then, unusual things began to happen.

The bomber's radar operator peered at his screen and spotted a blip that seemed to show something approaching from the right side of the aircraft. As the startled airman squinted at his equipment, the blip appeared to soar rapidly upward, then cross in front of the bomber before heading down the left side. It was almost as though some sort of craft was circling the RB-47. Shortly afterward, at 4:10 A.M., both pilot and copilot were startled to see an intense bluish white light streaking toward them from their left, apparently on a collision course. Later, the pilot would recall that the object appeared to be "as big as a barn." Before he could react, the blinding light changed course and disappeared from view, but it continued to radiate strong signals that were picked up by the bomber's electronic intelligence gear for the next eight minutes or so.

At 4:39, the pilot was again jolted by the appearance of a "huge" light about 5,000 feet below his flight path and just off to the right of the bomber's nose. Through the intercom the radarman reported new signals coming from the same location. The pilots then saw a glowing red object through the cockpit's bubble canopy. After receiving permission from ground controllers to give chase, the pilot nosed down, boosting his speed to about 550 miles per hour to pursue the bizarre light—which seemed to be accelerating away.

By this time the hurtling jet was approaching Fort Worth, Texas, and a ground-radar operator was picking up the strange object on his scope. Then, at 4:50, the speeding UFO seemed to make an abrupt stop in the sky. The RB-47 roared past, only to have its quarry in sight again two minutes later, when the light suddenly plunged to about 15,000 feet. Once more the air force pilot lost the capricious object, but found it six minutes later, twenty miles northwest of Fort Worth.

Finally, at 5:40, when the bomber was near Oklahoma City, the elusive light vanished and its signal faded away. Still mystified, the pilot flew back to land at Forbes. His cat-and-mouse game had covered as many as 700 miles of sky across four states.

The director of intelligence of the Fifty-fifth Strategic Reconnaissance Wing studied the episode and wrote that he "had no doubt the electronic D/F's [direction findings] coincided exactly with visual observations by aircraft commander numerous times, thus indicating positively the object being the signal source." Of course, that report left unanswered the question of just what the object might have been; other air force investigators, apparently seeking to downplay the significance of the darting light, concluded that it was a commercial airliner—leading some to wryly observe that the unsuspecting passengers on board the plane must have had the ride of their lives.

If the air force was hoping to throw cold water on the

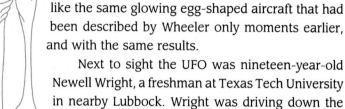

Although no scientifically confirmed photographs of aliens are known to exist, there are many sketches. The creatures on these two pages were drawn either by people reporting alien encounters or by artists sketching from the witnesses' accounts.

subject of unidentified flying objects, it was thwarted by cirumstances beyond its control. Reports continued to pour in through the rest of 1957, and not all of them involved objects that were as distant and elusive as the one spotted by the RB-47 crew. Indeed, before the year was out, several excited observers in the vicinity of Levelland, Texas, would describe one of the most impressive UFO events ever.

It began shortly before 11 P.M. on November 2, when patrolman A. J. Fowler of the Levelland police department received a bizarre telephone call. As a veteran police officer, Fowler had heard many strange stories, but none like the one told by a local farmhand named Pedro Saucedo.

Saucedo and a friend, Joe Salaz, had been in the cab of Saucedo's truck, driving along Route 116 a few miles

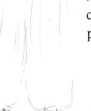

Short but fearsome, the beings who supposedly eluded the Suttons' shotgun attack in the 1955 Kentucky incident were said to look like this.

west of town, when they saw a bright flash of light in a field flanking the road. "Then it rose out of the field," Saucedo would recall later, "and started toward us, picking up speed. The lights of my truck went out and the motor died. I jumped out and hit the deck as the thing passed directly over the truck with a great sound and a rush of wind. It sounded like thunder, and my truck rocked from the blast. I felt a lot of heat." Saucedo watched the accelerating craft, a machine he described as "torpedo-shaped, like a rocket" and about 200 feet long, as it whipped through the late-night mist. When the strange object moved away from the men, the truck lights snapped back on, and the farmhand was able to restart the engine and drive to the nearest telephone. Fowler dismissed the call, believing that it had come from a drunk, but an hour later his phone rang again. This time the caller was a motorist by the name of Jim Wheeler, who reported that a glowing, 200-foot-long, egg-shaped object had blocked the road in front of him four miles east of town. Wheeler's engine and headlights had mysteriously failed. The driver

Some say the description of this fetuslike creature came from a doctor who performed an autopsy on its body during the early 1950s.

watched, dumbfounded, as the craft rose from the highway and continued its low-level flight. Once it had passed out of sight, Wheeler's automobile lights came back on by themselves.

Within five minutes of Wheeler's call, another report was phoned in, this one from the hamlet of Whitharral, located eleven miles north of Levelland. Jose Alvarez told Fowler of seeing what sounded like the same glowing egg-shaped aircraft that had been described by Wheeler only moments earlier, and with the same results.

Next to sight the UFO was nineteen-year-old Newell Wright, a freshman at Texas Tech University in nearby Lubbock. Wright was driving down the highway when his car engine quit and the headlights blinked out as though the battery cables had suddenly been disconnected. When Wright got out to inspect under the hood, he chanced to look up the road and saw the craft astride the highway. It was five minutes past midnight, and Wright was nine miles north of Levelland. He gaped at the huge object glowing bluish-green from what Wright assumed was an aluminum hull. Diving back inside the car, he frantically turned the ignition key, but to no avail. A few minutes later, the strange craft rose "almost straight up" and vanished. Wright started the engine and sped away. At first he was hesitant about reporting the incident "for fear of public ridicule," as he explained later.

The calls kept flooding in. Fowler alerted the sheriff, Weir Clem, who picked up his deputy, Pat McCulloch, and set off in search of the object, or objects, that were terrorizing motorists in the flat country around Levelland. The two men cruised the highways and farm roads around Levelland for more than an hour. Then, at 1:30 that morning, a few miles north of town, they joined the growing number of witnesses to the eerie phenomenon. About 300 yards ahead of them appeared "an oval-shaped light looking like a brilliant red sunset across the highway." The sighting was verified by a pair of police officers in a patrol car a few miles behind Clem's. Both men reported "a strange-looking flash [that] appeared to be close to the ground." The final sighting of that memorable night was made

In 1975, an English girl drew this "spacewoman" who, she said, visited her home.

68

at 2:00 by another law enforcement officer, Lloyd Ballen, who saw an object traveling in the darkened sky "so fast it looked like a flash of light moving from east to west." Within three hours, a dozen people had seen what appeared to be the same huge UFO, and another three reported an unexplained flash of light, all within a ten-mile radius of this northern Texas town. The sightings were made independently and were called in independently. Except for the police officers, the witnesses did not know each other, and the non-police sightings occurred while each of the witnesses was bound for some destination and not because they were consciously on the lookout for unidentified flying objects. The night was much too overcast for amateur sky watching, in any event.

Word of the Levelland lights made headlines in the nation's major newspapers (competing with the news that the USSR had put *Sputnik II* into orbit). Although the U.S. Air Force agreed to investigate the sensational series of sightings, it sent only one officer to the

A 1973 case in Pascagoula, Mississippi, involved this wrinkled creature.

scene—and he spent less than twenty-four hours in the area and talked to just six of the fifteen witnesses. The air force subsequently put out a press release explaining the sightings as a "weather phenomenon of electrical nature, generally classified as ball lightning or Saint Elmo's fire, caused by stormy conditions in the area, including mist, rain, thunderstorms and lightning." The mysterious failures that occurred in the electrical systems of all of the witnesses' vehicles were caused, according to the investigators, by "wet electrical circuits."

But, as many would point out, there were no thunderstorms or lightning in the area on the night of the sightings. Ball lightning has never been known to reach 200 feet in diameter nor to sit on a public highway and take off like a rocket, nor can it cause capricious failure of a vehicle's wiring. Whatever the air force's findings, UFO experts consider the Levelland

A British woman reported a 1979 visit from elfin aliens with iridescent wings.

lights a well-documented case that cannot be explained away.

It had now been a full ten years since Kenneth Arnold had spotted silvery vehicles zooming over the Cascade Mountains, and opinion continued to be marshaled along what could only be called pro-UFO and anti-UFO lines. In 1956 a new group had joined the Aerial Phenomena Research Organization and the less well-known Civilian Saucer Investigation in their fight to bring legitimacy to UFO investigation. This fledgling organization, which was known as NICAP, for National Investigations Committee on Aerial Phenomena, was founded by T. Townsend Brown, a former navy scientist, and its growing membership included a number of individuals who possessed unimpeachable credentials.

Among them were Rear Admiral Delmer S. Fahrney, former head of the U.S. Navy's guided missile program, two other retired admirals (including the first head of the CIA, R. H. Hillenkoetter); a retired three-star Marine Corps general; a physics professor; a professor of religion; two ministers; the noted radio and television commentator Frank Edwards; and eventually Senator Barry Goldwater, who was a

In 1970 schoolboys in Malaysia allegedly saw a tiny UFO land and disgorge three aliens, each three inches tall.

reserve air force pilot. The most outspoken of the members was feisty Donald E. Keyhoe, a retired Marine Corps officer, who became the crusading head of the committee. When APRO, CSI, and NICAP entered the arena, the air force was the only government agency investigating the UFO phenomenon. But its policy of downplaying sightings and its refusal to release its findings on grounds of national security left the public little better informed than it had been when the sightings began ten years earlier. Keyhoe believed that much of the government was in league with the air force to keep the lid on UFO findings. As early as 1954, he wrote: "Actually, the Air Force is

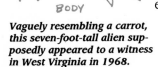

ROTATING EYES

EXPANDED AS IF BREATHING

LARGE FEET

ABOUT 7 FEET TALL

BODY

Vaguely resembling a carrot, this seven-foot-tall alien supposedly appeared to a witness in West Virginia in 1968.

not the only agency involved; the CIA, National Security Council, FBI, Civil Defense, all are tied in at top levels. The White House, of course, will have the final word as to what people are told and when."

Keyhoe took aim at the air force for its policy of secrecy, pointing to, as examples, Regulation 200-2, part of which prohibited release of UFO reports to the public, and Joint Army-Navy-Air Force Publication (JANAP) 146, which stipulated that public disclosure of any UFO sighting described on its pages was a criminal offense. He began to agitate for open congressional hearings on the whole subject of unidentified flying objects and air force secrecy.

rom the air force point of view, the time spent looking into UFO sightings was largely wasted and could have been better spent on the current cold war mission of monitoring the Soviet Union. Its research had turned up very little evidence for alien spaceships. Instead, air force investigators assumed that the flood of saucer sightings was the result of what was called Buck Rogers trauma, a phenomenon occasioned by the rapid advance of technology, unrelenting political tension, and such current science-fiction film fare as the popular *War of the Worlds.*

The lid refused to stay down on the simmering UFO controversy, however, and more close-encounter stories bubbled up after the bizarre events in Kentucky and Texas. Nor were these events confined to the North American continent, as became evident in 1959.

Nine thousand miles from the controversy in Washington, D.C., the island of New Guinea was undergoing its own wave of UFO sightings—more than sixty in all during ninety days of that southern-hemisphere winter. One of the most spectacular close-encounter stories came from the Reverend William Booth Gill, an Anglican priest, whose parish was in the territory of Papua on the Australian-controlled island.

It was about 6:45 on the evening of June 26, Gill later reported, and he had just stepped out of the mission house after finishing dinner. He looked up in the sky and "saw this sparkling object, which to me was peculiar because it sparkled, and because it was very, very bright, and it was above Venus, and so that caused me to watch it for awhile; then I saw it descend toward us." A mission teacher, Stephen Moi, joined Father Gill, and to get some idea of the size of the approaching object he put his arm straight out with his fist closed, observing that his fist covered "about half of the object." The two missionaries were soon joined by about thirty parishioners, all gazing at the astonishing sight, which was about to become more astonishing still.

Gill recorded that "men came out from this object and appeared on top of it, on what seemed to be a deck on top of the huge disk. There were four men in all, occasionally two, then one, then three, then four. . . . They seemed to be illuminated in two ways: by reflected light, as men seen working high up on a building at night caught by the glare of an oxyacetylene torch, and by this curious halo which outlined them, following every contour of their bodies."

At 8:29, nearly two hours into the sighting, a second and apparently smaller disk appeared over the ocean, and a third over nearby Wadabuna Village. The larger UFO, which Gill called the mother ship, was hovering overhead in the now-cloudy, now-clearing sky. The breathtaking spectacle held the attention of the viewers for another two and a half hours until 11:04 P.M., when a heavy Pacific rain began to fall, shutting down the aerial display.

The phenomenon returned at 6:00 on the following evening. The sun had just set, but the sky was still light. Once again the figures appeared on the upper deck of the spheroid. Father Gill, in a most human gesture, raised his arm and waved at the creatures atop the saucer. To his surprise, he reported, the four aliens responded by waving back. Later, when the sky turned dark, Gill sent for a flashlight and began signaling the craft with a series of long flashes. After a minute or two, the saucer "wavered back and forth like a pendulum"—which the witnesses interpreted as a friendly response to the signals from below. Two smaller saucers hovered overhead but did not respond to the flashlight beams.

The close encounters on that second night ended, ac-

The Oz Factor

Moviegoers can readily imagine the sense of displacement Dorothy must have felt when she was whisked out of Kansas and transported to the mysterious Land of Oz *(above)*. That feeling, says British ufologist Jenny Randles, may resemble the perceptions experienced by people who encounter—or at least believe they encounter—unidentified flying objects.

Randles says her studies show that many UFO witnesses experience what she calls the Oz factor, "a sense of timelessness and sensory isolation" in which "the witness feels the UFO has temporarily sucked him into a kind of void where only he and the phenomenon coexist." This might occur, she speculates, when a person who is in a state of consciousness below normal waking reality interprets some natural condition, object, or event—a bright planet, for instance—as being preternatural in origin.

Randles further theorizes that in some rare cases the witness's subjective impression is strong enough to manipulate objective reality. In other words, a person who is caught in the grip of the Oz factor may actually be able to photograph something that he or she sees, even though it does not, in a completely objective sense, exist.

Randles's theory—which is dismissed by most other researchers—does not rule out alien contact. On the contrary, the theory posits it as a possible source of the bizarre events that witnesses believe they experience. It may be, she says, that outworlders are contacting humans through consciousness alone rather than with sophisticated technology. These alien beings are somehow able to induce a subjectively real incidence of an encounter. If this is so, a particularly sensitive person might serve as a sort of radio receiver of cosmic messages.

*In the debris of an alleged 1948 UFO crash in Mexico lie charred remains
of an alien called Tomato Man by ufologists who doubt his extraterrestrial origins.
They point to the very earthly glasses near him.*

cording to Father Gill's log, at 7:45. "Evensong over," he wrote, "and sky covered with cloud. Visibility very poor. No UFOs in sight." The sightings had ceased, but the controversy was just beginning.

Gill and twenty-four other witnesses signed a statement attesting to what they had seen. The Royal Australian Air Force countered with a more naturalistic explanation: "An analysis of bearings and angles above the horizon," it reported, "does suggest that at least three of the lights were planets, e.g., Jupiter, Saturn and Mars." However, UFO

proponents point out in response that none of these planets is anywhere near large enough to cover half of a closed fist, nor does any slide back and forth on its axis in response to signals from the earth.

Investigator J. Allen Hynek later said that he found it difficult to believe that a well-educated Anglican priest such as Gill would fabricate the fantastic tale out of sheer intent to deceive. Indeed, Father Gill never made any attempt to convert his UFO encounter into cash, and he read no religious significance into it; he merely reported what he and the others there believed they had seen in the night skies.

Five years later, another tantalizing report of close-up sightings of humanoids emerged, this time from Socorro, New Mexico. The incident had begun at about 5:45 P.M. on April 24, 1964. On that spring evening, police officer Lonnie Zamora was in hot pursuit of a speeding car through the desert outside of Socorro when, as he later reported, he was jolted off the road by a sudden roar and a burst of blue-orange flame. Thinking that a nearby dynamite storage shack had blown up, Zamora bounced across the rugged terrain and stopped his patrol car at a gully, where he spotted an egg-shaped object squatting on the ground. Next to it he saw two figures who appeared to be wearing white coveralls. One of them "seemed to turn and look straight at my car and seemed startled—seemed to jump quickly somewhat." Thinking the vehicle might be an overturned automobile, Zamora informed the sheriff over his radio that that he was going to investigate an accident.

Hardly had he left his car, however, when he heard a loud blast. The shiny craft, ablaze underneath, started to lift off the ground. Fearing that the thing might explode, Zamora turned and ran to take cover behind his car, while the UFO continued to rise with an eerie whining and roaring. As it moved, Zamora noted some kind of red insignia about two feet square displayed on the side of the hull. "It appeared to

Onlookers await results as alleged contactee Daniel W. Fry tries to reach aliens with a multiple frequency radio device he built in the 1950s. It could send but not receive.

go in straight line and at same height—possibly 10 to 15 feet from the ground, and it cleared the dynamite shack by about three feet. . . . Object was traveling very fast. It seemed to rise up, and take off immediately across country."

New Mexico state trooper M. S. Chavez arrived on the scene shortly afterward, and he and Zamora discovered indentations in the earth and still-burning brush where the mysterious craft had apparently taken off. The place was soon crowded with investigators, who were measuring and documenting what they found. Four squarish imprints arranged in a trapezoidal pattern were assumed to be the marks of landing legs. Several smaller, shallow, circular indentations may have been the footprints of the beings in white coveralls.

Hynek personally investigated this encounter. He interviewed Zamora and confirmed the burned areas and the depressions. When he was finished, Hynek concluded that the report was one of the "major UFO sightings in the history of the air force's consideration of the subject." The air force reluctantly carried the Zamora sighting as "unidentified"—the only combination landing, trace, and occupant case listed as such in Blue Book files.

Plausible-sounding incidents such as the Gill and Zamora sightings made the air force's attitude seem unnecessarily harsh. However, the official stance was more understandable in the context of the many hoaxes and woolly claims that garnered publicity in the 1950s and 1960s. Between 1952 and 1956 alone, 3,712 UFO incidents were reported, but the general population had no way of separating fact from fantasy. Mixed in with well-documented reports were stories of alien encounters so unlikely that they generally cast a lurid light over the whole field. Such questionable tales may say more about public attitudes toward UFOs than they do about UFOs themselves.

One type of story that sprang up immediately following the Kenneth Arnold sightings was the saucer-crash/purloined-alien tale. Perhaps the most persistent of such reports grew out of the alleged crash of an unidentified flying object in Roswell, New Mexico, in 1947 *(pages 39-40)*. Some years afterward, a civil engineer named Grady Landon ("Barney") Barnett began telling his friends that on the day after the crash, he had noticed sunlight glinting from metal that was sitting motionless on the desert floor, 250 miles from Roswell. Thinking that it might be the wreckage of an aircraft, Barnett hurried to the site, where he was soon joined by some archaeology students who had been working in the area. Together, he related, they gazed at a startling and grisly still life baking in the morning sun.

The craft, described as oval and about thirty feet across, was split open like a ripe melon. Dead bodies littered the

ground; others were still in the craft. But the bodies were unlike any that Barnett and his companions had ever seen: hairless, with tiny eyes and huge heads, wearing one-piece gray coveralls with no belts or zippers. According to Barnett's friends, who spoke publicly of the incident after his death, a detail of soldiers arrived, cordoned off the area, told the civilians it was "their patriotic duty" not to mention the incident, and sent them away. What happened to the wrecked saucer and the remains of the aliens? Barnett reportedly told friends the U.S. Army took everything away in a truck. Thirty-three years after the event, authors Charles Berlitz and Wil-

liam Moore published a book on the subject, disclosing the alleged testimony of Barnett and others, and claiming that the carefully preserved bodies remained stored in a CIA warehouse in Langley, Virginia. Pronouncements of a government cover-up of this event continued to make the news well into the late 1980s—but attempts by investigators to find con-

vincing evidence or witnesses for the story have not been fruitful so far.

Publicity about the Roswell incident seemed to spawn similar reports. According to one such story, which began surfacing in certain UFO enthusiast circles in late 1978, a saucer-like craft had crash-landed in Mexico, about thirty miles from the Texas border, on July 7, 1948. Discovered in the wreckage was the charred body of an alien pilot. The debris from the accident was carted away by Mexican and American military units, but not before a young U.S. Navy photographer had taken numerous shots of the dead extraterrestrial. Supposedly, the photographer kept some of the negatives and decided thirty years after the event to make the pictures public—although he himself chose to remain anonymous. Most serious ufologists dismiss this account and the photographs as parts of a hoax; some theorize that the figure shown in the pictures *(page 72)* may actually be the burned body of a human pilot killed in a light-plane crash.

Errant saucer pilots apparently did not exclude the rest of the world when it came to disastrous landings. One crash was reported in the cold, rocky terrain of Spitsbergen, a group of arctic islands more than 500 miles to the north of Norway. Another space vehicle was said to have smashed into the earth in Poland, and its humanoid pilot was allegedly pulled from the wreckage still alive. The story claimed that the alien was rushed to a hospital, where doctors struggled to remove its metal flight suit, but when they succeeded in removing an armband, the alien expired. The body was purportedly shipped to the USSR.

Serious UFO investigators discount most such stories, which usually rely on hearsay rather than documented eyewitness accounts and whose scanty evidence is frequently shown to have been fabricated. However, many enthusiasts maintain to this day that not only are such reports true, but also the government, fearing widespread public panic, is hiding the facts about UFOs.

If the government indeed succeeded in obscuring the truth about physical evidence of alien craft and crews, it was not able to stem the increasing reports of alien creatures who were very much alive. These beings were said to seek out quite ordinary men and women and to choose them as their representatives, enjoining them to spread a kind of cosmic gospel among their fellow humans. The contactees told a

different kind of story from the relatively coherent close-encounter reports typified by the Zamora or Sutton cases. Their tales involved mystical meetings with saintly extraterrestrials and were generally contradictory, unscientific, and messianic. Few ufologists gave credence to contactees, but in spite of, or perhaps because of, this, such people often became cult figures. They wrote popular books about their experiences and appeared on radio and television talk shows beginning in the 1950s and continuing, although to a diminished degree, through to the present.

One of the first of the widely known contactees was a man by the name of George Adamski, an uneducated Polish immigrant who worked as a handyman for a small roadside restaurant near Mount Palomar in California. (Palomar, of course, is the home of the 200-inch telescope that has been probing the galaxies since 1948.) Adamski, a former cavalryman with the U.S. Army and a self-styled professor of oriental mysticism, claimed to have seen his first spacecraft in 1946. The next year, he said, he observed a large fleet of them, 184 in all, flying in neat squadrons of thirty or so each. But it was on November 20, 1952, when Adamski was sixty-one years old, that he struck extraterrestrial pay dirt.

ccording to Adamski, he and six friends were driving near Desert Center, California, when they spotted a cigar-shaped craft settling gently down on the earth about a mile from the road. Grabbing a pair of cameras, Adamski dashed off to investigate the spectacle and was soon greeted by an alien with shoulder-length blond hair wearing a kind of belted ski suit. Through telepathy and sign language, Adamski learned that the visitor was called Orthon and that he had journeyed from Venus in an attempt to get the squabbling nations of Earth to stop their testing of atomic weapons. The radiation, Orthon informed him, was interfering with the delicate ecological balance of the other planets in the solar system. The Venusian traveler told Adamski it was permissible to take pictures of his spacecraft but declined to be photographed himself, since he wished to remain incognito.

Then Orthon reboarded the metal cigar and zoomed off into space, while Adamski worked his cameras furiously.

Adamski noticed that Orthon's footprints remained in the sand. His friends just happened to have a supply of water and plaster of paris handy, and they made plaster casts for later study—though they were never able to decipher the hieroglyphics embedded in the Venusian shoe soles. Adamski's luck with his photographs of the departing spacecraft was not much better: They turned out as generally unrecognizable blurs.

At least in part because his evidence was skimpy, Adamski made no headway in bringing the practice of atomic weapons testing to a halt. His desert encounter with Orthon was only the beginning of his UFO odyssey, and he was soon making a comfortable living from lectures and books describing his fantastic voyages aboard spacecraft arriving from Mars, Jupiter, Saturn, and Venus. On one of these interplanetary excursions, Adamski said, his alien hosts flew him to the far side of the moon, where he gazed upon "cities, forests, lakes, snow-capped mountains, . . . even people strolling along the sidewalks." In 1959, when the Russians released satellite photographs of the far side of the moon that revealed its utterly barren, cratered face, Adamski had a ready rejoinder: The wily Soviets, he huffed, had retouched the prints "in order to deceive the United States."

Despite the obvious holes in Adamski's imaginative claims, he gained not only followers but imitators throughout the 1950s. Truman Bethurum, a fifty-six-year-old asphalt worker, entered the arena in 1954 with the publication of a book detailing his experiences with extraterrestrials. It all began, he said, with an encounter in the Mojave Desert. Bethurum was invited aboard a flying saucer that had been parked on the burning sands by eight, nine, or ten little men who introduced the dazed worker to their captain, a gorgeous female named Aura Rhanes who hailed from the planet Clarion. Clarion? Bethurum had never heard of it. Of course he had not—Clarion was unknown to earthly astronomers, the visitor explained, because "its orbit always placed it directly behind the sun."

The Ominous Men in Black

The visit reportedly came in 1976 while Dr. Herbert Hopkins was working as a consulting hypnotist on an alleged UFO abduction case in Maine. One night when he was home alone, the physician said, he got a telephone call from a man who claimed to represent a New Jersey UFO research group. (Hopkins would later discover that the group did not exist.) The caller asked to see Hopkins in order to discuss the abduction case with him, and the doctor assented. He would later reflect upon how odd it was that he had so readily agreed to share the matter.

At the time, however, Hopkins did not even find it odd that an extraordinary visitor was on his doorstep only seconds after the phone call ended. The man was hairless—bald, and without eyebrows or eyelashes. He wore a black suit, a black tie, and a gleaming white shirt—all immaculate and precisely pressed. "I thought, he looks like an undertaker," Hopkins said later. The man also had a dead-white face and wore what appeared to be lipstick.

Apparently put off by none of this, the doctor sat with the stranger and talked about the details of the case for some time. Eventually, Hopkins noticed that the man's speech seemed to be slowing and that his movements were unsteady as he rose to leave. His cryptic parting words to his host were, "My energy is running low. Must go now. Goodbye." Only after his guest had staggered off did Hopkins find himself shaken, cognizant at last of the incident's strangeness.

Despite certain anomalies, the mysterious visitor was not untypical of the fabled Men in Black, or MIB, as they are known—beings, outwardly human yet plainly not human, who are said to emerge as threatening presences in the lives of UFO witnesses or researchers. Since the late 1950s, MIB have become a curious adjunct of some UFO sightings and have attained near-mythic status in their own right.

Researchers have investigated more than thirty alleged MIB visits in detail. While some involve pale creatures such as the one Hopkins described, the MIB are more usually depicted as dark-skinned and somehow foreign looking, often with slanted eyes. Although they sometimes appear singly, they usually travel in threes. Many are said to show surprise and puzzlement at such mundane items as ballpoint pens and eating utensils. Nearly all have in common their somber attire of dauntingly neat black suits, black ties, and white shirts.

Some reportedly speak with peculiar accents, and their language is either excessively formal or prone to the jarring slang of dated Hollywood B movies. ("Look, boy, if you value your life and your family's too, don't talk any more about this sighting of yours," a UFO witness quotes one of the Men in Black as saying.) As reports have it, MIB personalities tend to be robotic; they usually seem neither warm nor malign. Nevertheless, they appear menacing. Some, such as the one who supposedly visited Dr. Hopkins, instill fear merely by their presence. Others supposedly intimidate their victims with threats of bodily harm, although there has never been a report of any MIB resorting to violence. In all cases, the MIB mission seems to be to dissuade people from talking about UFO experiences or seeking information about them. An early and persistent theory about the Men in Black was that they were government agents who were bent on obscuring truths about UFOs. That notion gradually lost currency, however—probably because the eccentricities of the MIB outstripped all but the most paranoid imaginings about nefarious federal conspiracies. Most present thinking is that either the encounters with MIB are illusions conjured by persons shaken by real or imagined encounters with UFOs, or they are hoaxes.

The laborer listened in wonderment as the skipper described the idyllic life lived by the Clarionites on their own planet. Why, then, he asked, would they want to visit Earth, with all its problems? Because, she explained, the Clarionites wished to reaffirm the values of marriage, family, and fidelity in the face of the "dreadful paganism" that was loose in the land. Like Orthon before her, Captain Rhanes greatly feared the possibility of atomic warfare, which would certainly create considerable confusion, as she put it, in outer space.

Bethurum was entranced by the visitors, finding them "very religious, understanding, kind, friendly and . . . trusting." By his own count, Bethurum met with his new friends on eleven separate occasions before they returned to their paradise somewhere behind the sun. George Adamski was one of the few to believe in Bethurum's tale, and he urged the contactee to rush into print with his story, which Bethurum subsequently titled *Aboard a Flying Saucer.*

With contactees and believers in extraterrestrial visitors proliferating, there arose a need on the part of these people for a gathering place, a need that was met by another contactee named George Van Tassel. During 1954 the forty-four-year-old Van Tassel was managing Giant Rock Airport in California's Mojave Desert north of Yucca Valley, and it was here that he began to construct a four-story-high domed machine he called the Integratron. Its purpose, he explained, was to "rejuvenate the old and prevent aging of the young." The intricate engineering design, which included an electrostatic armature fifty-five feet in diameter, was dictated to Van Tassel by the so-called Space People with whom he claimed to be in constant contact.

Van Tassel had twice been aboard alien craft as a guest, he said, and once had been whirled aloft to meet the Council of Seven Lights, which comprised former earthlings who were now living in a spaceship that was perpetually orbiting

Unarius leader Ruth Norman, also known as Uriel, shows an artist's rendering of the benign space fleet that, followers believe, will help solve the earth's problems.

the earth. When he hosted the first of the annual Giant Rock Space Conventions in the spring of 1954, more than 5,000 devotees appeared. During the day they listened to a nonstop series of speakers, and during the night they waited hopefully—and futilely—for the majestic sight of unidentified flying objects gliding across the sky to honor those gathered below. The conventions were attended by most of the well-known contactees, including Adamski and Bethurum, and resembled the religious camp meetings of the 1920s and 1930s.

Van Tassel enjoyed a long run with his new career as intermediary with the Space People. He died in 1970 after guest appearances on 409 radio and television programs, after writing five books on his out-of-this-world experiences, and after delivering 297 lectures in the United States and Canada. But to his great disappointment, no alien ever showed up at one of his space conventions—which ceased at his death—and the Integratron was never completed.

Still flourishing is the contactee cult called the Aetherius Society, founded in 1956 by George King, a former taxi driver, in London. King, who had an interest in Eastern mysticism, was sitting in a trancelike state one day when he allegedly received messages from extraterrestrial beings. Through them he learned, he said, that Jesus and several saints were alive and living on Venus.

King and the members of his society believe in "thought power" and "prayer power." They have built metal and wooden cosmic batteries, which are charged by the extended hands and prayers of the members. Because the batteries are said to work most effectively from mountains, Aetherians have trekked with their singular apparatus to several uplands, including Mount Kilimanjaro. They claim that their batteries have exerted a power for good in the world and have averted many catastrophes.

Even more flamboyant than the Aetherius Society is the

UFO-inspired Unarius Foundation, which is administered outside of San Diego, California, by self-described cosmic visionary Ruth Norman. Norman, also known by the name Uriel, claims that she has received transmissions from supercelestial beings and to have traveled to as many as sixty planets. Through her teachings, Norman says, earthbound humans can reach a higher spiritual plane, preferably in time to greet the thirty-three starships of the Interplanetary Confederation when they land in San Diego in the year 2001.

Bizarre as such claims may seem to the skeptical eye, they do reflect the social dimensions of belief in interplanetary UFOs. For the many followers of contactees, alien visitors apparently represent a last hope for a failing world. It is probably no coincidence that these stories first came to light in the 1950s, when society was preoccupied with the threat of the atomic bomb—nor, per-

haps, is it strange that such tales continue today.

More sinister than the contactee stories—and somewhat more respectable in the eyes of many investigators—are the tales of alien abduction and experimentation that began to spread during the 1960s. Possibly the most famous abduction tale of all was the one told by Betty Hill, age forty-one, and her thirty-nine-year-old husband, Barney.

The Hills' story began on the night of September 19, 1961, as the two were returning to their Portsmouth, New Hampshire, home from a vacation in Canada. While their car was traveling along U.S. Route 3, the couple noticed a bright, star-like object moving through the southwestern sky. Barney Hill stopped the car several times so his wife could gaze at the object through 7 × 50 binoculars. He thought it was a small airplane until it changed course and curved toward them. They were a little more than two miles from North Woodstock when the UFO slid around in front of the car and hovered to the right

Allegedly prompted by alien supporters, Gabriel Green ran for president in 1960 and 1972. He also ran for the U.S. Senate in California during 1962, garnering more than 171,000 votes. Founder-president of the California-based Amalgamated Flying Saucer Clubs of America, Inc., Green claimed both personal meetings and telepathic links with friendly extraterrestrials.

On Wimbledon Common, members of the Aetherius Society chant to charge a prayer battery with spiritual energy. Aetherians believe a so-called interplanetary parliament directs this energy toward averting catastrophes. Some have made journeys to place the batteries on mountaintops, where they are said to work best.

of the highway "eight or ten stories" (as the husband estimated) above the ground.

Barney Hill took the binoculars from his wife and stepped out onto the deserted highway for a closer look. The saucer-shaped UFO silently shifted to the left and approached the stopped car head on. Then Barney Hill got an enormous shock: Through the binoculars he could make out lit portholes along the side of the craft, and behind the portholes he could see the illuminated interior where from five to eleven humanlike figures were busily working. To Hill, the humanoids appeared to be wearing some kind of shiny black uniforms with billed caps. Their movements reminded him of German soldiers executing a military drill. From inside the car, Betty Hill could hear her husband exclaiming, "I don't believe it! I don't believe it! This is ridiculous!"

The Hills claimed that the craft came so close to them that it filled the field of view of the binoculars. Barney dashed back to the waiting car in a state of hysteria, as his wife remembered, and they took off down the highway. As they drove, a series of inexplicable beeps seemed to come from the trunk, sounds that caused the car to vibrate. The couple made it home without further incident, but those few minutes of fright and excitement were to haunt them for years.

Betty Hill began to dream nightly of a terrifying UFO experience. Barney Hill suffered from apprehension, insomnia, and a worsening of his duodenal ulcer. In reliving the incident in his own mind, Hill was disturbed when he realized that he was unable to account for more than two hours between the time they first encountered the UFO and the time they reached home. Where had the seemingly missing time

gone? What had happened?

As their anxieties grew, the Hills decided to get medical help. A local doctor recommended that they consult a prominent Boston psychiatrist, Dr. Benjamin Simon, to see if hypnotic regression could unravel the mystery surrounding the night of September 19 and allow them to pick up their lives again. The psychiatric treatments began in December 1963, more than two years after the alleged UFO encounter. It was while under deep hypnosis that Barney and Betty Hill narrated a tale much stranger than the one apparently lodged in their conscious minds. Dr. Simon kept his tape recorder going while Barney Hill described his abduction by alien captors.

Hill recounted being led up a ramp to the alien craft and ushered into an examination room. "I could feel them examining me with their hands. . . . They looked at my back, and I could feel them touching my skin . . ., as if they were counting my spinal column . . . and then I was turned over, and again I was looked at. My mouth was opened, and I could feel two fingers pulling it back. Then I heard as if some more men came in, and I could feel them rustling around on the left side of the table I was lying on. Something scratched very lightly, like a stick against my left arm. And then these men left.

"Then my shoes were put back on, and I stepped down. I think I felt very good because I knew it was over. . . . I went down [the ramp] and opened my eyes and kept walking. I saw my car . . . and Betty was coming down the road, and she came around and opened the door."

Betty Hill told a similar story of physical examination. It seemed to her that the aliens were taking samples for later

Betty and Barney Hill (top) hold a copy of The Interrupted Journey, an account of their alleged abduction by aliens in New Hampshire in 1961. At right is a sketch by an artist who heard Barney Hill describe the mysterious visitors.

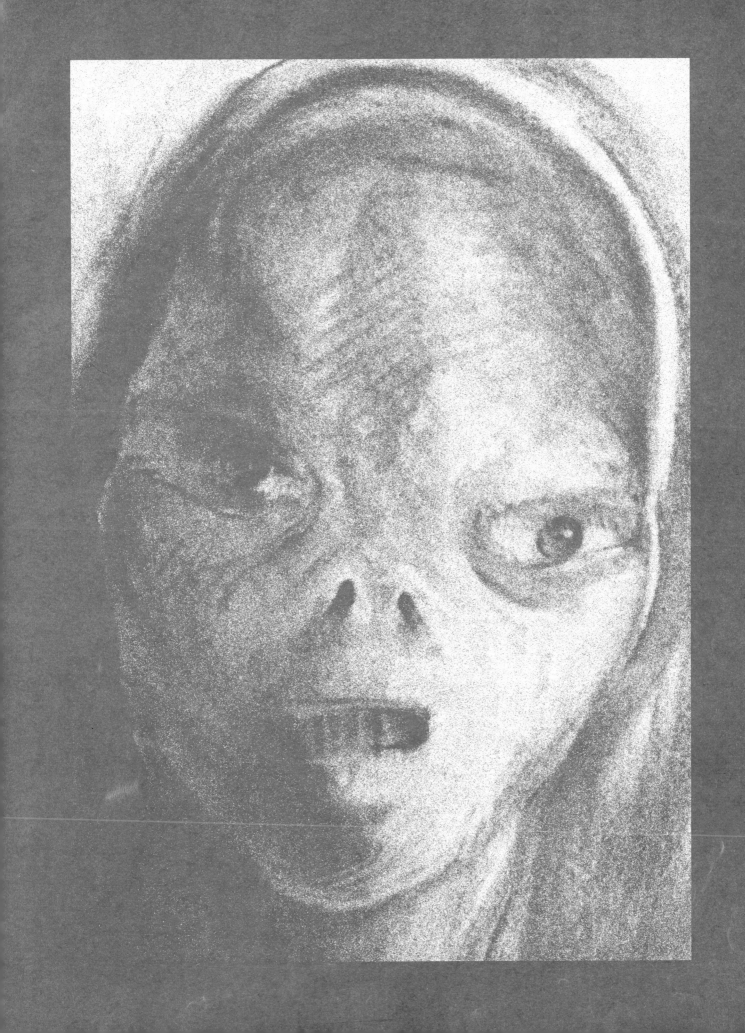

Brazilian student Antonio Villas Boas, who claimed he was abducted by aliens in 1957, recalled a bold inscription (below) that appeared over a door inside the visitors' spacecraft.

analysis. "I go into this room," she began, "and some of the men come in the room with this man who speaks English. They stay a minute—I don't know who they are; I guess maybe they're the crew . . . and another man comes in. I haven't seen him before. I think he's a doctor. They bring the machine over . . . it's something like a microscope, only a microscope with a big lens. I had an idea they were taking a picture of my skin. "Then they took something like a letter opener—only it wasn't—and they scraped my arm here . . . there was something like a piece of cellophane or plastic, or something like that, they scraped, and they put this that came off on this plastic."

Betty Hill said she asked the apparent leader where his ship had come from, and he showed her the location on a star map. Then she was escorted back down the ramp so she could return to the car.

The psychiatric examination of Betty and Barney Hill lasted six months; at the end of that time, Dr. Simon delivered his professional opinion: "The charisma of hypnosis has tended to foster the belief that hypnosis is the magical and royal road to TRUTH. In one sense, this is so, but it must be understood that hypnosis is a pathway to the truth as it is felt and understood by the patient. The truth is what he believes to be the truth, and this may or may not be consonant with the ultimate nonpersonal truth." Simon concluded that the abduction part of the Hills' story was a fantasy, absorbed by Barney from Betty's retelling of her dreams following the encounter along the lonely New Hampshire road.

Barney Hill recovered his health but died at the age of forty-six from natural causes. Years afterward, Betty Hill claimed to see UFOs again, sometimes as many as 50 to 100 a night in what she called "a special area" of New Hampshire. But she never again claimed to be the target of kidnappers from other planets.

Two particular aspects of the Hills' account have helped to give it a certain amount of credibility in the eyes of many investigators. The first of these is a star map that Betty Hill drew following her hypnotic sessions. The chart was based, she said, on the one shown to her by the alien leader. In the late 1960s, an elementary-school teacher and amateur astronomer named Marjorie Fish read of the Hills' story and decided to see if Betty's map could be matched to any nearby star system. After building a scale model of the stars within a radius of thirty-three light-years from the earth, based on the 1969 *Catalogue of Nearby Stars,* she discovered that the map corresponded closely—though not exactly—to a view of our sun and neighboring stars from a few light-years beyond the Zeta Reticuli star system.

Several astronomers verified the accuracy of Fish's model. Intriguingly enough, a number of these stars were unknown (to earthlings, at least) until the 1969 catalogue was published—in other words, eight years after the Hills' experience. To be sure, critics have argued that the match between the model and Betty Hill's star map was a lucky coincidence, but proponents of the Hills' UFO account maintain that the odds for this appear to be slim.

The second significant feature of the Hill story is that their abduction experience, unlikely as it was, came over the years to be echoed by more and more people around the world, many of them purportedly remembering the details of these traumatic events only under hypnosis. Apparently sincere and frightened people reported abductions that usually followed the consistent pattern of car failure on a lonely road, the approach of alien creatures, paralysis and transport onto an unidentified flying object, medical examination, and return to the car *(pages 57-63).*

For example, members of the Avis family were driving back to their home in Aveley, England, a town in the county of Essex, east of London, one night in 1974 when they saw a pale blue light accompanying their car. As they entered a lonely stretch of road, they passed through an eerie green mist that seemed to jolt the car. When they arrived home, they found that they had somehow lost three hours. Although they had no memory of the missing time, subsequent hypnosis brought out a tale of abduction and medical experimentation by four-foot-tall aliens.

Echoing the Avis story, with some extraordinary contactee elements thrown in, was the tale recounted by a New

84

England woman, Betty Andreasson, in the mid-1970s. Her account was so bizarre, and yet so sincere, that it thoroughly baffled an investigating team that consisted of a hypnotist, a psychiatrist, a physicist, an aerospace engineer, and others who looked into her case for a year.

Like many abductees, Betty Andreasson claimed to have only a fragmentary memory of her experience until the whole story emerged under hypnosis, many years later. According to this subsequent recollection, it all began in the winter of 1967. Betty Andreasson and her seven children were going through trying times in their home in South Ashburnham, Massachusetts, a small, wooded town in the northern part of the state. Her husband had been badly hurt in an automobile accident the previous month and was hospitalized, so Betty Andreasson's parents had joined the household to help out. The woman's main support, however, was her strong Christian faith.

On January 25, the warm air of an early thaw wrapped the little town in fog. That night, the lights in the Andreasson house flickered and went out. At the same time, a pink glow pulsed into the house through a kitchen window. Betty Andreasson's father, looking into the backyard, witnessed something amazing. According to his signed statement: "These creatures that I saw through the window of Betty's house were just like Halloween freaks. I thought they had put on a funny kind of headdress imitating a moon man . . . the one in front looked at me and I felt kind of queer. That's all I knew."

At that point, Betty Andreasson said later, her entire family fell into a sort of suspended animation. But she remained awake to see small alien beings enter her house, passing right through a closed door. She described

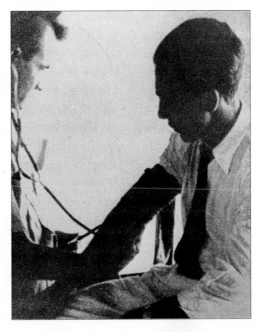

Four months after his alleged abduction, Villas Boas was examined by Dr. Olavo T. Fontes, who said the student might have suffered radiation poisoning.

the intruding creatures as short and gray skinned, with huge, slanted, catlike eyes. Their hands each had only three fingers, and their bodies were clothed in shiny, form-fitting uniforms.

The aliens communicated with the woman telepathically. They asked her, she said, to follow them so she could help the world. When she reluctantly agreed, feeling as though she was being hypnotized, the creatures led her to their oval craft in her backyard.

Like Betty and Barney Hill, Betty Andreasson reported being subjected to an unpleasant medical examination on board the craft. At one point the aliens inserted needlelike wires into her nose and navel, relieving some of the ensuing pain merely by placing their hands on her forehead. When they were finished with the exam, she said, her captors led her through a long black tunnel and into a room where she was encased in a glassy canopy. A gray fluid flowed into the canopy, covering Betty Andreasson and apparently protecting her while she and the aliens traveled to another world.

When they arrived, more tunnels led the woman and two aliens from the vehicle into an eerie, lifeless landscape. Shimmering red light surrounded them as they glided along a floating track between square buildings. Betty Andreasson was horrified to see headless creatures that resembled lemurs swarming over some of the structures—but she and her captors passed safely among them.

After moving through a circular membrane, the woman found herself amid new scenery: The atmosphere was now green, and the travelers were flanked on either side by misty bodies of water. Ahead of the party appeared a pyramid and an array of airborne crystals, which were reflecting a brilliant light. The light source lay at the end of the path, but blocking their view of it was an even more astonishing sight. A huge bird that looked like an eagle but was twice as tall as a human loomed in front of her, radiating an intense heat. Even as the woman watched, half blinded by the light, the bird vanished. In its place was a small fire, dying down to ashes; from the ashes crawled a thick gray worm.

A loud voice to her right called Betty Andreasson's name. It told her that she had been chosen, although her mission was not to be revealed to her then. When the woman proclaimed her faith in God, the voice told her that was the reason why she was chosen. No more information was given to her, and the woman's alien companions brought her back through the green and red realms to the room with the glass canopies. The apparent leader of the creatures, whose name seemed to be Quazgaa, told her that he would impart to her certain formulas that could help humanity, but only when people learned to look within the spirit.

 he return voyage, if such it was, resembled the first trip, and Betty Andreasson and her captors soon emerged into her fog-shrouded backyard. It was still nighttime, and Andreasson's family was still frozen in position inside the house. The aliens led them all to their beds and departed. In the morning, the woman said later, she remembered little of the experience. It was not until eight years afterward, when she saw an article about J. Allen Hynek's studies of unidentified flying objects, that she wrote to investigators.

Betty Andreasson could provide no corroborating evidence for her story other than the fleeting impressions of her family. She was unable to explain her phoenixlike vision or relate the message that had supposedly been implanted in her memory. Voice-stress tests and psychiatric examinations confirmed both her sanity and her sincerity, however, and those looking into her case could conclude only that she appeared to be a reliable person who believed in the truth of her experience.

Almost as bizarre was the tale told by Antonio Villas Boas, a Brazilian student who often helped out on his father's farm. He claimed to have been plowing a field by the lights of his tractor one night in 1957, when an egg-shaped UFO landed about fifteen yards away from him. The tractor's engine failed, and although Villas Boas attempted to run away, four humanoids managed to seize him and drag him struggling into their spacecraft. The creatures spoke to each other with odd barking noises while they took a blood sample and removed the young man's clothes. Villas Boas, who was already disoriented by these invasive procedures, was further astonished when the humanoids departed and another creature, who was described as a small, naked, and beautifully blond "woman," entered the room.

After some encouragement by the speechless alien, the student reported, he felt compelled to have sex with her; following this she pointed to her belly and then to the sky, leading Villas Boas to believe that she would bear his child. The humanoids then allowed him to dress, gave him a tour of the craft, and finally deposited him back in his fields as dawn was approaching.

Villas Boas felt increasingly nauseous over the next few days, and he discovered unusual wounds on his body. The doctor who examined him a few months later recorded a number of strange scars as well as symptoms resembling those typical of radiation poisoning. This medical evidence, together with the young man's reputation for honesty, has led some researchers to study the case seriously, despite the fact that its details sound incredible.

The disconcerting and frequently outlandish close encounter, contactee, and abduction stories that began to crop up in the 1950s did little to boost the credibility of UFO tales in scientific circles or in the eyes of the U.S. government. But continued sightings of a less fantastic sort fueled public interest in flying saucers until, in time, the air force would acknowledge widespread concern and sponsor an independent study of the UFO phenomenon. Unfortunately, though, the investigation would eventually stimulate the very controversy it was designed to quell, and the struggle to separate fact from fiction would persist.

Project Blue Book

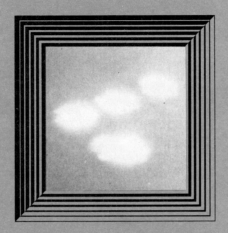

For more than twenty years, from 1948 through 1969, the United States Air Force was charged with investigating UFO reports. During most of that period, the responsibility lay with a task force code-named Project Blue Book.

Project Blue Book evolved from two previous air force studies— Projects Sign and Grudge—that had been formed to investigate UFO reports but had floundered because of inexperience and disorganized procedures. With the rash of UFO sightings in 1952, the need for a more systematic study of UFOs became apparent, and Project Blue Book was inaugurated. Led by Captain Edward J. Ruppelt, staffers developed quick, concise methods of evaluating sightings. Witnesses received an eight-page questionnaire, photographs and negatives were analyzed, and field interviews were conducted. Investigators consulted astronomical data, monitored aircraft flights, and checked weather records.

On the whole, the Project Blue Book team successfully weeded out UFO reports that were obvious hoaxes or could be attributed to natural phenomena. But the group operated under an undisguised bias that UFOs did not exist. Thus, for the small percentage of cases not readily solved, investigators had two choices: admit they had failed to identify the object or embrace any remotely feasible explanation. Both options were exercised. On the following pages is a representative sampling of Project Blue Book cases, including some of the original documentation with names deleted by the air force for reasons of confidentiality.

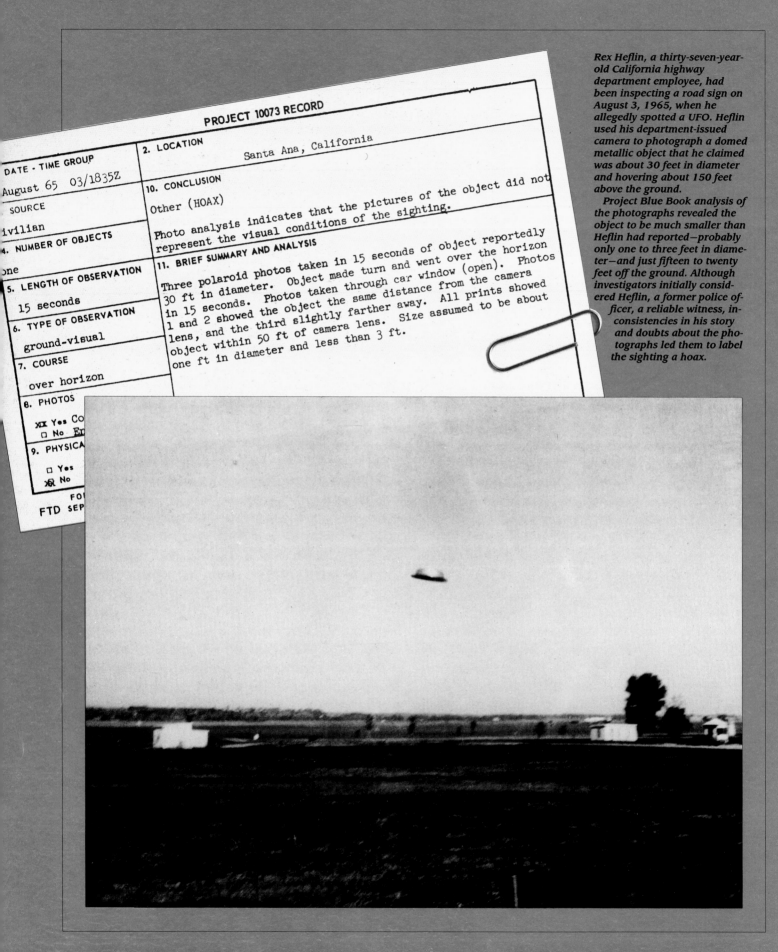

PROJECT 10073 RECORD

DATE - TIME GROUP	2. LOCATION
August 65 03/1835Z	Santa Ana, California

SOURCE

ivilian

10. CONCLUSION

Other (HOAX)

4. NUMBER OF OBJECTS

one

Photo analysis indicates that the pictures of the object did not
represent the visual conditions of the sighting.

5. LENGTH OF OBSERVATION

15 seconds

11. BRIEF SUMMARY AND ANALYSIS

6. TYPE OF OBSERVATION

ground-visual

Three polaroid photos taken in 15 seconds of object reportedly
30 ft in diameter. Object made turn and went over the horizon
in 15 seconds. Photos taken through car window (open). Photos
1 and 2 showed the object the same distance from the camera
lens, and the third slightly farther away. All prints showed
object within 50 ft of camera lens. Size assumed to be about
one ft in diameter and less than 3 ft.

7. COURSE

over horizon

8. PHOTOS

XX Yes Co
☐ No Er

9. PHYSICA

☐ Yes
XX No

FO
FTD SEP

Rex Heflin, a thirty-seven-year-old California highway department employee, had been inspecting a road sign on August 3, 1965, when he allegedly spotted a UFO. Heflin used his department-issued camera to photograph a domed metallic object that he claimed was about 30 feet in diameter and hovering about 150 feet above the ground.

Project Blue Book analysis of the photographs revealed the object to be much smaller than Heflin had reported—probably only one to three feet in diameter—and just fifteen to twenty feet off the ground. Although investigators initially considered Heflin, a former police officer, a reliable witness, inconsistencies in his story and doubts about the photographs led them to label the sighting a hoax.

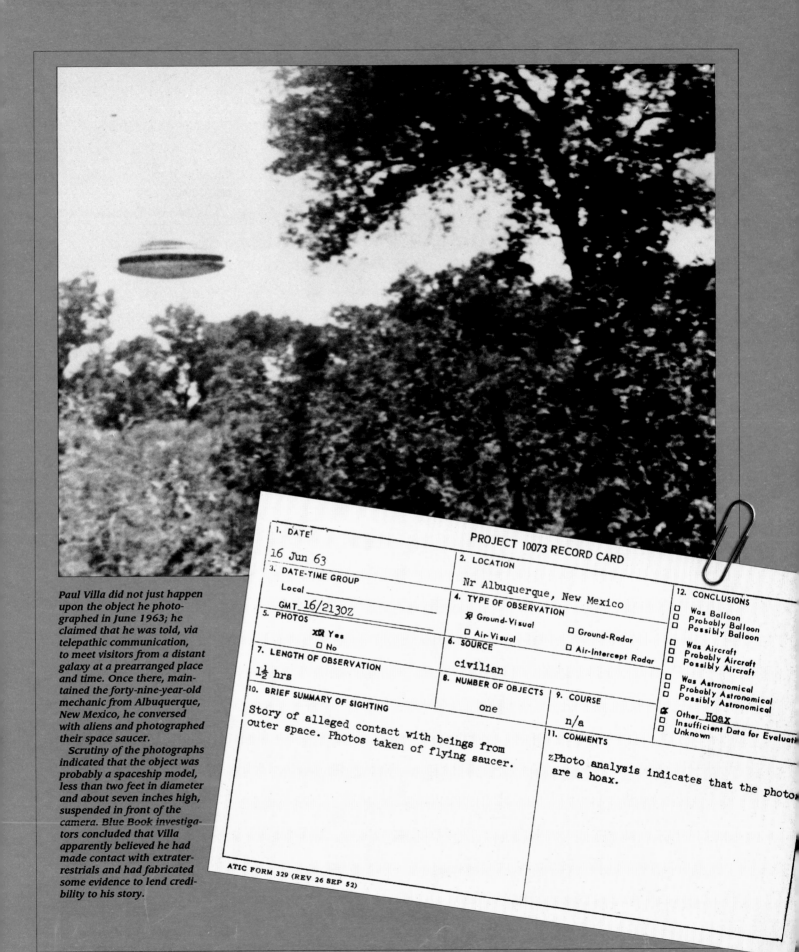

Paul Villa did not just happen upon the object he photographed in June 1963; he claimed that he was told, via telepathic communication, to meet visitors from a distant galaxy at a prearranged place and time. Once there, maintained the forty-nine-year-old mechanic from Albuquerque, New Mexico, he conversed with aliens and photographed their space saucer.

Scrutiny of the photographs indicated that the object was probably a spaceship model, less than two feet in diameter and about seven inches high, suspended in front of the camera. Blue Book investigators concluded that Villa apparently believed he had made contact with extraterrestrials and had fabricated some evidence to lend credibility to his story.

PROJECT 10073 RECORD CARD

1. DATE 16 Jun 63	**2. LOCATION** Nr Albuquerque, New Mexico
3. DATE-TIME GROUP Local ____ GMT 16/2130Z	**4. TYPE OF OBSERVATION** ☒ Ground-Visual ☐ Air-Visual ☐ Ground-Radar ☐ Air-Intercept Radar
5. PHOTOS ☒ Yes ☐ No	**6. SOURCE** civilian
7. LENGTH OF OBSERVATION 1½ hrs	**8. NUMBER OF OBJECTS** one **9. COURSE** n/a

10. BRIEF SUMMARY OF SIGHTING
Story of alleged contact with beings from outer space. Photos taken of flying saucer.

11. COMMENTS
zPhoto analysis indicates that the photos are a hoax.

12. CONCLUSIONS
☐ Was Balloon
☐ Probably Balloon
☐ Possibly Balloon
☐ Was Aircraft
☐ Probably Aircraft
☐ Possibly Aircraft
☐ Was Astronomical
☐ Probably Astronomical
☐ Possibly Astronomical
☒ Other Hoax
☐ Insufficient Data for Evaluation
☐ Unknown

ATIC FORM 329 (REV 26 SEP 52)

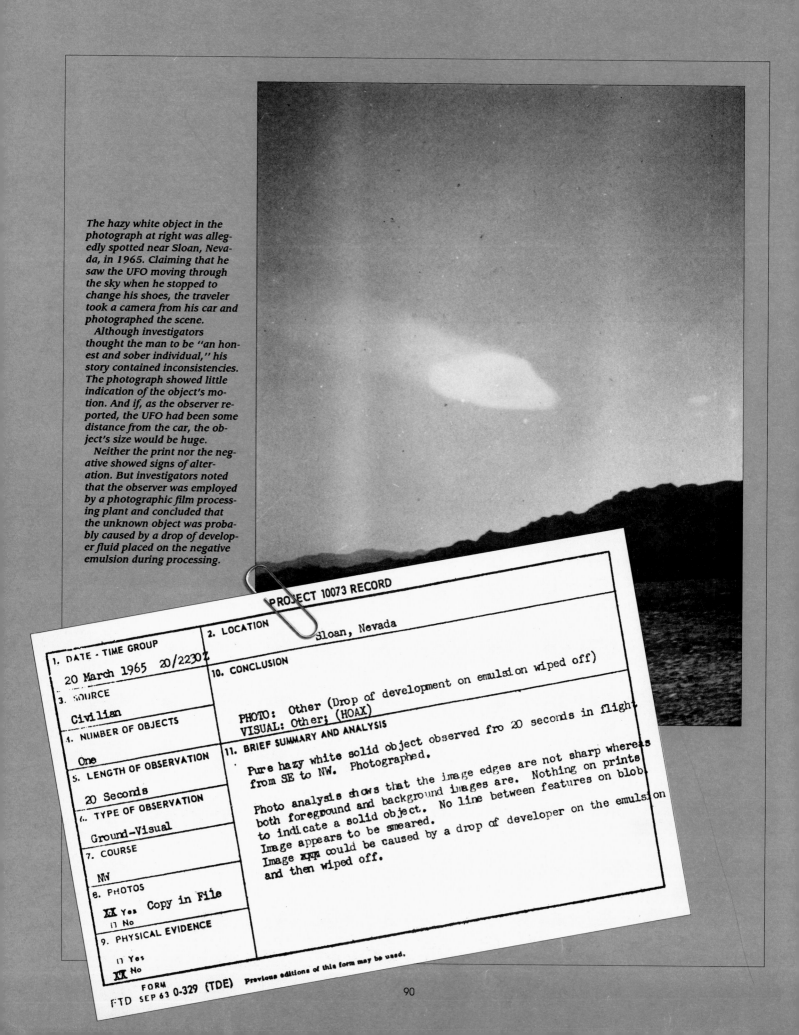

The hazy white object in the photograph at right was allegedly spotted near Sloan, Nevada, in 1965. Claiming that he saw the UFO moving through the sky when he stopped to change his shoes, the traveler took a camera from his car and photographed the scene.

Although investigators thought the man to be "an honest and sober individual," his story contained inconsistencies. The photograph showed little indication of the object's motion. And if, as the observer reported, the UFO had been some distance from the car, the object's size would be huge.

Neither the print nor the negative showed signs of alteration. But investigators noted that the observer was employed by a photographic film processing plant and concluded that the unknown object was probably caused by a drop of developer fluid placed on the negative emulsion during processing.

PROJECT 10073 RECORD

1. DATE - TIME GROUP 20 March 1965 20/2230Z	**2. LOCATION** Sloan, Nevada
3. SOURCE Civilian	**10. CONCLUSION** PHOTO: Other (Drop of development on emulsion wiped off) VISUAL: Other; (HOAX)
4. NUMBER OF OBJECTS One	**11. BRIEF SUMMARY AND ANALYSIS** Pure hazy white solid object observed fro 20 seconds in flight from SE to NW. Photographed.
5. LENGTH OF OBSERVATION 20 Seconds	Photo analysis shows that the image edges are not sharp whereas both foregpound and background images are. Nothing on prints to indicate a solid object. No line between features on blob.
6. TYPE OF OBSERVATION Ground-Visual	Image appears to be smeared. Image xxx could be caused by a drop of developer on the emulsion and then wiped off.
7. COURSE NW	
8. PHOTOS XX Yes Copy in File ☐ No	
9. PHYSICAL EVIDENCE ☐ Yes XX No	

FORM
FTD SEP 63 0-329 (TDE)   Previous editions of this form may be used.

90

PROJECT 10073 RECORD CARD

1. DATE
26 Sep 60

2. LOCATION
Italy

3. DATE-TIME GROUP
Local 1400
GMT 26/1300Z

4. TYPE OF OBSERVATION
☒ Ground-Visual
☐ Air-Visual
☐ Ground-Radar
☐ Air-Intercept Radar

5. PHOTOS
☒ Yes
☐ No

6. SOURCE
Civilian

7. LENGTH OF OBSERVATION
---

8. NUMBER OF OBJECTS
three

9. COURSE
---

12. CONCLUSIONS
☐ Was Balloon
☐ Probably Balloon
☐ Possibly Balloon
☐ Was Aircraft
☐ Probably Aircraft
☐ Possibly Aircraft
☐ Was Astronomical
☐ Probably Astronomical
☐ Possibly Astronomical
☒ Other Prob Hoax.
☐ Insufficient Data for Evaluation
☐ Unknown

10. BRIEF SUMMARY OF SIGHTING
Photos taken on 9-26-60 at 1400. Shape was round, about 15 meters in diameter. Photographed with a shutter of 6.5, time 1/250, distance infinite.

11. COMMENTS
Too little information to allow valid conclusion. Photo analysts state: objects either very small and close to camera or moving rapidly due to their being out of focus. Due to objects being much darker than other dark areas, negative or original print was possibly retouched. In one print, objects size increased, indicating they were closer to camera than in other print. However, other objects in print also increased in size, indicating that camera was moved toward background. Also in this print background appears overexposed, but objects are just as dark. Probably result of someone attempting a hoax.

ATIC FORM 329 (REV 26 SEP 52)

Photographs of supposed UFOs sometimes arrived at Project Blue Book headquarters with only the sparsest information about the sighting. While this made it difficult for investigators to reach a solid conclusion, each such case was usually given at least a cursory examination. One of these involved a photograph taken in Italy in September 1960.

According to the cover letter, the three domed objects in the photograph were round and about fifty feet in diameter. But after noting that the alleged UFOs were much darker than anything else in the print, and not in focus, photo analysts decided that the negative may have been retouched. The sighting was ruled a probable hoax.

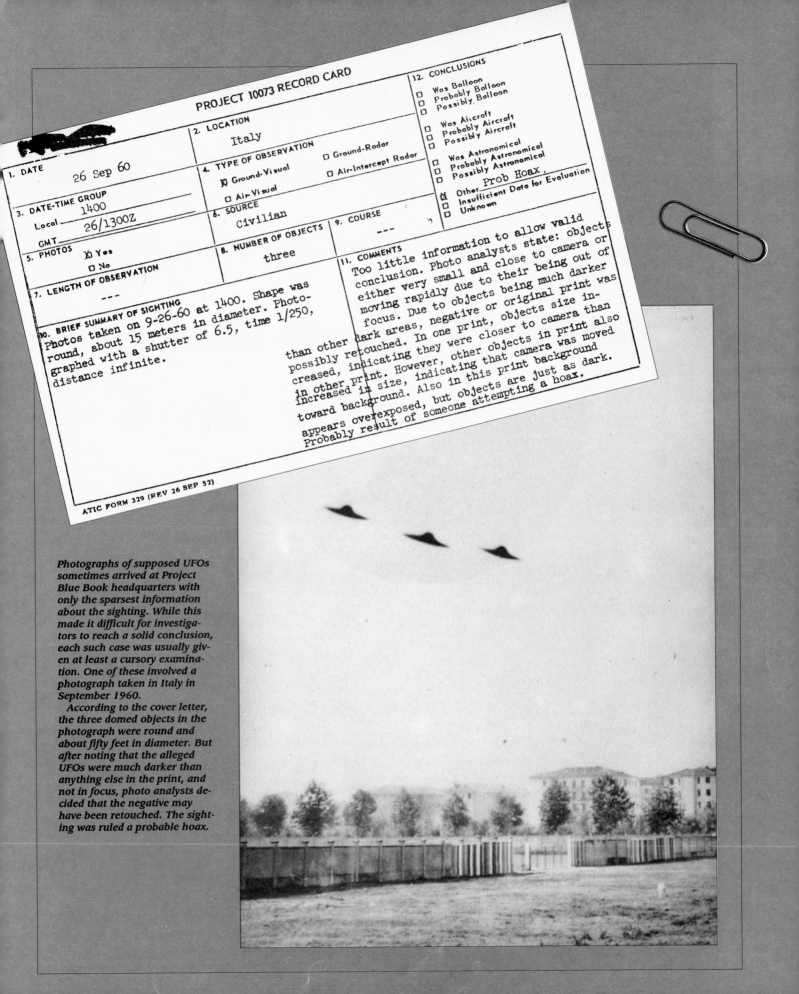

PROJECT 10073 RECORD CARD

		12. CONCLUSIONS
1. DATE 18 Mar 59	**2. LOCATION** Denville, NJ	☐ Was Balloon ☐ Probably Balloon ☐ Possibly Balloon
3. DATE-TIME GROUP Local 2050 EST GMT 19/0150Z	**4. TYPE OF OBSERVATION** ☒ Ground-Visual ☐ Ground-Radar ☐ Air-Visual ☐ Air-Intercept Radar	☐ Was Aircraft ☐ Probably Aircraft ☐ Possibly Aircraft ☐ Was Astronomical ☐ Probably Astronomical ☐ Possibly Astronomical
5. PHOTOS ☒ Yes ☐ No	**6. SOURCE** Civilian	☒ Other Static Electric ☐ Insufficient Data for Evaluation ☐ Unknown
7. LENGTH OF OBSERVATION N/A	**8. NUMBER OF OBJECTS** 34 **9. COURSE**	
10. BRIEF SUMMARY OF SIGHTING Photograph submitted w/34 objs appearing to race away fm the moon. Objs were not noticed until after film was developed.		**11. COMMENTS** Static electric discharge was arrived at as the cause by photo analysis section.

On a clear, crisp March evening in 1959, amateur astronomer Jesse Wilson decided to photograph the moon through his telescope. He noticed nothing unusual as he peered through the camera's viewfinder, fitted against the telescope's eyepiece. Later, however, he discovered that one print from the roll of film revealed a string of thirty-four bright objects, arcing in a line away from the moon.

Wilson had his equipment checked for light leaks, and he studied the print and negative under magnification. Finding no mechanical reason for the spots, he sent the photograph to Project Blue Book.

Photographic experts considered and ruled out many explanations, including static electricity in the camera. Unable to find a logical cause for the objects, however, Project Blue Book ultimately settled on static electricity as the culprit.

The brilliant illumination of their Island Park, New York, home roused a sleeping couple one night in August 1965. They looked out a window into the cloudless sky, where, they later reported, they saw four lights appearing one by one. The lights remained visible for two hours, ample time to capture them on film. Although the lights looked round to the observers, they appeared as odd linear shapes in the resulting photograph. Air force investigators concluded that the irregular shapes were due to camera movement. The lights themselves could not be positively identified and were arbitrarily attributed to ground lights reflected in the night sky.

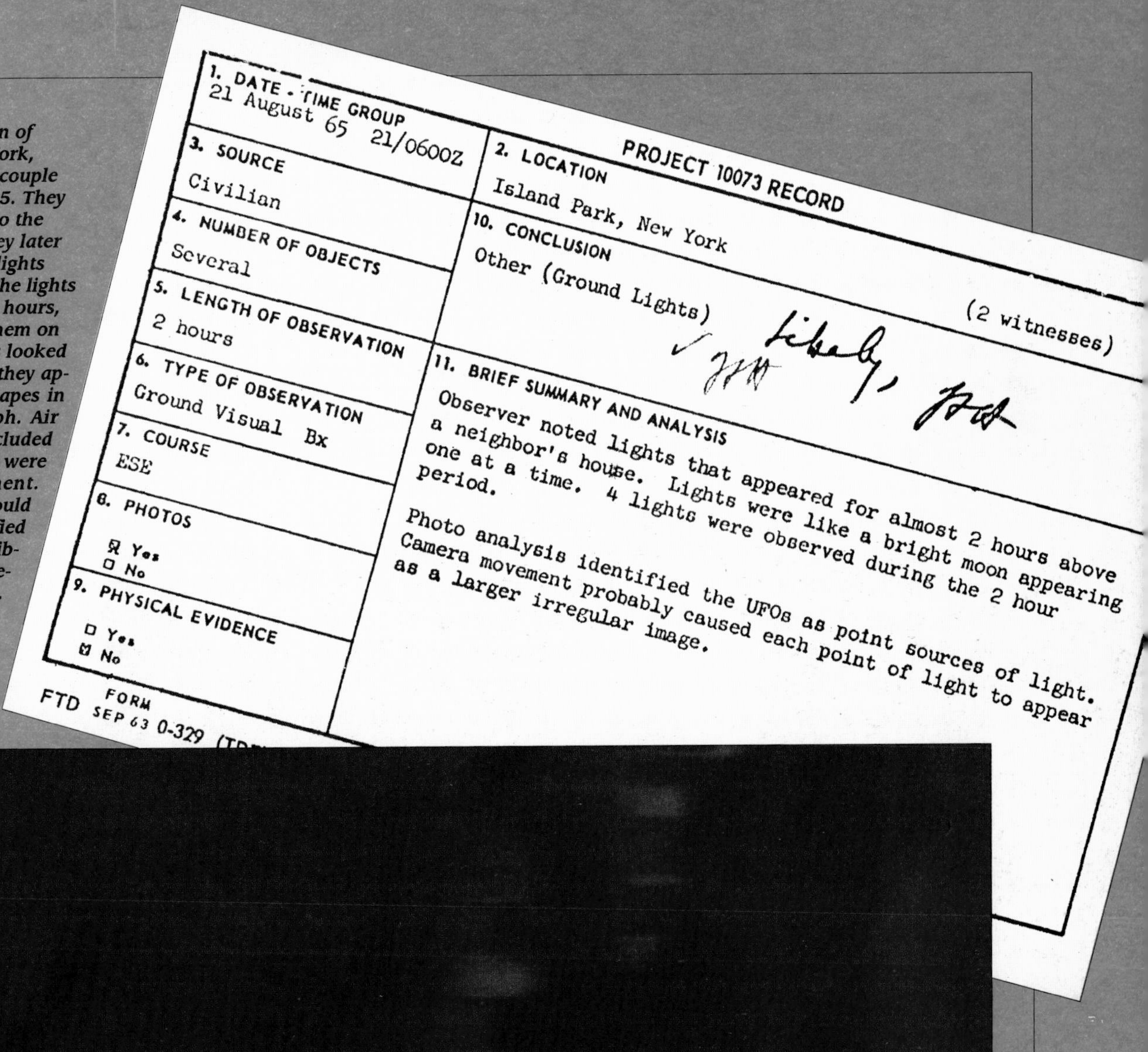

PROJECT 10073 RECORD

1. DATE - TIME GROUP 21 August 65 21/0600Z	2. LOCATION Island Park, New York
3. SOURCE Civilian	10. CONCLUSION Other (Ground Lights)
4. NUMBER OF OBJECTS Several	(2 witnesses)
5. LENGTH OF OBSERVATION 2 hours	*Likely, ...*

11. BRIEF SUMMARY AND ANALYSIS

6. TYPE OF OBSERVATION
Ground Visual Bx

7. COURSE
ESE

8. PHOTOS
☒ Yes
☐ No

9. PHYSICAL EVIDENCE
☐ Yes
☒ No

FORM
FTD SEP 63 0-329 (TD...

Observer noted lights that appeared for almost 2 hours above a neighbor's house. Lights were like a bright moon appearing one at a time. 4 lights were observed during the 2 hour period.

Photo analysis identified the UFOs as point sources of light. Camera movement probably caused each point of light to appear as a larger irregular image.

93

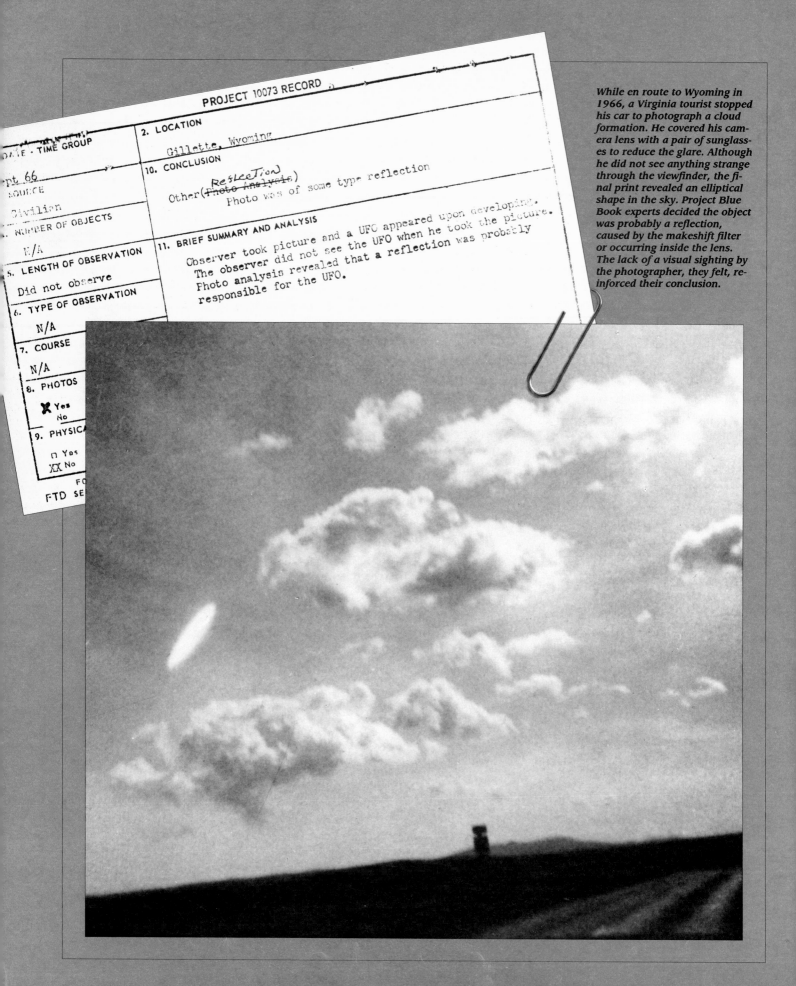

PROJECT 10073 RECORD

DATE - TIME GROUP	**2. LOCATION**
pt. 66	Gillette, Wyoming
SOURCE	**10. CONCLUSION**
Civilian	Reflection Other (~~Photo Analysis~~) Photo was of some type reflection
NUMBER OF OBJECTS	
N/A	**11. BRIEF SUMMARY AND ANALYSIS**
5. LENGTH OF OBSERVATION	Observer took picture and a UFO appeared upon developing.
Did not observe	The observer did not see the UFO when he took the picture.
6. TYPE OF OBSERVATION	Photo analysis revealed that a reflection was probably
N/A	responsible for the UFO.
7. COURSE	
N/A	
8. PHOTOS	
X Yes No	
9. PHYSICA	
☐ Yes XX No	

FTD SE

While en route to Wyoming in 1966, a Virginia tourist stopped his car to photograph a cloud formation. He covered his camera lens with a pair of sunglasses to reduce the glare. Although he did not see anything strange through the viewfinder, the final print revealed an elliptical shape in the sky. Project Blue Book experts decided the object was probably a reflection, caused by the makeshift filter or occurring inside the lens. The lack of a visual sighting by the photographer, they felt, reinforced their conclusion.

When teenage brothers Dan and Grant Jaroslaw photographed a suspended spaceship model near their Michigan home in 1967, they had no idea how far the joke would go. Their mother, thinking the pictures were real, alerted the newspapers; Project Blue Book came to call soon afterward. Scrutiny of the prints failed to identify the object, and even scientific consultant J. Allen Hynek was baffled. "Analysis so far does not show any indication of an obvious hoax," Hynek told reporters.

Reluctant to admit they were stumped, investigators stamped the case "insufficient data for evaluation." Nine years later the case was closed when the Jaroslaw brothers confessed their prank.

1. DATE - TIME GROUP	PROJECT 10073 RECORD	
9 Jan 67 1930Z	2. LOCATION	
3. SOURCE	Mt. Clemens, Michigan	
Civilian	10. CONCLUSION (2 witnesses)	
4. NUMBER OF OBJECTS	PHOTO (INSUFFICIENT DATA FOR EVALUATION, ORIGINAL PHOTOGRAPHS NOT RECEIVED)	
One	VISUAL: INSUFFICIENT DATA FOR EVALUATION	
5. LENGTH OF OBSERVATION	The measurement of the image does not substantiate the description given by the witnesses.	
Ten minutes	11. BRIEF SUMMARY AND ANALYSIS	
6. TYPE OF OBSERVATION	Two witnesses watched a dark gray colored, disk shaped object hover at a low altitude and finally move off very fast to the southeast. Photograph was taken of the alleged UFO; however detailed investigation of copies of the original indicated a possible hoax.	
ground visual		
7. COURSE		
Southeast	The case is being carried in Air Force files as insufficient data for evaluation since the original photographs were never analyzed by the Air Force.	
8. PHOTOS ☒ Yes Original negatives not received ☐ No		
9. PHYSICAL EVIDENCE ☐ Yes ☒ No		
FORM FTD SEP 63 0-329 (TDE) Previous editions of this form may be used.		

95

In 1962, Project Blue Book investigators were asked to review a UFO report filed by three young boys in Sheffield, England. The boys, allegedly intending to photograph a pet dog, claimed to have spied five peculiar objects in the sky and recorded them instead. Investigators from the British Air Ministry had uncovered no evidence that the photograph or negative had been altered.

Project Blue Book experts confirmed the photograph's authenticity and were at a loss to explain the objects. Rather than admit defeat, however, they cited a lack of sufficient information about the case. Ten years later, it was revealed that the objects were actually shapes painted on a windowpane.

1. DATE - TIME GROUP	2. LOCATION
4 March 62	Sheffield, England
3. SOURCE	10. CONCLUSION
Civilian	INSUFFICIENT DATA FOR EVALUATION
4. NUMBER OF OBJECTS	Negatives not with prints. No request made for phot
Multiple	Insufficient data for evaluation.
5. LENGTH OF OBSERVATION	11. BRIEF SUMMARY AND ANALYSIS
Not Stated	Photos submitted with letter requesting evaluation.
6. TYPE OF OBSERVATION	
Ground-Visual	
7. COURSE	
N/A	
8. PHOTOS	
XX Yes	
☐ No	
9. PHYSICAL EVIDENCE	
☐ Yes	
XXX No	

FORM
FTD SEP 63 0-329 (TDE) Previous editions of this form may be used.

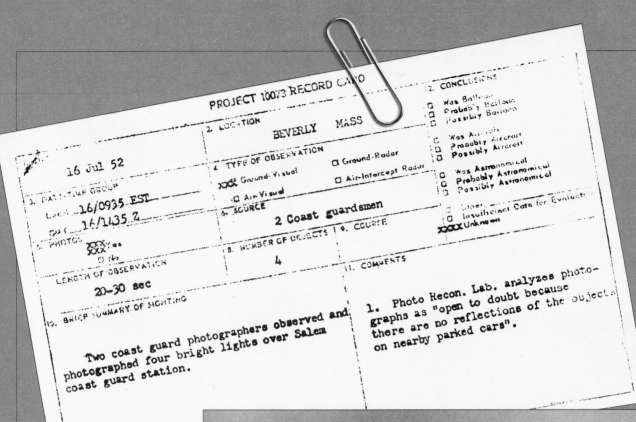

One case investigated during Project Blue Book's busiest month—July 1952—involved a Coast Guard photographer named Shell Alpert in Salem, Massachusetts. Alpert claimed to have seen four brilliant lights through his office window; they suddenly dimmed as he prepared to photograph them. He went to fetch a colleague, and as the two men entered the room, the lights shone again. Alpert snapped his picture; then the lights disappeared.

Analysts believed that the photograph had probably been faked by means of double exposure. Perhaps dissatisfied with their hasty first evaluation, investigators reviewed the case again eleven years later. They discounted the possibility of a hoax and concluded that the lights were, in fact, interior reflections on the window glass.

CHAPTER 4

A Deepening Controversy

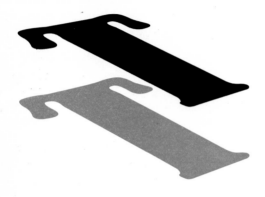

he 1960s were, to say the least, a turbulent time for the United States. There was unprecedented prosperity—never had an economic boom gone on so long—yet at the same time violent protests against poverty and racial segregation convulsed such major cities as Los Angeles and Detroit. The perceived threat of nuclear war with the Soviet Union eased, but America's entanglement in Vietnam was costing more in money and blood than anyone had intended, and seemingly could not be controlled. Science progressed dramatically as humankind reached for the moon, while a lengthening list of political leaders fell victim to assassins' bullets. Along with it all, beginning in 1965, came one of the great waves of UFO sightings. Since 1958, the number of cases reported to Project Blue Book had been averaging 514 per year; there were nearly that many in the summer alone of 1965.

The air force had long demonstrated that it did not want this job. The entire national program was being run out of Wright-Patterson Air Force Base in Ohio by an officer, a sergeant, and a secretary. Its usual response to a sighting was to dispatch an officer from the nearest air force base to take a cursory look around, then issue an immediate explanation—one that often had little or no credibility even with the casually interested—or refuse to comment. UFO enthusiasts continued to mutter darkly of a massive cover-up on the part of the U.S. government.

Far larger numbers of people thought the subject deserved better research. With astronauts virtually commuting to outer space, and the moon about to become a landing field for human explorers, public expectations of a complete explanation of the stubborn mystery of UFOs steadily escalated.

The pressure could not be bottled up indefinitely. During the next few years, matters seemed to come to a head: The U.S. Congress, sensitive to the growing public dissatisfaction, responded with two separate investigations; the air force contracted with the University of Colorado for an impartial, scientific review of the whole subject; and American journalists, finding all this irresistible, wrote copiously about the sightings, the investigators, and the investigations of the investigators. Surely no mystery, even one as intractable as UFOs, could withstand such sophisticated attention.

The flurry began early on the morning of September 3, 1965, in southeastern New Hampshire, not far from that state's minuscule share of the Atlantic shore. Norman J. Muscarello, eighteen, was hitchhiking home to the small town of Exeter from Amesbury, Massachusetts, about twelve miles away. Few cars were traveling Route 150 through the countryside after midnight; Muscarello had to walk most of the way. He had only about two miles to go when he saw it.

An enormous sphere rose like a red moon from behind some trees. But it was no moon. It pitched forward and hovered over a nearby house belonging to Clyde Russell, illuminating it with brilliant red light. Muscarello reckoned the thing was eighty or ninety feet long, much bigger than Russell's house, and noted a belt of blinking red lights around its girth. He had no idea what it was, but he knew it was no ordinary aircraft, for it yawed and careened clumsily and generated no engine noise. Suddenly, it appeared to lurch toward him, and Muscarello dived into the ditch for cover. But the craft disappeared behind the trees.

Muscarello got up, ran to the Russell house, and pounded frantically on the front door, screaming for help. There was no response. He saw headlights coming up the road, dashed out, and flagged down the car. It stopped, and the couple in it gave him a ride into Exeter. At 2:25 A.M., a badly shaken Muscarello stumbled into the Exeter police station and began babbling about having seen a UFO.

The patrolman on desk duty, Reginald Toland, listened to the scrambled

story and asked the youth how many beers he had had to drink. "Look," Muscarello pleaded, "I know you don't believe me. I don't blame you. But you got to send somebody back out there with me!" Toland put no stock in the story but could see that the boy was genuinely scared, and it was a slow night. He called in a patrol car.

Minutes later, officer Eugene Bertrand arrived at the station. And it turned out that he had something to add to Muscarello's story. An hour or so earlier, while patrolling the outskirts of Exeter, he had spotted a car parked alongside a highway. Upon checking, he found a woman sitting in it, too distraught to drive. She told Bertrand she had been followed for about twelve miles from Epping, New Hampshire, by a glowing red object. It hovered over her car until she reached Exeter, then shot straight up and disappeared. Bertrand had dismissed her story, not even bothering to report it to the station. Now, listening to Muscarello, he began to wonder.

Bertrand drove Muscarello back to the field where the boy claimed to have seen the UFO. It was a clear night with very little wind. The moon had gone down sometime before midnight, and the stars shone brightly. Bertrand parked the cruiser near a telephone pole and told Toland by radio that he could not see anything unusual. But Muscarello was still upset.

The patrol officer walked with him toward the woods, across a farm field owned by Carl Dining. When they reached a horse corral, Bertrand flicked his flashlight around and tried to persuade Muscarello that

A giant oval looming over a field bathes the New Hampshire landscape in a blood-red glow. This UFO, o.

...others like it, was seen by many local witnesses in 1965 in what came to be known as the "Exeter incident."

he had probably seen a helicopter. Muscarello protested that he knew aircraft and how they flew, and that what he had seen was definitely not a helicopter or one of the aircraft stationed at Pease Air Force Base about ten miles to the northeast. Then, as Bertrand told it later, the horses in the corral began kicking and whinnying, dogs in the nearby yards began howling, and Muscarello screamed, "I see it! I see it!"

Bertrand whirled and saw, rising slowly from behind the trees, a brilliant, round object. Silently, it wobbled toward them as a leaf flutters from a tree, bathing the landscape in

Officers David Hunt (left) and Eugene Bertrand of the Exeter police department stand by a squad car on Route 150 in southern New Hampshire, where, in September 1965, they allegedly saw a UFO.

crimson light. Bertrand, an air force veteran who had served aboard KC-97 tankers, was so frightened that he reflexively grabbed for his revolver. Then he thought better of that and ran with Muscarello back to the cruiser.

"My God!" Bertrand yelled into his radio, "I see the damn thing myself!" Then he and Muscarello watched, enthralled, as the object hovered eerily about 100 feet above the ground, 300 feet away from them. It rocked silently back and forth, its brilliant red lights flashing sequentially. They were so bright, Bertrand said later, that he could not determine the exact shape of the object; it was, he said, "like trying to describe a car with its headlights coming at you."

Another patrolman, David Hunt, had been listening to the radio traffic and had decided to have a look. As he pulled up and jumped out of his car, he said later, "I could see those pulsating lights. I could hear those horses kicking out in the barn there. Those dogs were really howling. Then it started moving, slow-like, across the tops of the trees, just above the trees. It was rocking when it did this. A creepy type of look. Airplanes don't do this."

Bertrand was unwilling to believe his eyes. "Your mind is telling you this can't be true, and yet you're seeing it," he said later. "I kept telling Dave, What is that, Dave? What do you think? He'd say, I don't know. I have never seen an aircraft like that before, and I know damn well they haven't changed that much since I was in the service." The object finally moved out toward the ocean. "We waited awhile," said Hunt. "A B-47 came over. You could tell the difference. There was no comparison."

Shortly after the overwrought message from Bertrand, Officer Toland received another call back at the station—this one from a night telephone operator in Exeter. "Some man had just called her," Toland reported later, "and he was so hysterical he could hardly talk straight. He told her that a flying saucer came right at him, but before he could finish, he was cut off." The caller had been at a pay phone in Hampton, about seven miles east of Exeter. Toland notified the Hampton police and Pease Air Force Base.

The hysterical man was never located, but that night and for several days afterward, other people reported similar sightings. The next day two air force officers interviewed Muscarello, Bertrand, and Hunt, then returned, tight-lipped, to the base. Under air force regulations, official comment could be made only from the office of the secretary of the air force in Washington. No one knew when that might come.

But because of the number of witnesses involved, their credibility, and the convincing detail of their reports, the story could not be ignored. It was picked up by the national news services, and among the people intrigued by it was John Fuller, a columnist for the magazine *Saturday Review*. Fuller published his own carefully researched version of what came to be known as the "Exeter incident," then decided to investigate even more extensively.

He was hardly alone. The National Investigations Committee on Aerial Phenomena (NICAP), headquartered in Washington, D.C., had already assigned one of its investigators to the case. Despite its imposing name, NICAP had no official status; it was an organization of private citizens who were convinced that UFO sightings were not being properly studied. A volunteer NICAP investigator from Massachusetts, Raymond E. Fowler, visited Exeter, collected signed statements from the witnesses, and compiled a thorough eighteen-page report. Fowler was impressed by the quality of the sighting. He told Fuller that "both the officers are intelligent, capable, and seem to know what they're talking about." Others were not so impressed. A local reporter who knew that a pilot often flew around the Exeter area towing an illuminated advertising sign suggested that that was what everyone had been seeing. Aside from the fact that there was no resemblance between the sign and the descriptions of the object, it was later confirmed that the aircraft and the sign had been on the ground when the sightings occurred.

Then there was the air force. It took its usual uninterested stance, despite the proximity of these reported aerial phenomena to Pease Air Force Base—a Strategic Air Command bomber base, home to B-47s and B-

Veteran news reporter Virginia Hale was washing dishes one evening in 1965 when she glanced out her kitchen window in Hampton and reportedly saw a glowing saucer-shaped object in the twilight sky.

Among the first to see a UFO during the Exeter incident was Norman Muscarello. He was hitchhiking before dawn on September 3 when, he said, a huge object with pulsing red lights appeared in the sky.

52s. Several witnesses reported having observed, in addition to the big red UFO, a number of jet fighters in the sky that night. Area residents were used to seeing bombers but not fighters; the presence of interceptors suggested that they had been sent up from other bases to investigate the UFOs, although the air force emphatically denied this.

There was other evidence, however, that the air force was intensely interested in the incident at Exeter. Air force officers were seen for a time prowling the roads where the sightings had taken place. Two of them—a colonel and a major—got into an angry exchange with some local residents when the colonel insisted that what everyone had taken for a UFO was just the glare of landing lights at the base. In the face of vociferous denials, the colonel sent the major off to have the runway marker lights and approach strobes (which provide visual assistance to pilots in all kinds of weather) turned on and off for a fifteen-minute period. Neither the colonel nor anyone else present saw a thing. In due course, the air force issued its official pronouncement on the Exeter sightings. In fact, the statement made at the Pentagon on October 27, 1965, offered several explanations, all of them natural. To begin with, said a spokesman, multiple aircraft had been in the area because of a Strategic Air Command training exercise. Moreover, there had been a weather inversion, in which cold air is trapped between warm layers of air, causing stars and planets to "dance and twinkle." In conclusion, he said, "We believe what the people saw that night were stars and planets in unusual formations." He offered no specifics about these so-called unusual formations.

 ater checking revealed that the training exercise, which had been run out of Westover Air Force Base at Springfield, Massachusetts, more than 100 air miles from Exeter, was over by 2:00 A.M., well before officers Bertrand and Hunt had observed the UFO. As to the dancing planets in unusual formations, there was nothing to check. Patrolmen Bertrand and Hunt, deeply embarrassed by the belittling official explanation of their frightening experience, wrote a letter of protest to the air force. Approximately three months later, they received an apology of sorts. Signed by a lieutenant colonel in an air force public-information office, it said: "Based on additional information you submitted to our UFO investigation office at Wright-Patterson Air Force Base, Ohio, we have been unable to identify the object you observed on September 3, 1965."

But, it went on to say, virtually all such reports in the past had turned out to be man-made objects, or the product of atmospheric conditions, or meteors. And, in conclusion, "Thank you for reporting your observation to the Air Force." John Fuller's book *Incident at Exeter* stimulated a third and more serious attempt to explain what all those people had seen. The book was read carefully by, among many others,

Philip J. Klass—an electrical engineer and senior editor of the technical journal *Aviation Week & Space Technology.* He was preparing to debunk UFOs at a 1966 symposium sponsored by the Institute of Electrical and Electronics Engineers.

Klass was struck by several prominent themes present in most of the Exeter sightings—the spherical shape, erratic flight, bright glow, and humming or hissing sound of the objects. Klass knew of something in nature that had all these characteristics: ball lightning. This little-known kind of lightning is usually oval in shape and an intense red, is often heard to sizzle, and moves around with unpredictable vigor, sometimes hanging motionless, at other times darting about at high speeds with instantaneous changes in direction. Of course, Klass had problems trying to make a complete match between the Exeter UFO sightings and ball lightning. The objects seen around Exeter were larger, and remained visible longer, than any confirmed examples of ball lightning. And, of course, the big objection was that ball lightning is a product of thunderstorms, and the Exeter sightings were not accompanied by any. Unwilling to give up on a promising line of research, Klass delved deeper. Ball lightning is one example of what physicists call a plasma—a region of ionized gas (in this case, air) created by a strong electrical charge.

Plasmas, which behave differently from ordinary gases, are regarded as a fourth state of matter; their study has become a separate branch of physics. They are being researched for use in controlling thermonuclear reactions and as the potential driving force for interstellar travel. Saint Elmo's fire, often seen on ships and aircraft during thunderstorms, is a plasma. But it is not only static electricity that produces plasmas; high-voltage power lines are sometimes spangled with moving globes of light called coronas—another form of plasma. And many of the Exeter UFO reports included references to nearby electric transmission lines.

Perhaps, Klass said, the corona of the high-tension lines had somehow produced a special, previously unknown kind of luminous plasma—a larger, more long-lived form of ball lightning originating from power lines instead of thunderstorms. No such phenomenon had ever been witnessed or

Philip J. Klass says that all UFO reports are amenable to natural explanation. The author of UFOs—Identified believes ball lightning and related phenomena account for most sightings.

produced in a laboratory, but it seemed far more plausible—to Klass, at least—than the alternate explanation that the objects were alien spaceships.

Klass extended his study to 746 other sightings documented by NICAP. In almost every case, he found the reported UFOs displayed the characteristics typical of plasmas: color, shape, erratic movement, hissing. The strong electrical charge of a plasma could also explain the frequent reports of interference with radios, lights, and automobile electrical systems in the vicinity of UFOs. Since a plasma has little mass and is responsive to electromagnetic fields, its erratic flight and high-speed reversals of direction posed no theoretical problem. Moreover, plasmas reflect radio waves, so they cannot be ruled out when UFOs appear on radar screens. Klass made limited, but insistent, claims for his hypothesis. It may, he wrote, "explain many sightings of lower-altitude 'unidentified flying objects.' " Another writer quoted him as believing his explanation was "susceptible to confirmation by scientific experiment." After examining the NICAP literature, Klass made a stronger statement of his belief: "Hundreds of 'un-

identified flying objects' exhibit characteristics that clearly identify them as plasmas."

Klass received scant encouragement. Traditional scientists had little reason to pursue his hypothesis; those who had already made up their minds about UFOs were uninterested or openly hostile. *Newsweek* called his theory "one of the most persuasive explanations of all" but added that the air force was "noncommittal" and that UFO buffs were "unimpressed." One skeptic sarcastically described Klass's theory as "a freak of nature—hitherto unknown to science: a clear-weather plasma, akin to 'ball lightning,' caused by an electrical discharge from nearby high-tension power lines, which was somehow able to detach itself, grow to tremendous size, and cavort about the countryside under its own power." As Klass put it, somewhat ruefully, a few UFO buffs "seemed to appreciate my attempt to explain the UFO mystery rationally, but most of them acted as though I had shot Santa Claus or spat upon my country's flag."

Whatever he had done, he had not answered all the questions about the Exeter incident, which would remain

classified as unexplained. Meanwhile, another rash of sightings of mysterious objects in the sky occurred, prompting another less-than-convincing explanation.

The next widely publicized cluster of UFO sightings—around Ann Arbor, Michigan, during March 1966—gained notoriety as the "swamp gas affair" and embroiled the Congress of the United States in the UFO controversy.

The first episode to gain national attention took place on March 14, when citizens and police officers in three counties reported that they had seen lit objects flashing across the predawn skies. According to one deputy sheriff, "these objects could move at fantastic speeds, make very sharp turns, dive and climb and hover with great maneuverability." Three days later, a similar display of aerobatics was widely reported in the same area. On Sunday, March 20, near the town of Dexter, twelve miles from Ann Arbor, Frank Mannor, a forty-seven-year-old truck driver, went outside at about 7:30 P.M. to

quiet his dogs. "When I turned back I saw this meteor," he said later. "It stopped and settled to the ground, then rose again. It was about a half mile away. I called my wife and my kids out, and we watched it for fifteen minutes."

Then Mannor and his son, Ronnie, walked toward the object. "We got to about 500 yards of the thing. It was sort of shaped like a pyramid, with a blue-green light on the right-hand side and on the left a white light. I didn't see no antenna or porthole. The body was like a yellowish coral rock and looked like it had holes in it—sort of like if you took a piece of cardboard box and split it open. You couldn't see it too good, because it was surrounded with heat waves, like you see on the desert. The white light turned to a blood red as we got close to it, and Ron said, 'Look at that horrible thing.' " At that point the object disappeared.

In the meantime, Mannor's wife, Leona, had called the police, using the family's multiparty telephone line. "We've

106

87 Coeds Saw a Flying Object Near a Dormitory in Michigan

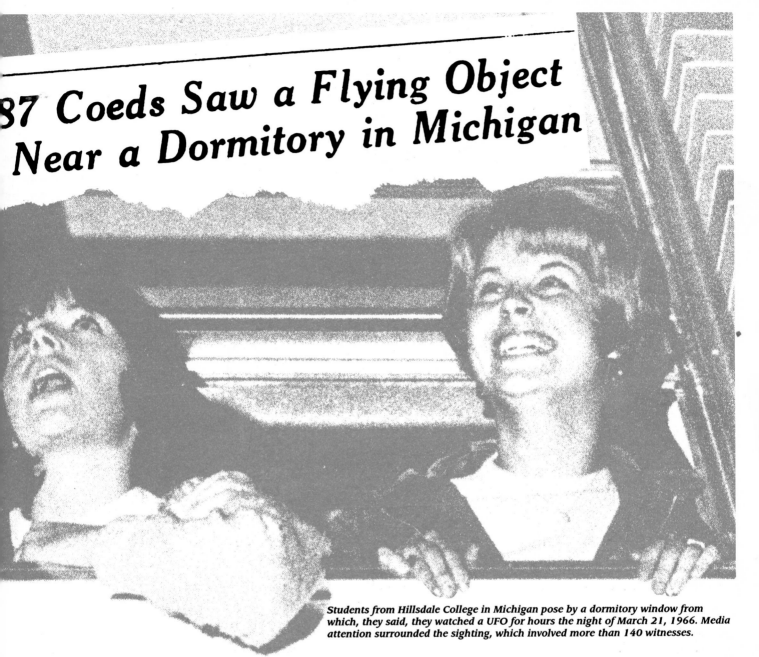

Students from Hillsdale College in Michigan pose by a dormitory window from which, they said, they watched a UFO for hours the night of March 21, 1966. Media attention surrounded the sighting, which involved more than 140 witnesses.

got an object out here that looks like what they call a flying saucer,'' she reported while several neighbors listened in. ''It's got lights on it down in the swamp.'' By the time six cruisers arrived, the road past the Mannor house was jammed with sightseers' cars. More than fifty people reported they had seen the object in the swamp that Sunday evening, including several police officers. And later, on the way back to Ann Arbor, police in one squad car spotted a UFO in the sky and pursued it at high speed, fruitlessly.

The next day, another fifty people, including twelve policemen, saw an object near Ann Arbor that resembled the one the Mannors had described. That evening, eighty-seven female students at Hillsdale College, sixty-five miles southwest of Ann Arbor, watched an object flying around and

flashing bright lights in a swampland for a period of about four hours. With them was a local civil defense director and a college dean, who was also a former newspaper reporter. They said that the object was shaped like a football; that it swayed, wobbled, and glowed in flight; and that it once darted straight toward a dormitory window before stopping suddenly. The entire area, indeed much of the state of Michigan, was in a frenzy that was magnified by the national news media. Beseeched by state and local officials to do something, the air force dispatched Project Blue Book's consultant, J. Allen Hynek, to Ann Arbor to investigate the sightings.

''The situation was so charged with emotion,'' Hynek said, ''that it was impossible for me to do any really serious investigation.'' Even when he decided to focus only on the

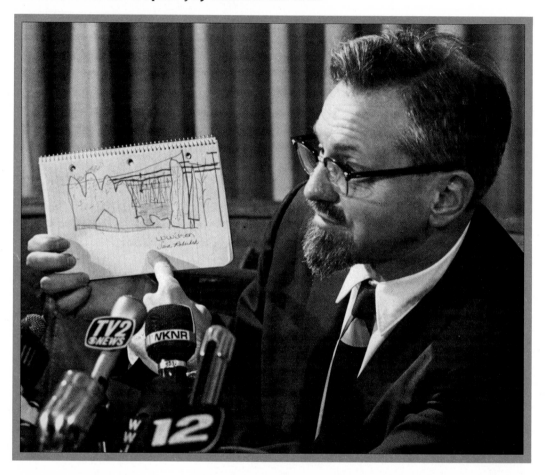

At a hastily called news conference in March 1966, J. Allen Hynek shows a sketch made by a witness in the Michigan UFO sightings. Hynek's suggestion that the UFOs might be swamp gas touched off a furor he later termed the "low point of my association with UFOs."

sightings of March 20 and 21, Hynek found that his work was obstructed by "clusters of reporters," and he received no assistance whatsoever from the air force.

Though he was a scientist and a skeptic, Hynek found himself caught up in what he described as the "near hysteria" that gripped the area. He was with the police one night when a sighting was reported; several squad cars converged on the spot, radios crackling with such excited messages as, "I see it!" or "There it is!" or "It's east of the river near Dexter!" Hynek later confessed that "occasionally even I thought I glimpsed 'it.'"

Finally the squad cars met at an intersection and officers spilled out, pointing excitedly at the sky and saying, "See—there it is! It's moving." But, Hynek wrote later, "it wasn't moving. 'It' was the star Arcturus, undeniably identified by its position in relation to the handle of the Big Dipper. A sobering demonstration for me."

Then, to add to this already chaotic situation, peremptory orders were issued by the air force: Hynek was to hold a news conference on March 25—only four days after the sighting. As he recalled, his instructions were to release "a statement about the cause of the sightings. It did me no good to protest, to say that as yet I had no real idea what had caused the reported sightings in the swamps. I was to have a press conference, ready or not."

Hynek had nothing to go on until he remembered a phone call from a botanist at the University of Michigan who had "called to my attention the phenomenon of burning 'swamp gas.'" This was a substance better known to folklore and legend—as jack-o'-lantern, fox fire, and will-o'-the-wisp—than to science. It is a gas caused by decaying vegetation, consisting mainly of methane; under certain circumstances it can ignite spontaneously and cast a brief, flickering light. Little else was known about it, but it suited Hynek's need perfectly: "After learning more about swamp gas from other Michigan scientists, I decided that it was a 'possible' explanation that I could offer to the reporters."

To his credit, Hynek made repeated, strenuous qualifications in his statement. "I am not making a blanket statement to cover the entire UFO phenomenon," he wrote; "I emphasize in conclusion that I cannot prove in a Court of Law that this is the full explanation of these sightings."

But most of his statement was an exposition of swamp gas as the probable cause of the sightings at Dexter and Hillsdale: "The flames go out in one place and suddenly appear in another place, giving the illusion of motion. No heat is felt, and the lights do not burn or char the ground. They can appear for hours at a time and sometimes for a whole night. Generally there is no smell, and usually no sound, except the popping sound of little explosions." To Hynek's dismay, however, the news conference "turned out to be no place for scholarly discussion; it was a circus. The TV cameramen wanted me in one spot, the newspaper men wanted me in another, and for a while, both groups were actually tugging at me. Everyone was clamoring for a single, spectacular explanation of the sightings. They wanted little green men. When I handed out a statement that discussed swamp gas, many of the men simply ignored the fact that I said it was a 'possible' reason. I watched with horror as one reporter scanned the page, found the phrase 'swamp gas,' underlined it, and rushed for a telephone.

"Too many of the stories the next day not only said that swamp gas was definitely the cause of the Michigan lights but implied that it was the cause of other UFO sightings as well. I got out of town as quickly and as quietly as I could."

Despite Hynek's dismay, which was expressed only later, his swamp gas hypothesis quickly became as famous as the Michigan sightings themselves; both received national coverage to an extent unprecedented in the long history of the UFO controversy. The staid *New York Times,* historically leery of UFO stories, carried several reports on the Michigan sightings, reproduced Frank Mannor's sketch of what he had seen, and even hazarded a cautious editorial. Its breezy conclusion: "The flying saucer enthusiasts demonstrate human frailties that are likely to sail on forever." A few days later, *New York Times* columnist Russell Baker dished out a typically sardonic observation: "The possibility of flying saucers is a healthy antidote for human boredom. Zoo keepers in Pittsburgh and New York have recently been seeking a similar antidote for their caged gorillas." The *New Yorker* magazine

ran an extensive piece in April, discussing what it called the "saucer flap" with an air of genteel derision.

Newsweek carried a full summary, and *Life* magazine weighed in with a more gaudy but no less carefully qualified article titled "Well-Witnessed Invasion—by Something." Summing up, the editors said: "Call them what you will: flying saucers, Unidentified Flying Objects (UFOs), optical illusions, or the first symptoms of the silly season. They are back again—and seen by more people than ever before. Last week the manifestations seemed almost to have reached the proportions of an invasion." But the amused detachment with which many reporters viewed the sightings was not shared by the hundreds of people who had seen the Ann Arbor UFOs or knew people who had. They were offended by the way Hynek's explanation was reported and accepted, and their feelings spread throughout Michigan.

ne of the state's representatives in Congress, House minority leader Gerald Ford, returned to Washington in late March to issue a call for a "full-blown" congressional investigation. At about the same time, there were calls for action from respected publications and observers not previously heard from on this issue. The *Christian Science Monitor,* for one, said in an editorial that the Michigan sightings had "deepened the mystery" of UFOs, adding, "It is time for the scientific community to conduct a thorough and objective study of the 'unexplainable.'" Syndicated columnist Roscoe Drummond called on Congress to "take charge" and order an investigation. If the air force believed it could ignore such demands, Congress was under no such illusion. Like it or not, it would have to act.

Thus it was that the first congressional hearing on UFOs began as a closed session of the House Committee on Armed Services, chaired by Representative L. Mendel Rivers of South Carolina, on April 5, 1966. The previous week, Rivers had received a letter from Congressman Ford—who, observed Rivers, "has a pretty good sized stature in the Congress." Ford cited widespread dissatisfaction with the official response to the Ann Arbor sightings and concluded: "In the firm belief

UFO sightings in the 1960s produced many witnesses willing to report what they saw. On these two pages are sketches made either by witnesses or by artists who based their work on witnesses' accounts. The drawings are among hundreds collected during the decade, some by the federal government and others by private UFO research groups. These sketches are similar in depicting craft roughly elliptical or round in shape.

Several Oklahomans described this object with rotating "ports" in 1967.

that the American public deserves a better explanation than that thus far given by the Air Force, I strongly recommend that there be a committee investigation" of the UFO phenomenon. Ford did not get the wide-ranging inquiry that he had hoped for. He had asked that members of the executive branch of government and people who had seen UFOs be invited to testify; instead, Rivers summoned just three men to brief the committee: Secretary of the Air Force Harold Brown; the director of Project Blue Book, Major Hector Quintanilla, Jr.; and Blue Book's scientific consultant, J. Allen Hynek. "See if you can shed some light on these highly illuminated objects," drawled Rivers. "We can't just write them off. There are too many responsible people who are concerned."

Secretary Brown responded with pride that of 10,147 UFOs investigated since 1947 by the air force, 9,501 had been identified as "bright stars and planets, comets and meteors," and the like by "carefully selected and highly qualified scientists, engineers, technicians and consultants"—implied experts—using "the finest Air Force laboratories, test centers, scientific instrumentation and technical equipment." In the other 646 cases, he said, "the information available does not provide an adequate basis for analysis."

Spotted in Illinois in 1967, this UFO was described as yellow-orange with red lights.

He had reached a confident conclusion: "The past 18 years of investigating UFOs have not yet identified any threat to our national security, or evidence that the unidentified objects represent developments or principles beyond present-day scientific knowledge, or any evidence of extraterrestrial vehicles." But despite the utter lack of results thus far, the air force would remain steadfast and, he said, "continue to investigate such phenomena with an open mind." Congressman Rivers was apparently reassured by Brown's stance; he suddenly saw no reason to continue in executive session and admitted the crowd of reporters that had gathered in the halls. Brown repeated his testimony for their ben-

efit; then Rivers asked Hynek for his views. Hynek was a good deal more ambivalent than Brown, and in fact, more so than he had been in the past. In 1948, when he was first involved with Project Blue Book, he had stated that "the whole subject seemed utterly ridiculous" and had expected the fad to pass quickly. Instead, UFO sightings had become more widespread and frequent. The attention of the national news media waxed and waned, he said, but "the underlying concern about UFOs, fed by a continuous trickle of reports, is indeed growing in the mind and sight of the public." It was time, asserted Hynek, for a thorough, scholarly approach to what he called the "UFO problem." The air force had approached all UFO reports, he continued, with the assumption "that a conventional explana-

A Texas family reportedly saw this domed craft and its white trail in February 1967.

tion existed, either as a misidentification or as an otherwise well-known object or phenomenon, a hallucination, or a hoax. This has been a very successful and productive hypothesis." Yet there were incidents for which that approach did not work; Hynek had collected twenty that he could not explain.

"In dealing with the truly puzzling cases, we have tended either to say that, if an investigation had been pursued long enough, the misidentified object would have been recognized, or that the sighting had no validity to begin with." Hynek admitted to being increasingly uncomfortable with the air force's confident approach. "As a scientist, I must be mindful of the lessons of the past; all too often it has happened that matters of great value to science were overlooked because the new phenomenon simply did not fit the accepted scientific outlook of the time." During a brief, rambling discussion peppered with jokes about Martians, committee members asked about a particularly spectacular sighting that had been covered by *Life*

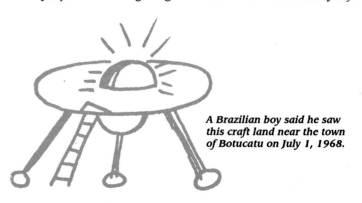

A Brazilian boy said he saw this craft land near the town of Botucatu on July 1, 1968.

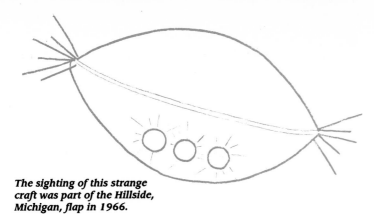

The sighting of this strange craft was part of the Hillside, Michigan, flap in 1966.

magazine. Major Quintanilla, who spoke only when directly questioned, said Project Blue Book had not investigated that case. And then, just an hour and twenty minutes after commencing, the congressional investigation was over.

Virtually nothing had been accomplished, except that some additional impetus was given to a proposal for a different kind of study. In an attempt to patch its badly frayed credibility on the subject, the air force had already convened what it called a scientific advisory board ad hoc committee to review Project Blue Book. After a one-day examination of Blue Book, the advisory committee reported in February 1966; Secretary Brown used some of its findings in his statement to Rivers's House committee. The full advisory committee report, however, directly contradicted Brown on one point.

In 1965, an Oklahoma witness said he saw this low-flying UFO in front of a tree. Whereas he had noted that highly qualified experts and sophisticated equipment had been brought to bear on UFO investigations, the advisory committee concluded that the resources assigned to Blue Book "(only one officer, a sergeant and secretary) have been quite limited." The committee recommended that skilled teams, including clinical psychologists and physical scientists, be recruited from various universities to investigate selected UFO sightings. It was an intriguing idea, and one that was made to seem all the more reasonable by the air force's handling of a spectacular sighting that occurred less than two weeks after the hearing.

Before dawn on April 17, 1966, two sheriff's deputies, Dale Spaur and Wilbur L. Neff, were wrapping up an accident investigation near Ra-

venna, in eastern Ohio. At 4:50, the Portage County dispatcher told them to be on the lookout for a low-flying UFO reported to be heading their way from the west. They drove in that direction, then spotted an abandoned car and stopped. They left their cruiser and approached the empty car. That was when Spaur—an air force gunner during the Korean War—noticed a glowing object about 1,000 feet above the trees and to the west. The two watched as it grew larger and moved south. Then it came toward them, illuminating the roadside. "I had never seen anything this bright before in my life," Spaur said later. They ran back to the squad car. Spaur grabbed the microphone and described for the dispatcher what they were seeing:

"It's about fifty feet across, and I can just make out a dome or something on the top, but that's very dark. The bottom is real bright; it's putting out a beam of light that makes a big spot underneath. It's like it's sitting on the beam. It was overhead a minute ago, and it was bright as day here: Our headlights didn't make nearly as much light as it did. And this is no helicopter or

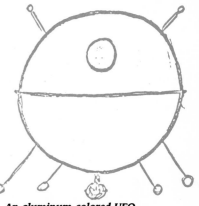

An aluminum-colored UFO was reported hovering over a highway in 1967 by a West Virginia merchant.

anything like that; it's perfectly still and it just makes a humming noise." The dispatcher sent out a car with camera equipment and told Spaur and Neff to keep the UFO in sight. The object moved; they followed and were soon barreling along at nearly ninety miles per hour. Because of their speed and some confusion about their location—they were on Route 14, but the dispatcher thought they were on 14A—the camera unit never found them.

As Spaur and Neff raced toward Pennsylvania, another police officer, Wayne Huston of East Palestine, Ohio, was listening to their radio traffic. He pulled up at an intersection in their path and soon saw the UFO pass, traveling at more than eighty miles per

This helmet-shaped object allegedly was sighted by some English boys at Parr, Merseyside, during 1963.

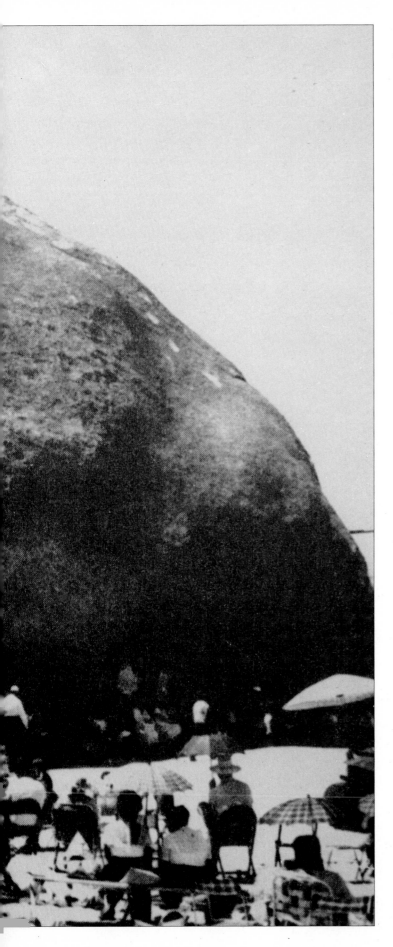

hour and at an altitude of about 900 feet. Huston joined the chase. "It was a funny thing," he recalled later, "but when the object got too far ahead of us it appeared to stop and wait." The UFO crossed the state line into Pennsylvania, and Huston notified the state police. One of their officers contacted the Greater Pittsburgh Airport to see if the UFO was visible on radar, but the air traffic controllers said they had no such object on their screens.

The pursuit cars were now near Conway, eighty-five miles from where the chase had started. Spaur's was running low on gas. He noticed another police cruiser at a service station, pulled in, and screeched to a halt, with Huston right behind him. There they met patrolman Frank Panzanella of the Conway police department, who had been tracking the UFO. The four officers stood together, watching the object hover to the east. The moon was to its right and the planet Venus to the right of the moon. As the object moved higher, a commercial aircraft (later identified as United Airlines flight 454) flew underneath it. Panzanella had a request put through to the Pittsburgh airport tower: Could it instruct the airline flight crew to look for the object?

The operator who made the call radioed back that airport radar operators had picked up the UFO on their screens, but this report was later denied. At that point the object shot upward at great speed and disappeared. Another policeman on duty later reported that he had seen two jet-fighter aircraft aloft, not following but being followed by a bright object shaped like a football.

Before Spaur and Neff returned to Ohio, they were asked to call an air force reserve officer at the Pittsburgh airport, who talked with them briefly and said a report would be filed with Project Blue Book. On their return to Ravenna, the deputies found reporters waiting for them; the news wires had been monitoring the police radio transmissions. With public interest in UFOs still high, the story was avidly picked up and, before the day was over, was being talked about all over the country. Spaur was willing to discuss it; Neff filed his report, went home—"real white, almost in a state of shock," his wife said later—and refused to talk to anyone.

Major Hector Quintanilla, Jr., of Project Blue Book called Spaur the next day and spoke with him for a few minutes. As before, the air force had a ready explanation for the sighting, which it announced five days later. In fact, the air force explained, the policemen had first pursued a communications satellite called Echo, and then the planet Venus.

Once again the air force's account produced outrage; a judge and former Congressman called it "ridiculous" and added, "the air force has suffered a great loss of prestige in this community." Ohio Congressman William Stanton was equally blunt. "The air force failed in its responsibility," he said on May 5. "Once people entrusted with the public welfare no longer think the people can handle the truth, then the people, in turn, will no longer trust the government."

In response, Major Quintanilla traveled to Ravenna and conducted a brief, personal interview with deputy Spaur. Quintanilla apparently knew nothing about the other officers involved in the chase and made no attempt to talk to the corroborating witnesses. He also denied that the air force had dispatched any jets during the incident. He soon left, and the official conclusion remained unchanged: Spaur and the others had been chasing the satellite and the planet Venus.

Further efforts by Congressman Stanton and others to get the air force to change its conclusion from "satellite-Venus" to "unidentified" were unavailing. Several months later, Project Blue Book's consultant, J. Allen Hynek, publicly

disagreed with the official verdict. But the air force was unmoved; according to its version, at least five experienced police officers, one of them a veteran air crewman, had conducted an hours-long, high-speed chase of the morning star. The effect of the experience on some of the police officers was devastating. Deputy Spaur soon resigned from the sheriff's department and was divorced from his wife. A reporter found him in October living in poverty in a seedy motel, eking out a house painter's existence. "If I could change all that I have done in my life," he said, "I would change just one thing, and that would be the night we chased that damn saucer."

Deputy Neff refused to discuss the incident any further. "If that thing landed in my backyard," he told his wife after the hubbub died down, "I wouldn't tell a soul." Another officer involved in the chase reportedly moved to Seattle, Washington, where he went to work as a bus driver. "Sure I quit the force because of that thing," the unidentified ex-police officer was quoted as saying. "People laughed at me— and there was pressure. You couldn't put your finger on it, but the pressure was there."

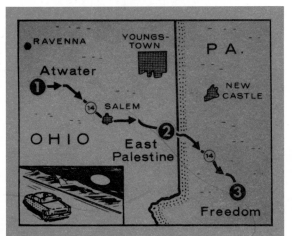

Dale Spaur's sketch of the UFO he chased (above) shows a disk with a rudderlike appendage on top and a cone-shaped beam of light beneath. The map below shows the chase route.

There had been pressure on the government, too. Just a month after the Ohio-Pennsylvania chase and the congressional hearing, the air force announced that it was indeed going to contract with an American university to conduct an investigation of UFOs. It was to be done wholly outside the jurisdiction of the air force; the scientists involved were to have access to the files of Project Blue Book and complete freedom of inquiry. On paper, it sounded as if it was precisely what UFO enthusiasts had been demanding for years. A long silence followed, while the air force tried to find a university that would take on a job that one academic vice president described as "elusive and controversial." Several prominent schools, including Harvard University, the Massachusetts Institute of Technology, the University of North Carolina, and the University of California at Berkeley, refused. Hynek wanted the job to be given to Northwestern University, where he had moved in 1961; James E. McDonald, an atmospheric physicist at the University of Arizona, wanted it to go to his school. Both of the schools were ruled out because these two men had taken strong public positions on the subject of UFOs—Hynek as a skeptic and McDonald as a believer in their extraterrestrial origins. Five months later, the University of Colorado announced it had taken the project and Edward U. Condon— professor of physics and Fellow of the Joint Institute for Laboratory Astrophysics—would serve as chairman of the group.

The sixty-four-year-old Condon was a well-known figure. In the late 1920s, after taking his Ph.D. in physics at the University of California, he had spent two years in Germany working with several of the world's preeminent physicists. He had held teaching positions at Princeton and the University of Minnesota before becoming associate director of Westing-

Edward U. Condon sits behind a UFO model and his committee's controversial report debunking flying saucers.

house Research Laboratories, and he had earned wide respect for his contributions to the development of both radar and the atomic bomb. After World War II Condon had served as the director of the U.S. Bureau of Standards.

Thus, there was great optimism on all sides as the Condon committee undertook to solve the mysteries of UFOs. With twelve members who were specialists in various fields and the eager cooperation of such civilian organizations as NICAP, things appeared to be progressing well. The committee assembled a library, established investigative teams, and devised a method to study reported UFO sightings. But before long, hopes for an objective study evaporated, at least in the eyes of UFO enthusiasts.

Such hopes were dashed largely by Condon himself. The day after his appointment, he was quoted as saying that there was "no evidence that there is advanced life on other planets." And just three months later, he irritated his committee staff and his critics alike by announcing at a public meeting: "It is my inclination right now to recommend that the government get out of this business. My attitude right now is that there's nothing to it, but I'm not supposed to reach a conclusion for another year." To many observers, this did not sound like the impartiality that was to have been the principal criterion for committee membership.

Then came the disclosure of what many UFO researchers regarded as a smoking gun—a memorandum written while the University of Colorado was considering the air force's proposal. In what subsequently became known as the "trick" memo, Robert Low—an academic dean who was to become project coordinator of the Condon committee—discussed how the university might take on the project without losing respectability in the academic world.

"The trick would be, I think," wrote Low, "to describe the project so that to the public, it would appear a totally objective study, but, to the scientific community, would present the image of a group of nonbelievers trying their best to be objective, but having an almost zero expectation of finding a saucer." Publication of the memo further damaged the committee's already damaged credibility and disrupted its work; the two members who had found and discussed the memo were fired. NICAP formally withdrew its support, and its director, Donald Keyhoe, indignantly called for a new government inquiry and said that NICAP's investigations would be intensified to offset what he called "the Colorado failure."

While the Condon investigation floundered in controversy, the Congress decided to take another, expanded look at the subject of UFOs. This was in the form of a symposium conducted by the House Committee on Science and Astronautics. One of its members, Representative J. Edward Roush of Indiana, had become impressed with the arguments of Arizona's James McDonald, who was emerging as a leading advocate of the alien-spacecraft hypothesis.

McDonald was a tireless UFO investigator who lectured continually about his conclusions. After studying thousands of cases and interviewing hundreds of witnesses, he wrote, he had concluded that "the extraterrestrial hypothesis is the least unlikely hypothesis to account for the UFO." Influenced by McDonald's credentials and reasoning, Congressman Roush scheduled the symposium for July 29, 1968, and asked McDonald to select the witnesses.

As a result, the tone of the symposium was far different from that of the 1966 hearing. It was addressed by six distinguished scientists and academics associated with major universities: astronomer J. Allen Hynek, physicist James

McDonald, sociologist Robert L. Hall, engineers James A. Harder and Robert M. Baker, and astrophysicist Carl Sagan. They all agreed not to discuss the troubled Condon committee or to criticize the beleaguered air force.

Hynek, the veteran UFO debunker and Blue Book apologist, led off with a statement that confirmed his continuing change of attitude. The UFO problem, he said, "has been made immensely more difficult by the supposition held by most scientists, on the basis of the poor data available to them, that there couldn't possibly be anything substantial to UFO reports in the first place, and hence that there is no point to wasting time or money investigating." This, of course, was precisely the position that had been held by the air force, and by Hynek, for the previous twenty years.

But this attitude, Hynek now said, was no longer acceptable: "Can we afford not to look toward UFO skies; can we afford to overlook a potential breakthrough of great significance? And even apart from that, the public is growing impatient. The public does not want another 20 years of UFO confusion. They want to know whether there really is something to this whole UFO business—and I can tell you definitely that they are not satisfied with the answers they have been getting." Nor was Hynek. He confessed that he had been forced to a reluctant conclusion by "the cumulative weight of continued reports from groups of people around the world whose competence and sanity I have no reason to doubt, reports involving unexplainable craft with physical effects on animals, motor vehicles, growing plants and on the ground." The choice, he now believed, was clear: "Either there is a scientifically valuable subset of reports on the UFO phenomenon or we have a world society containing people who are articulate, sane and reputable in all matters save UFO reports."

Hynek's call for more serious research was echoed by McDonald: "My position is that UFOs are entirely real and we do not know what they are, because we have laughed them out of court. The possibility that these are extraterrestrial devices, that we are dealing with surveillance from some advanced technology, is a possibility I take very seriously." McDonald pleaded for a more strenuous scientific approach to the subject, with the involvement of the National Aeronautics and Space Administration.

James Harder, an engineering professor from the University of California at Berkeley, was even more blunt in his opinion: "On the basis of the data and the ordinary rules of evidence, as would be applied in civil or criminal courts, the

Public skepticism made Condon and his report the butt of several cartoons, including this one by Pat Oliphant.

"STAY CALM, DR. CONDON—JUST TELL THEM YOU DON'T BELIEVE IN THEM!"

117

physical reality of UFOs has been proved beyond a reasonable doubt."

There was, of course, dissent. Donald H. Menzel, the distinguished astronomer, former director of the Harvard College Observatory, and relentless UFO debunker, submitted a written statement that fairly dripped scorn. "The believers," he declared, "are too eager to reach a decision. Having no real logic on their side, they resort to innuendo as a weapon and try to discredit those who fail to support their view."

Menzel's logic was that if alien pilots had been "bugging us for centuries," as he put it, "why should one not have landed and shown himself to the President of the United States, to a member of the National Academy of Sciences, or at least to some member of Congress?" Menzel's conclusion about unidentified flying objects was unequivocal: "Natural explanations exist for the unexplained sightings."

But the consensus of the symposium was clearly that UFOs merited serious study and should be given closer, more objective attention. The proceedings, however, had been merely a discussion, not a prelude to any congressional action, and had little impact. And five months later the symposium sank even further into obscurity as the country turned its attention to the formal report of the Condon committee.

Major Hector Quintanilla, Jr., of Project Blue Book stands amid supposedly extraterrestrial artifacts that all proved earthly. He holds a copper shell filled with radio parts. The disks in the foreground are pancakes.

Despite the controversy that had dogged its preparation, the report appeared to be an exhaustive review of the whole subject of UFOs by first-rate scientists. It was physically impressive: 1,465 pages crammed with charts, photographs, and dense academic exposition. It seemed that no effort had been spared; thirty-six authors had contributed analyses and explanations, and the cost had exceeded half a million dollars.

The National Academy of Sciences had reviewed the report and announced its approval. Walter Sullivan, the respected science reporter for the *New York Times,* wrote an admiring introduction in which he said: "The report is a memorable document. While the case histories read like detective stories, it is also a scientific study." Few people, however, waded through the hundreds of pages of analysis. Most read only the first section, titled "Conclusions and Recommendations," and the second, "Summary of the Report." Both were written by Condon himself.

"Our general conclusion," declared the ever-skeptical committee chairman, "is that nothing has come from the study of UFOs in the past 21 years that has added to scientific knowledge. Careful consideration of the record leads us to conclude that further extensive study of UFOs probably can

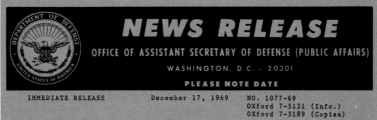

NEWS RELEASE

OFFICE OF ASSISTANT SECRETARY OF DEFENSE (PUBLIC AFFAIRS)

WASHINGTON, D.C. - 20301

PLEASE NOTE DATE

IMMEDIATE RELEASE   December 17, 1969   NO. 1077-69
                                                 OXford 7-5131 (Info.)
                                                 OXford 7-3189 (Copies)

AIR FORCE TO TERMINATE
PROJECT "BLUE BOOK"

Secretary of the Air Force Robert C. Seamans, Jr., announced today the termination of Project Blue Book, the Air Force program for the investigation of unidentified flying objects (UFOs).

In a memorandum to Air Force Chief of Staff General John D. Ryan, Secretary Seamans stated that "the continuation of Project Blue Book cannot be justified either on the ground of national security or in the interest of science," and concluded that the project does not merit future expenditures of resources.

The decision to discontinue UFO investigations was based on:

- An evaluation of a report prepared by the University of Colorado entitled, "Scientific Study of Unidentified Flying Objects."

- A review of the University of Colorado's report by the National Academy of Sciences.

- Past UFO studies.

- Air Force experience investigating UFO reports during the past two decades.

Under the direction of Dr. Edward U. Condon, the University of Colorado completed an 18-month contracted study of UFOs and its report was released to the public in January, 1969. The report concluded that little if anything has come from the study of UFOs in the past 21 years that has added to scientific knowledge, and that further extensive study of UFO sightings is not justified in the expectation that science will be advanced.

The University of Colorado report also states that, "It seems that only so much attention to the subject (UFOs) should be give as the Department of Defense deems to be necessary strictly from a defense point of view....It is our impression that the defense function could be performed within the framework established for intelligence and surveillance operations without the continuance of a special unit such as Project Blue Book, but this is a question for defense specialists rather than research scientists."

A panel of the National Academy of Sciences made an independent assessment of the scope, methodology, and findings of the University of Colorado study. The panel concurred in the University of Colorado's recommendation that "no high priority in UFO investigations is warranted by data of the past two decades." It concluded by stating that, "On the basis of present knowledge, the least likely explanation of UFOs is the hypothesis of extraterrestrial visitations by intelligent beings."

Past UFO studies include one conducted by a Scientific Advisory Panel of UFOs in January, 1953 (Robertson Panel); and, a review of Project Blue Book by the Air Force Scientific Advisory Board Ad Hoc Committee, February-March, 1966 (Dr. Brian O'Brien, Chairman). These studies concluded that no evidence has been found that any of the UFO reports reflect a threat to our national security.

As a result of investigating UFO reports since 1948, the conclusions of Project Blue Book are: (1) no UFO reported, investigated, and evaluated by the Air Force has ever given any indication of threat to our national security; (2) there has been no evidence submitted or discovered by the Air Force that sightings categorized as "unidentified" represent technological developments or principles beyond the range of present-day scientific knowledge; and (3) there has been no evidence indicating that sightings categorized as "unidentified" are extraterrestrial vehicles.

Project Blue Book records will be retired to the USAF Archives, Maxwell Air Force Base, Alabama. Requests for information will continue to be handled by the Secretary of the Air Force, Office of Information (SAFOI), Washington, D.C. 20330.

END

In December 1969, the Defense Department issued a news release announcing that the air force was disbanding Project Blue Book. The document marked the formal demise of governmental involvement in the investigation of unidentified flying objects.

not be justified in the expectation that science will be advanced."

The air force, Condon continued, had been correct in its handling of UFO reports and had never attempted to conceal its findings. "It has been contended that the subject has been shrouded in official secrecy. We conclude otherwise. We have no evidence of secrecy concerning UFO reports. What has been miscalled secrecy has been no more than an intelligent policy of delay in releasing data so that the public does not become confused by premature publication of incomplete studies of reports."

In general, the report—or, more accurately, Condon's summary of the report—was greeted as the authoritative final word on the entire UFO controversy. Headlines proclaimed that "Flying Saucers Do Not Exist—Official" or, more bluntly, "UFOs are Bunk." But dissent was quick to appear. On the very day the report was released to the public, David R. Saunders, one of the men fired earlier by Condon for releasing the so-called trick memo, published a book titled *UFOs? YES! Where the Condon Committee Went Wrong.*

Saunders and other critics pointed out that what Condon had written was a summary not of the findings of the committee but of his own preexisting beliefs. Among other things, Condon ignored the fact that some 30 percent of the ninety-one cases his committee analyzed remained unsolved. This was a jarring statistic in view of the fact that Project Blue Book had classified as "unidentified" only about 5 percent of reported sightings. Moreover, the ninety-one cases had been selected from among thousands of possibilities, presumably with the intention of giving each one of them intensive—and conclusive—study.

Thus the massive "Scientific Study of Unidentified Flying Objects," in the end, gave skeptics the ammunition they wanted to dismiss UFO reports altogether. At the same time, it contained enough loose ends and mysteries for enthusiasts of the UFO phenomenon to continue to proclaim that there had been bias at best or, at worst, a cover-up.

Apparently, the air force—which, after all, had paid for the study—got what it wanted as well. In December 1969 it announced that it was disbanding Project Blue Book and, as Condon had recommended at the very beginning of his effort, was getting out of the UFO business. The very determined would be able to discover thereafter that the Department of Defense had given responsibility for future UFO reports to something called the Aerospace Defense Command. But to the general public, it seemed that the government wanted nothing more to do with UFO reports.

CHAPTER 5

The Enduring Enigma

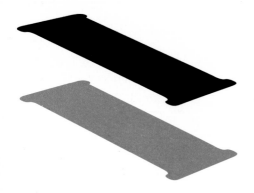

t happened on July 20, 1969. A silvery object, twinkling against inky blackness, hurtled through space at an astonishing rate of speed. A small, vaguely buglike craft disengaged from the object and descended smoothly, landing in a cloud of fine, light-colored dust. A trapdoor inched open; a ladder descended, and two humanlike, white-clad figures clambered down. Lumbering about the surface, they peered this way and that with what appeared to be enormous, single, insect eyes that reflected everything before them.

The creatures—whose names were Neil Armstrong and Edwin (Buzz) Aldrin—were the first humans to leave their blue-green home planet behind and travel to the moon. Space travel, for so long the province of visionaries and science-fiction writers, was a fact. Flying objects really were capable of visiting alien worlds. It had become slightly less heretical to suggest that space travel was not necessarily a one-way street or that reports of anomalous flying objects deserved serious scientific study.

But just as the age of space travel was dawning, the era of the UFO seemed to be coming to an end. The Condon report had said there was nothing to the persistent stories about UFOs; in 1969 the air force slammed shut the doors of Project Blue Book. Meanwhile, the number of sightings had dwindled, and the news media seemed to have lost interest. Many people were ready to assign the records of the UFO phenomenon to some back shelf.

During the ensuing two decades, however, only twelve men would visit the moon, while thousands of people all over the world would continue to see UFOs. In the United States, they would have to wonder where to report their sightings. Ignored by the air force, the government, and the scientific establishment, these startled and often frightened people would have to seek out organizations of interested civilians in order to report what they had seen and get information about other UFO sightings.

Ironically, the resulting investigations would in many cases be more complete, and more rigorously conducted, than any the air force had done. The 1970s and 1980s would be marked by new themes and directions in UFO research, thoughtful new methods for collecting data, fascinating new speculations about the nature of the phenomenon, a decreased tolerance for automatic acceptance—or automatic debunking—of UFO reports, and some of the most thoroughly reported and mystifying sightings and alleged alien encounters on record.

That the combined weight of the Condon committee and the air force was not enough to quash scientific interest in UFOs was due in large measure to the enduring curiosity of J. Allen Hynek. During his twenty-one-year association with air force UFO investigations, he had become increasingly dissatisfied with their shortcomings and, in the late 1960s, increasingly outspoken in his criticism.

Nonetheless, while employed by the air force he had remained a team player, nudging the service toward better performance, all the while collecting evidence and cases that eluded explanation. The good cases cried out for serious study, he maintained; they needed far more intensive investigation by trained scientists than they were getting. The information thus gathered needed to be standardized, shared, and made available to manipulation by computers so that common attributes—such things as colors, shapes, velocities, and geographic concentrations—could be analyzed.

Freed of the air force connection, secure in his position as chairman of Northwestern University's astronomy department, Hynek began to speak out ever more forcefully in the 1970s for better work on UFO reports. In his 1972 book, *The UFO Experience,* he outlined a method for collecting complete information about sightings—a kind of

taxonomy of UFO reports. And shortly thereafter, he founded an organization, the Center for UFO Studies (CUFOS), dedicated to putting his ideas into practice.

In Hynek's scheme, sightings were to be organized into six categories. Of lower magnitude were three kinds made at a distance: nocturnal lights, daylight disks, and visual sightings confirmed by radar. An example of the last kind occurred near Fairbanks, Alaska, in late 1986, when a Japan Air Lines pilot not only saw a strange, illuminated craft approach his plane but picked it up on his in-flight radar. Later reports showed that Federal Aviation Administration radar on the ground had also tracked the UFO in the vicinity of the Japanese airliner. Hynek also defined three kinds of close-up sightings, for which he coined a term that soon became part of the language: close encounters. A close encounter of the first kind was a sighting made from within 500 feet of the object. A sighting was to be labeled the second kind, he said, when investigation revealed some "measurable physical effect" on land or objects—for example, scorched grass, frightened animals, malfunctioning electrical systems, or stalled engines. One such event took place in the south of France in January 1981. A retired man named Renato Nicolai reported that at 5:00 one evening, a metallic object about eight feet in diameter landed in his backyard. It soon took off again, he said, leaving a circle about six feet across on the ground. Investigators from the government-sponsored French UFO study organization later reported that something had deformed the ground by "mass, mechanics, a heating effect, and perhaps certain transformations and deposits of trace minerals." Most startling of all, perhaps, was that the young plants near the circle all lacked 50 percent of their normal amount of chlorophyll.

A close encounter of the third kind is a sighting that includes allegations of occupants seen in or around the UFO. Hynek intended this classification mainly for events where no physical contact between the witness and the occupants is claimed. For example, scores of people around the world have reported seeing a UFO land at a distance and watching while occupants watched back or disembarked briefly.

Hynek was at pains to differentiate encounters of the third kind from reports of the so-called contactees who say they communicate with extraterrestrial creatures regularly, accompany them on long rides in their spacecraft, and return with extraterrestrial messages of cosmic importance to humankind. Scientist that he was, Hynek viewed such stories as incredible and did not wish to dignify them with a category of their own.

He also devised a strangeness-probability chart to determine which UFO reports deserved further investigation. As fanciful as many UFO reports may seem, they actually contain a fairly narrow range of variables. Indeed, as Hynek put it, there is even "a sort of monotony" to them. Reports of bright lights in the sky that move in extraordinary ways are common; only the reported velocities and maneuvers are strange. On the other hand, an account of a weird craft that swoops down next to an automobile, at which point the car's engine stops and its lights go out, has several unusual at-

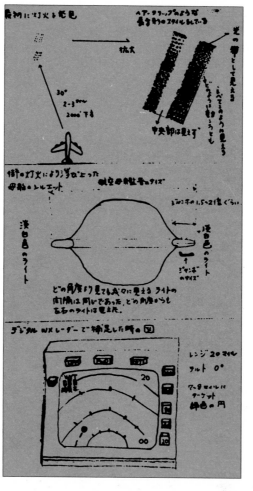

tributes. So, an investigator, as Hynek showed, can rank UFO reports on a somewhat rigorous scale of strangeness.

Probability can also be scaled, he said, depending mostly on the nature of the witness. An event observed independently by three witnesses of good character and normal behavior is more likely to have occurred than one seen by a single witness with a background of erratic activity. If witnesses pass lie-detector and psychological testing, the probability of their report is further raised. Thus, the higher the strangeness-probability rating assigned to a UFO report, the more worthy it is of additional study.

Hynek's book may have elevated UFO reporting to a new level of sophistication, but interest in UFOs continued to fade. As before, the standard response of established science (and the established press) to UFO reports was derisive. Harvard astronomer Donald H. Menzel, for example, relishing his self-described role as the "man who killed Santa Claus," continued his single-minded debunking, saying that all such reports were foolishness. But there were also some new and more thoughtful approaches to the subject.

In 1972, the same year that Hynek's book appeared, Cornell University published the proceedings of a 1969 symposium on the UFO phenomenon. Organized under the auspices of the American Association for the Advancement of Science by astronomers Carl Sagan and Thornton Page, the symposium was controversial, with many of the association's members claiming that merely to hold a formal discussion gave far too much credence to UFOs. The proceedings, titled *UFO's—Scientific Debate,* included the expected statements from the regular debaters: Hynek argued for serious scientific study and Menzel jeered. But there were other points of view as well.

For example, a University of Chicago sociologist, Robert L. Hall, addressed the role that so-called hysterical contagion might play in the reporting of UFOs. This explanation, often invoked when a wave of sightings occurs, holds that accounts of UFOs are self-propagating because they encourage other people to imagine similar experiences. While this may contribute to a large number of sightings, Hall said, "documented cases of hysterical contagion," such as the one following Orson Welles's 1938 broadcast of a fictional invasion from Mars, usually last only a few days. According to Hall, "the continuation of UFO reports over at least decades and their spread over all parts of the world would both be unprecedented for a case of hysterical contagion." He also pointed out that most people will not come forward with reports that defy conventional wisdom and expose them to suspicion and ridicule. Upon considering the reports that remain unexplainable even after thorough investigation, Hall concluded that either something is there that physicists cannot presently explain or something is there that psychologists and social scientists cannot presently explain.

Carl Sagan's contribution to the symposium was an attack on the belief that UFOs are piloted by extraterrestrial beings. Applying several logical assumptions, Sagan calculated the possible number of advanced civilizations capable of interstellar travel to be about one million. Continuing with what he called his mathematical "entertainment," he projected that any civilization

Japan Air Lines pilot Kenju Terauchi describes an alleged encounter with three UFOs over Alaska during a 1986 JAL flight. Terauchi's sketch (opposite page) shows how the largest craft dwarfed his plane. It also estimates the UFOs' positions relative to the plane, and on his radar screen, when they were first sighted.

wishing to check on all the others on a regular basis of, say, once a year would have to launch 10,000 spacecraft annually. Not only does that seem like an unreasonable number of launchings, he said, but it would take all the material in one percent of the universe's *stars* to produce all the spaceships needed for all the civilizations to seek each other out.

To argue that the earth was being chosen for regular visitations, Sagan said, one would have to assume that the planet is somehow unique in all the universe. And that assumption, he continued, "goes exactly against the idea that there are lots of civilizations around. Because if there are lots of them around then the development of our sort of civilization must be pretty common. And if we're not pretty common then there aren't going to be many civilizations advanced enough to send visitors."

This argument, which some called "Sagan's paradox," helped to establish a new school of thought in science: the belief that extraterrestrial life exists but has nothing to do with UFOs. Sagan, among others, was convinced that given the number of stars in the universe—"billions and billions," as he became noted for saying—the odds were very high that not just life, not just merely intelligent life, but highly advanced civilizations must exist. He simply doubted that emissaries from these civilizations were in the habit of buzzing remote farmhouses or touching down on desert highways, as popular reports so often had them doing.

The new belief system had a salutary effect on UFO studies. It helped separate researchers who wanted to identify unidentified flying objects from those who wanted to identify the pilots. And it gave scientists opportunities to search the universe for intelligent life unencumbered by the stigma associated with UFOs. Indeed, the 1970s saw an increasing amount of scientific energy applied to what became known as SETI, the search for extraterrestrial intelligence.

rowing awareness of the possibility of other life in the universe was symbolically acknowledged in 1972, when the United States made a singular gesture to its hypothetical neighbors in the galaxy. It sent them a cryptic message, inscribed on a six-inch by nine-inch plaque of gold-anodized aluminum affixed to the antenna support struts of a space probe dubbed *Pioneer 10*. Another followed the next year on *Pioneer 11*. Designed by Carl and Linda Sagan, the messages provided clues with which an alien civilization could figure out where the message came from and what sort of beings sent it.

By the late 1980s, the probes had made their silent way out of the solar system, past the dark and frigid region inhabited by Pluto—wistful messages in bottles cast into a limitless ocean. There is virtually no chance that these messages will find their way to any civilization out there, but they were inexpensive and romantic gestures, and they enchanted otherwise hard-boiled scientists; in 1980, another space-bound probe carried a golden phonograph record containing greetings from Earth in fifty-four languages.

Others took a more systematic approach to the search for extraterrestrial intelligence. Indeed, one such effort had been undertaken as long ago as 1960 by astronomer Frank Drake, then with the National Radio Astronomy Observatory. Drake was to become, and remain for more than a quarter of a century, a leader in the search for what he called the "diamonds of civilization" that he believed must be scattered among the far-flung galaxies. The way to find them, he was convinced, was to listen to radio.

The universe is alive with radio transmissions, a constant buzz of signals given off by stars, galaxies, and even the cosmic dust of interstellar space. These signals are the products of physical processes, not transmitters, and although radio astronomers have learned from the signals a great deal about their sources, they have found no evidence of any deliberate broadcasts. Still, since radio waves travel at the speed of light and are easily shaped to carry messages, it seems logical to assume that any contact between civilizations might first be made by radio.

But the roar of the heavens is continuous, comes from every direction at once, and sprawls across the whole spectrum of radio frequencies. With limited time, equipment, and money for listening, choices had to be made. Drake and his colleagues thought it reasonable to narrow their search to the radio frequencies given off by hydrogen (H), the oxygen-hydrogen molecule (OH), and water (H_2O), since hydrogen is the most abundant element in the universe and water is the material most basic to life as we know it. Radio astronomers refer to the frequency band of these emissions—1,000 to 40,000 megahertz—as the water hole.

Drake further limited his initial search to the vicinity of two stars that are relatively close and similar in mass to the earth's sun. He spent 200 hours gathering signals—the emissions are so weak that it takes time to accumulate enough energy to be distinguishable—and then combed through the noise looking for the imprint of intelligence among the random signals. There was no such imprint.

More modern equipment, such as the enormous radio telescope in Arecibo, Puerto Rico, with its twenty acres of collecting area, can duplicate Drake's 200-hour search in seconds. Since 1960, Drake and his successors have made more than a million searches—probes in a single direction, at as many frequencies as the receiver can detect—without success. Yet this can hardly be regarded a failure. Given the enormous number of possibilities, what has been examined so far amounts to only a few stalks in the celestial haystack. It has been accomplished with telescope time snatched from other projects—such as the search for black holes—that have

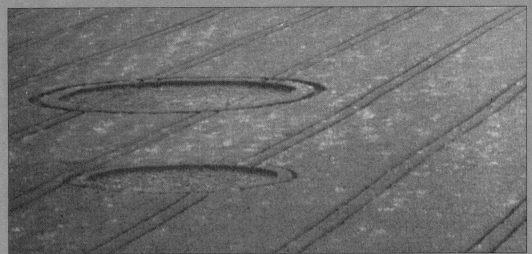

Some ufologists believe these topographical oddities mark UFO landing sites: mysterious circles (left) that appeared in a Hampshire, England, cornfield in an area called the Devil's Punchbowl, July 1986; a horseshoe-shaped ring (below, left) of whitish, crystalline soil found following a reported UFO sighting at Delphos, Kansas, in 1971; a circular patch of dead soybean plants (below, right) discovered in an Iowa soybean field after a 1969 sighting; and an oval of flattened reeds (bottom) in a swamp near Nishikawa-cho in northern Japan, found in 1986 after a night of reported electrical disturbances.

better funding and higher probabilities of success.

Devotees of the search earnestly hope for more substantial funding and even more sophisticated equipment. In the 1960s they proposed an ambitious approach

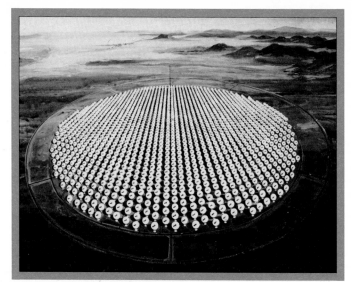

An artist conceptualizes Project Cyclops, a cluster of huge radio telescope antennae. This project to search out intelligent extraterrestrial life was never begun.

dubbed Project Cyclops, which involved the construction of an array of 1,000 radio telescopes, each with a diameter longer than a football field. Operating in unison, they would have the power to detect an ordinary television broadcast originating hundreds of light years away. But the cost of the array was put even at that time at a staggering $10 billion, and it has yet to be built.

Meanwhile, a number of more modest equipment advances have been made, and avid scientists continue to listen in to the water hole with the hope that one day something will pop out of the meaningless noise and announce that humanity is not alone in the universe. And although such activities and hopes may raise the eyebrows of the orthodox, they have evoked nothing like the ridicule reserved for people interested in UFOs. That derisive commentary would continue to dog the search for extraterrestrial intelligence as it proceeded at its erratic pace through the 1970s.

The first major wave of UFO sightings to be reported in the United States since 1965 occurred in 1973—coincidentally enough, the year after publication of Hynek's book and Sagan's report and the launching of *Pioneer 10*. Thousands of reports of every imaginable kind of sighting came from every part of the country, shattering any hope that the weight of the Condon Report and the air force disengagement had crushed the UFO phenomenon. Among the most famous cases of this wave was a reported close encounter of the third kind that happened at Pascagoula, Mississippi; in their account, two distraught shipyard workers claimed they had been abducted and examined by creatures aboard a UFO. The air force conducted an investigation, which it promptly classified.

Seven days later, on October 18, a close encounter that became just as famous was reported and—because of the technical sophistication of the subjects—was much more difficult to dismiss. A crew of three under the command of Army Reserve Captain Lawrence J. Coyne took a Bell UH-IH helicopter on a routine flight between Columbus and Cleveland, Ohio. At about 10:30 P.M., a crew member spotted a red light to the east that seemed to be flying at the same altitude and speed as the helicopter. He notified Coyne, who said, "Keep an eye on it." The crew tried to call air traffic control, but their radio would not transmit. Suddenly the light approached at a "terrifically fast" speed, an estimated 700 miles per hour. "It's going to ram us," Coyne remembered thinking. "Oh God, this is it!" He seized the controls and tried to descend. Swiftly they dropped below the object—which, to their astonishment, had stopped dead in the air and was now hovering over them in the clear, starlit sky.

"It was shaped like a fat cigar," said Coyne later, and had "a big, gray, metallic-looking hull about sixty feet long." In front was a glowing red light, on the center section a dome, and to the rear both a white and a green light. Presently, the green light aft swiveled like a spotlight. "It was shining brightly through the bubble canopy . . . turning everything inside green," Coyne recalled.

Then the object turned abruptly and accelerated toward the horizon, its white rear light winking out. Coyne insisted that he had the controls set for descent but the chopper was in fact rising—at a rate of 1,000 feet per minute for about 100 seconds. Also, his compass was spinning wildly (and had to be replaced later). When the crew regained control over the helicopter, the radio began to transmit again, and they went on to land at Cleveland. Each crew member filed a separate Operation Hazard Report with the FAA.

Subsequent investigations turned up no conventional explanation for the sighting. Coyne stuck to his story but at the same time said, "I don't believe in UFOs." Some local commentators theorized that the UFO was a spaceship that had somehow canceled out gravity locally, causing the chopper to rise despite its own controls. Meanwhile, the tirelessly skeptical Philip Klass suggested that the crew had been mesmerized by a fireball associated with the Orionid meteor showers—which are common that time of year and in 1973 peaked on October 21, three days after the incident—and that the entire event had taken only seconds rather than the four minutes reported by the crew.

The air force managed to keep its distance from—and its silence on—the subject of UFOs during the extensive flap, which finally dwindled away in 1974. But it could not put an end to its involvement with the bedeviling lights in the sky. In fact, with what almost seemed like deliberate perversity, the next UFO controversy was focused on air force bases.

On October 27, 1975, Staff Sergeant Danny Lewis was on security duty at Loring Air Force Base in Maine, near the Canadian border. His mission was to patrol the munitions storage area, which was dotted with igloolike huts containing nuclear weapons. At 7:45 P.M. Sergeant Lewis spotted an aircraft flying low along the northern edge of the base. Its altitude was about 300 feet. As he watched it enter the restricted air space over the base, he noted that it bore a red

The radio telescope at Arecibo, Puerto Rico, began operating in 1974 with a message beamed to stars 24,000 light years away.

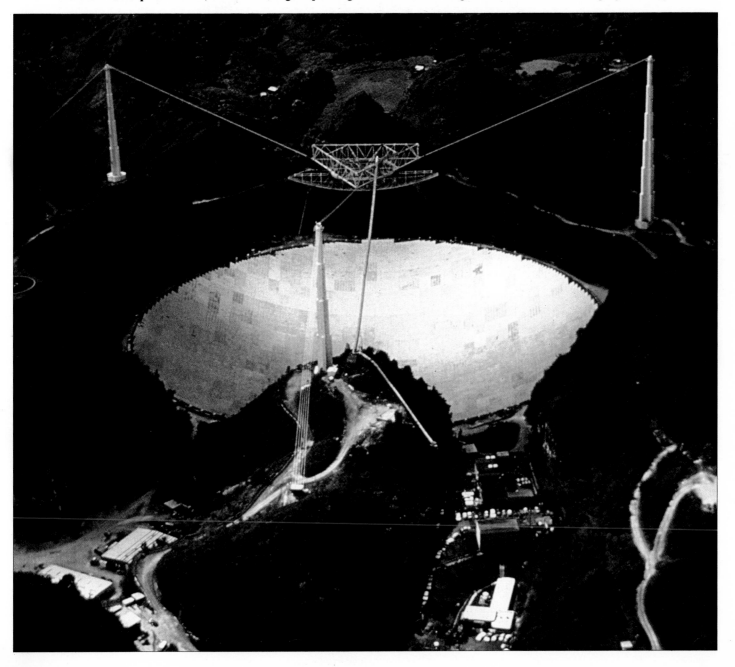

light and a blinking white strobe. At about this time, the control tower picked up a radar image of an aircraft some ten miles northeast of the base. Attempts to contact it by radio failed as the craft neared the base, circling low above the storehouse containing nuclear warheads. Alarms sounded as the base was put on alert. Security police began to scour the weapons storage area for intruders, while the tower kept the craft—presumably a helicopter—under radar surveillance. Abruptly, the craft stopped circling and disappeared.

The next night, a craft displaying a white flashing light and an amber light was observed, for thirty-five minutes, north of the base by Lewis and several other security officers. The sighting also was confirmed by radar. At one point the object, hovering 150 feet above the runway, shut off its lights and reappeared 150 feet above the munitions dump. A B-52 flight crew on the ground later reported they had observed a red and orange object in the air nearby. Shaped like a stretched-out football, it hovered, disappeared, and then reappeared, moving jerkily. The crewmen said they leaped into their truck and drove to within 300 feet of the object; it seemed to be about five feet off the ground and four car lengths long. One of the crew said later: "There were these waves in front of the object, and all the colors were blending together. The object was solid, and we could not hear any noise coming from it."

Suddenly the base came to life with sirens and lights. The object's lights went out and it streaked toward Canada, tracked briefly by radar as it went. The next night, National Guard helicopters were deployed to track any intruding craft, but during the next few weeks, there were only occasional reports and radar sightings. Whenever the base helicopters went to the place where ground personnel were seeing or hearing the object, they found nothing.

Some of these events were reported in the local press, along with a number of UFO sightings by civilian residents of the area. But most of the official account remained unread by the public until the 1980s, when two UFO researchers, Lawrence Fawcett and Barry Greenwood, extracted some documents from the air force by invoking the Freedom of

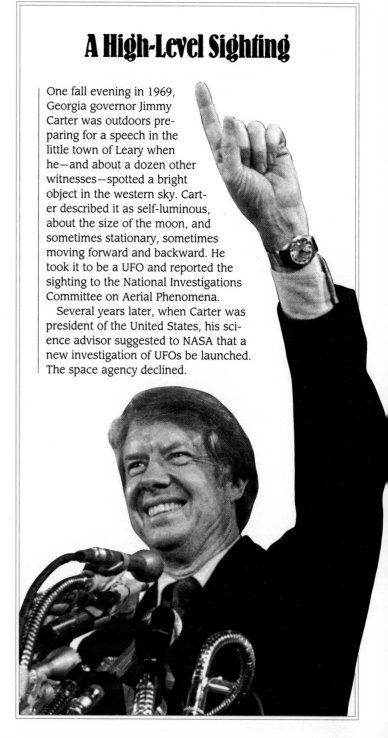

A High-Level Sighting

One fall evening in 1969, Georgia governor Jimmy Carter was outdoors preparing for a speech in the little town of Leary when he—and about a dozen other witnesses—spotted a bright object in the western sky. Carter described it as self-luminous, about the size of the moon, and sometimes stationary, sometimes moving forward and backward. He took it to be a UFO and reported the sighting to the National Investigations Committee on Aerial Phenomena.

Several years later, when Carter was president of the United States, his science advisor suggested to NASA that a new investigation of UFOs be launched. The space agency declined.

Information Act, which provides broad public access to government records. They also discovered that another, even more bizarre event had been reported on October 27, the night Sergeant Lewis first saw the object at Loring.

That evening, two young men, David Stephens and Glen Gray, were driving along a road about forty miles from Loring when, they said, their car was seized by an "unknown force" and whisked at well over 100 miles per hour to a field eleven miles away in the town of Poland, Maine. There the terrified men saw two bright lights: a truck, they thought. Then a cigar-shaped object about 100 yards long with red, blue, and green lights rose into the air from the field, and the two men drove away in fear. But when they looked back from a quarter of a mile away, they reported later, a bright light struck their car and they blacked out, reawakening hours afterward.

They tried to flee, only to lose control of the car again. The UFO then propelled them to the vicinity of a pond, where it was joined by two other craft. In moments all three objects disappeared. The hour was almost dawn.

The men soon noticed that their hands and feet were swollen and their teeth were loose. They also had severe chills, and red rings had appeared around their necks. Later, a doctor, Herbert Hopkins of Old Orchard Beach, Maine, treated Stephens with hypnosis in order to discover what had occurred during the missing time. Stephens recalled that he had been in a dome-shaped room when a humanlike creature entered.

"He was four and a half feet tall, dressed in a dark robe," Stephens said. "His head was shaped like a big lightbulb. He had slanted eyes, no hair, and no mouth." In due course, five such beings put Stephens on a table and examined him, using a machine with an extension arm. They took skin, blood, and hair samples and injected him with a brown liquid they said was a sedative. When Stephens eventually woke up, he found himself in his car next to his friend.

Aside from the symptoms reported by the two men, there was no evidence to support their dramatic story, although it would at length be seen to fit an emerging pattern in such accounts of close encounters of the third kind. In fact, a similar encounter allegedly took place a week later—this time on the other side of the continent.

On November 5, 1975, seven men were driving a pickup truck near Heber, Arizona, when they spotted an object hovering near the road, about fifteen feet off the ground. They stopped to look. One of the men, twenty-two-year-old Travis Walton, got out and approached the object. Suddenly, the men reported, a beam of light flashed from the UFO, struck Walton in the chest, and sent him sprawling ten feet back. His companions fled. They returned shortly afterward, when the UFO lifted off and disappeared, but Walton was gone.

ot until November 10, five days after the reported sighting, did Walton reappear, claiming he had been taken on board the craft and examined twice by small humanoids with large hairless heads, whitish skin, and oval eyes. Later, he said, he found himself on a road twelve miles from his abduction point, watching the UFO disappear overhead.

Researchers were quick to note the similarities in descriptions of aliens claimed to have been seen at different times and places by different observers. Meanwhile, another pattern—one involving the appearance of UFOs at Strategic Air Command installations—was also becoming apparent.

Three days after the first sighting at Loring, for example, much the same thing occurred over Wurtsmith Air Force Base in Michigan. Unknown craft with white and red lights were seen approaching. The base was put on alert, and a pilot was ordered to check out a reported UFO over the munitions dump. He spotted the object and, while pursuing it at a distance of only one mile, verified it on his radar before it zipped over Lake Huron. "I know this might sound crazy," he reported (in a memorandum dictated four years later, in 1979), "but I would estimate that the UFO sped away from us doing approximately 1,000 knots [1,150 miles per hour]."

One week later, an alarm went off at Malmstrom Air Force Base in Montana, the site of launching facilities for Minuteman missiles, and the electronic warning apparatus flagged one missile site. A Sabotage Alert Team (SAT) headed

immediately for the site, reporting by radio that they saw a glowing orange disk the size of a football field hovering over the area. It began to rise, and North American Air Defense Command radar picked it up when it reached an altitude of 1,000 feet. Two F-106 jet fighters were dispatched from Great Falls, Montana, to intercept the craft, but before the fighters arrived, it disappeared from the radar screens.

On November 8, there were more sightings—both visual and electronic—over the base. According to SAT teams, each time the F-106 jets screamed into the area, the UFOs shut off their lights, which reappeared only after the jets left. In the next eight months, 130 similar reports were logged at the base and in the surrounding county.

The air force had a ready explanation for the UFO reports: The intruders were helicopters. There was no explanation, however, of how or why they had breached base security, nor was there discussion of how so many experienced air force personnel—highly trained, carefully screened, with heavy responsibilities for the nation's missile defenses—had been fooled by ordinary helicopters.

Unsurprisingly, the official explanation did not satisfy some people who had first-hand knowledge of the events. One helicopter pilot who had been on alert at Malmstrom said later: "People were reporting a craft at low level they thought

was a helicopter. . . . Well, the weather was so bad when the report came in that it would have been impossible to fly a helicopter, with the icing and so forth. We couldn't fly, but this craft had no trouble flying in this weather."

The Strategic Air Command-base incidents ended, as had so many others, with some people fascinated by the reports, others dissatisfied with the official explanation, and no one sure exactly what had happened. Soon, however, more data would become available, and more investigators would be enlisted in the effort to solve the UFO mystery.

In the mid-1970s, usually under pressure from suits filed under provisions of the Freedom of Information Act by small, private UFO groups, various branches of the government released information about previous sightings and investigations. Numerous documents began to appear in public from such organizations as the CIA, the State Department, the Coast Guard, and the U.S. Army, Navy, and Air Force. These records indicated that the government had taken a more serious and widespread look than had been previously admitted. The new information added credibility to some long-forgotten sightings and attracted the attention of some newcomers to the study of the UFO phenomenon.

One of those whose interest was piqued was Bruce

Maccabee, a research physicist and teacher at American University in Washington, D.C. Maccabee—who in 1979 founded an organization called the Fund for UFO Research—was outraged by the seemingly cavalier attitude scientists had taken toward UFOs. "Although the sighting information is now available," he would observe, "it has been largely ignored" by the scientific community. "Evidently there is a general feeling that the 'UFO problem' was put to sleep long ago."

Seeking to remedy what he saw as the failings of most scientists, Maccabee took to debunking the UFO debunkers. Among his favorite targets was the skeptic Donald Menzel, who had proposed natural explanations, some of them tortuous, for any UFO report he came across. For some he offered several explanations—as he did for Kenneth Arnold's famous 1947 sighting, which marked the start of the modern UFO phenomenon in America.

As Menzel had it, the array of saucers that Arnold spotted was an illusion created by "billowing blasts of snow ballooning up from the tops of ridges" on Mount Rainier, reflecting the sun like a mirror. But Maccabee—knowledgeable about atmospheric optics—determined that such snow clouds do not reflect the sun anywhere near as brightly as a mirror. He also pointed out that there were no winds sufficient to propel the clouds at the estimated speed of the objects—between 1,200 and 1,700 miles per hour.

Lest the snow-cloud hypothesis fail to stand up, Menzel had proffered no fewer than six other atmospheric explanations for the sighting. But Maccabee proceeded to refute every one. "The UFO phenom-

enon," he wrote in conclusion, "is considered to be a trivial scientific problem, and therefore any explanation is acceptable to the science community."

While such figures as J. Allen Hynek and Maccabee pressed for more serious and objective study of unidentified flying objects, other scientists trotted out new hypotheses to explain the entire phenomenon. Some argued that it was a psychological problem; it was said, for example, that most people who observe UFOs are presumably status deficient, meaning that their position in life does not measure up to their expectations and that reporting sightings may give them gratifying importance. Others observed in rebuttal that this perceived syndrome is greatly overstated and, in any case, has no firm link to UFO sightings.

While scientists sought an acceptable, natural explanation for the UFO phenomenon, the more avid UFO enthusiasts strained to pinpoint the origins of the presumptive pilots of the ships. Some believers, expanding considerably on the old legends of lost Atlantis—and departing widely from mainstream ufologists—proposed that UFOs belong to an undersea civilization as yet undetected by oceanographic exploration. Others speculated that the vehicles come from a hollow portion of the earth that geophysicists are confident does not exist. Still others suggested the UFOs are piloted by creatures living nearby in space but capable of hiding in thin air—or, to use the modern jargon, in hyperspace.

Other explanations seek to link UFOs and international politics. Jacques Vallee, a French computer scientist who became interested in

UFOs in the early 1960s, has proposed a fanciful conspiracy theory that attributes the entire phenomenon to an international organization that has been operating in deep secrecy since the end of World War II. According to Vallee's elaborate scenario, this singular agency uses something called psychotronic technology—a combination of hypnotism and suggestion—to preprogram susceptible people to have UFO experiences. (At the same time, Vallee maintains that UFOs are real.) The purpose, as Vallee tells the tale, is to bring about major social change and avoid World War III.

 allee's perceived plot is a variation of the theory that UFOs are sophisticated weapons being developed by one of the great powers. The Cash-Landrum incident of 1980—in which the UFO was reportedly surrounded by what appeared to be U.S. military helicopters—raised this issue again. And so did a mysterious event that took place at about the same time in a British woodland. Shrouded in secrecy for some time, it gradually became one of the better publicized cases of a purported close encounter of the second—and perhaps third—kind.

Rendlesham Forest, near Ipswich in East Anglia, is a fourteen-square-mile expanse of pines managed by the British Forestry Commission for both timber harvesting and recreation. It is a damp place, the forest floor lushly blanketed by ferns. The area around it is, for Great Britain, sparsely populated, its largest settlements being the town of Woodbridge, west of the forest; the Woodbridge Royal Air Force Base, on the forest's western boundary with its main runway extending into the heart of Rendlesham; and the Bentwaters Royal Air Force Base, four miles away, just north of the forest.

The Bentwaters and Woodbridge bases were leased to the U.S. Air Force as part of the defense network of the North Atlantic Treaty Organization, or NATO. The British base commander acted merely as a caretaker; operations at both bases were under the control of an American colonel and his deputy.

Reports on the events of the night of December 27,

1980—if indeed that was the night they occurred—were pieced together later by a few investigators. The story remains murky, with the contradictory testimony providing footing as precarious as that found in the bogs that surround Rendlesham Forest.

A memorandum written more than two weeks after the event by the deputy base commander, Charles I. Halt, (and extracted from the air force much later by a request under the Freedom of Information Act) details the parts of the story on which there is little disagreement. Around 3:00 A.M. on December 27, wrote Halt, "two USAF security police patrolmen saw unusual lights outside the back gate at RAF Woodbridge. Thinking an aircraft might have crashed or been forced down, they called for permission to go outside the gate to investigate." Permission was granted.

Apparently a local farmer also saw a bright light go down into the forest at this time, assumed it was an aircraft, and called the security police at Bentwaters. A three-man patrol went out to investigate the odd light, which was still visible. When they approached the light they found a UFO. This was attested to by an American airman—who later said he was present and who insisted on anonymity yet identified himself as the acting commander of security at the base.

"The thing had a pulsating red light on top of it, and several blue lights underneath it," the informant told a civilian investigator. "Every time we got close to it, it would move away from us through the trees, then we'd try to catch up to it again." Colonel Halt, notified of the situation by radio, soon arrived with more help.

Members of the security force brought up portable floodlights operated by gasoline-powered generators; the engines would not start. As the search continued in the dark forest, the men came across what the nameless informant described as "a yellow mist on the ground, like nothing I'd ever seen before." They also heard a commotion from some animals on a nearby farm. And then they saw the UFO.

"Suddenly the object was just there," recalled the informant. "It was a dark silver-colored metal, with plenty of rainbow-colored lights on it. It was a tremendous size. We

Watchers at the Windows

The Yakima Indians have a legend that, in ages past, a red-eyed man with great healing powers came to live with the tribe. In due course he grew old, and one day he asked the Indians to take him to a particular place where he wished to die. Soon after his death, an object from the sky set down on the earth, took his body on board, and flew back into the heavens.

This story may be only a quaint bit of folklore, but some ufologists think otherwise. They contend that the Yakima Indian Reservation, a million acres of rugged terrain in south central Washington state, is a so-called window—a location frequented by unidentified flying objects. In recent years, a number of researchers have conducted studies at Yakima and other window sites in hopes of documenting and explaining the elusive lights and disks that seem to appear there.

The Yakima reservation is five miles south of Mount Rainier, where Kenneth Arnold's flying saucer sighting in 1947 started the modern UFO controversy. Between the years 1964 and 1984, there were 186 reports of UFO sightings on the reservation. Most of these came from fire lookouts, whose task it was to watch over the area's vast forests. In the main, their stories concerned red-orange or white nocturnal lights that behaved erratically, sometimes hovering, sometimes skittering about the sky with an agility belying terrestrial origin.

Intrigued by the reservation's mystery, the noted astronomer and UFO investigator J. Allen Hynek acquired backing for a study of the Yakima phenomena. Heading the project was an electrical engineer and volunteer UFO investigator by the name of David

The leader of a window watch in Norway, Leif Havik, sits outside a shelter used by field researchers in the snow-covered Hessdalen Valley. Around him are cameras used to capture some of the lights appearing in the area.

Akers. His equipment included a variety of cameras for both motion and still shots, one of which was fitted with a grating to analyze light wavelengths. He also had a magnetometer to record changes in magnetic fields, as well as instruments for measuring nuclear and infrared radiation and ultrasound frequencies. Akers began a two-week stakeout of the reservation on August 19, 1972. During that period he managed to get several still photographs of distant, anomalous lights, but the images were indistinct. However spirited it may have been, the work at the Yakima site was inconclusive.

The same could be said for Project Identification, a far more elaborate window watch centering on the town of Piedmont, Missouri. The project was initiated by physics professor Harley D. Rutledge of Southeast Missouri State University. Curious about a rash of UFO sightings in Piedmont early in 1973, Rutledge visited the town and saw twelve of the mysterious celestial lights himself. The eventual result of his experience there was a seven-year study that began in 1973 and involved a total of forty scientists, engineers, students, and laypeople, along with nearly $40,000 worth of equipment—everything that David Akers had used at the Yakima reservation and more.

Along with sophisticated cameras, the gear brought to Piedmont included four telescopes, a spectrum analyzer, and a gravimeter, which could be used to measure changes in gravitational field strength. Project Identification registered 157 sightings involving 178 UFOs. Professor Rutledge claimed to have made 160 personal sightings. But again, for all their labor, the researchers came away rich in long-distance photographs but poor in new knowledge about the nature and origin of unidentified flying objects.

Windows at overseas locations have

been equally grudging with their secrets. In a two-part study spanning two weeks each in 1984 and 1985, hardy Scandinavian researchers braved the arctic night to probe reports of UFOs over the Hessdalen Valley of Norway, five miles below the Arctic Circle. In December 1981, villagers there began seeing scores of strange objects in the sky. During a five-week period in January and February 1984, they reported as many as 188 sightings of amorphous lights, ovals, and cigar-shaped objects.

Like the Piedmont researchers, Project Hessdalen crew members were well equipped, having, among other

These mysterious lights were photographed by Leif Havik at Hessdalen two years before Project Hessdalen officially began.

items, radar and seismographic gear. They managed to pick up several UFOs on their radar, even when the objects themselves were not visible in any other way, and got some long-distance photographs. The crew also reported strange lights that had no discernible source. There was, for instance, a laser-thin red light that moved along the snow at ground level, playing around the feet of a villager who had been helping the crew, before it suddenly died out. Again, however, the

window watch fell short of identifying the local phenomena or explaining why unidentified flying objects seem to congregate in certain places.

While all this research was going on, a theory was advanced to explain not only windows but UFOs in general. Largely the brain child of Canadian psychophysiologist Michael A. Persinger, the theory proposed that geophysical processes that are associated with faults—or subsurface cracks in the earth's crust—created "earth lights" mistaken by some people for spaceships. Persinger posited that tectonic activity—underground movement of the earth along fault lines (Yakima, Piedmont, and Hessdalen are all located in fault zones)—compresses quartz crystals in rock, thereby releasing a form of energy known as *piezoelectricity.* This in turn, said Persinger, could produce balls of light capable of long duration and unpredictable behavior. Moreover, the theory went, the same energy could interfere with electrical impulses in the human brain, leading some people to misinterpret earth lights as UFOs. Many scientists, however, doubt the capacity of compressed quartz to produce enough energy to mimic unidentified flying objects. Also in question is whether the electricity could influence thought processes to any marked degree.

Window watchers also discount the Persinger theory. Rutledge has said that earth lights could not have constituted even one percent of the sightings recorded at Piedmont. Hessdalen is riddled with faults, but researchers there recorded no seismic activity during the project.

Intriguingly, researchers at all three of the window projects felt they were not just observing the UFOs but interreacting with them too. There were reports of objects that seemed to react to their being watched with binoculars or telescopes or having lights shined at them. Sometimes the mysterious objects allegedly flashed their own lights in apparent response or disappeared suddenly, as though they were shy of being scrutinized. It was even said that some of the UFOs seemed to know, perhaps through intercepting radio messages or through telepathy, the schedules of the watchers.

As Professor Rutledge maintained in his summing up of the Piedmont experiment: "More was involved than the measurement of physical properties of UFOs by dispassionate observers. A relationship, a cognizance, between us and the UFO intelligence evolved. A game was played."

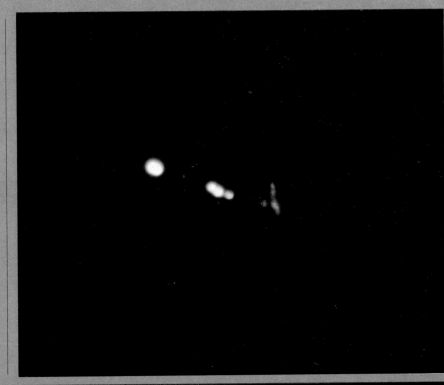

At the Yakima reservation, a sixty-second time exposure (right) shows one UFO in short bursts of motion from left to right; a light (below) seen from Piedmont, Missouri, was reported to have hovered for thirty minutes before it sped away.

were ordered to form a perimeter around the object at about fifteen-foot intervals between patrol members." Two British police officers, apparently investigating the strange lights, were off to one side taking photographs. The informant said that, on orders of Colonel Halt, he and another airman confiscated the film from the cameras. Meanwhile, two air force security officers continuously took pictures, he said.

After about half an hour, the craft vanished. "It was gone in a flash," said the alleged witness, "almost like it just disappeared. When it left, we were hit by a cold blast of wind which blew toward us for five or ten seconds. It was a really scary feeling. My life actually passed in front of my eyes."

"The next day," Colonel Halt's later memo continued in its second paragraph, "three depressions 1½ inches deep and 7 inches in diameter were found where the object had been sighted on the ground." Other observers told of scorched treetops in the area and damaged lights off the end of the nearby runway. "Later in the night," Colonel Halt went on, "a red sun-like light was seen through the trees. It moved about and pulsed. At one point it appeared to throw off glowing particles and broke into five separate white objects and then disappeared. Numerous individuals, including the undersigned, witnessed the activities in paragraphs 2 and 3."

hus Colonel Halt denied that he had seen the UFO itself. It was also denied that the base commander, Colonel Gordon Williams, was even present. But persistent rumors would later have it that Colonel Halt had not only ordered the craft guarded and protected from photographers, but also that Colonel Williams had met and talked with three occupants of the craft who stood before him enveloped in shafts of light. They were—or so the stories went—about three feet tall. As surprising allegations came to light, investigators tried to account for the extraordinary reports—in the face of official denials or silence. One suggestion was that the alien craft had crashed, that the air force personnel had been there while the craft was repaired and watched it depart. Another was that the craft had been taken by the air force and shipped secretly back to the United States.

Much later, an American UFO investigator associated with the private Mutual UFO Network (MUFON), Raymond Boeche, obtained documents related to the incident, including Halt's memo, and took them to Nebraska's Senator J. James Exon, who was at the time a member of the Senate Armed Services Committee. The senator agreed—somewhat reluctantly, Boeche thought—to look into the matter.

Later, according to Boeche, Senator Exon's staff told him the senator had indeed spent a great deal of time calling and writing people, including Colonel Halt. A staff member reportedly told Boeche, "I think he talked to just about everybody in DOD [Department of Defense] that there was to talk to. I've never seen him do the whole thing himself like this—it's just unusual." Whatever the senator found, he evidently never discussed it with his staff or anyone else. He told Boeche merely that there was "no government cover-up."

No cover-up of what? What did occur at Rendlesham Forest? To some ufologists, of course, it remains—and will always remain—an officially confirmed UFO landing and alien contact. Not long after news of the incident first appeared in a British tabloid in the fall of 1983, the British science writer Ian Ridpath conducted an on-the-scene investigation that suggested a more ordinary explanation.

According to Ridpath, who was shown around the area by a local forester, those who reported having seen a flashing UFO were in fact staring into the brilliant beam of a lighthouse, five miles away on the Suffolk coast. From the site of the alleged landing, observed Ridpath, the beam seemed to move and hover just a few feet off the ground, and its light seemed to be only a few hundred yards away. As for the so-called landing marks left behind by the departing craft, Ridpath's forester guide—who had seen shallow depressions—said that he had recognized them as rabbit diggings. The supposed burns on nearby trees were identified as resin-blotched axe cuts made by foresters to mark trees for harvesting. Ridpath also checked local police records and found that the event had actually occurred the night before the date given in Halt's memo, written two weeks afterward. And on the night of the incident, Ridpath discovered, an excep-

136

These dramatic pictures were taken by a Swiss laborer named Eduard Meier, who in the 1970s became one of ufology's most controversial figures. Meier lived in the village of Hinwil, southeast of Zurich. Considered eccentric because of his inexplicable visits to forests near his home, Meier eventually disclosed that he was communing there with extraterrestrials from the Pleiades star cluster. He took hundreds of photographs of what he said were their spaceships. Still other pictures allegedly were shot in outer space during jaunts there with his alien friends. Meier has attracted many believers, and even his detractors concede that his pictures, if fakes, are remarkably clever.

Trial by Computer

Mrs. Paul Trent was feeding rabbits in her backyard when the saucer appeared. According to the McMinnville, Oregon, woman, she glanced up from her task on the evening of May 11, 1950, to see a huge, metallic disk gliding silently through the overcast sky. She called her husband, fetched a camera, and watched as he snapped two pictures of the craft before it accelerated into the west.

Those two photographs became fa-mous in the annals of ufology. For decades afterward they were scrutinized by a variety of investigators ranging from U.S. Air Force officials to *Life* magazine photographers. Most of those who studied the pictures agreed with the conclusions of 1969's skeptical Condon Report: "The simplest, most direct interpretation of the photographs confirms precisely what the witnesses said they saw." More recently, William H. Spaulding of Ground Saucer Watch Inc., a group devoted to the scientific study of UFOs, has subjected the pictures to a computer analysis that yielded even more evidence about the much-handled photographs—evidence that seems to indicate that they are not a hoax.

Spaulding and his colleagues have used their computer to study more than 1,000 UFO photos, including the Trent pictures. First, they scan each photograph with a television-type camera that breaks the picture down into almost a quarter of a million pixels, or picture cells. The scanner measures the brightness of each pixel and assigns it a numerical rating. These values are entered into the computer's memory; the original picture can then be reproduced and manipulated on a computer screen.

Formerly difficult feats are easy with the computer. A technician can identify two points on the screen and ask the computer to calculate the exact distance between them, using a program that analyzes known points of reference in the photo. The user can also enlarge tiny details, revealing in some cases the telltale Frisbee trademark on a supposed UFO. Per-

One of Paul Trent's 1950 snapshots (left) reveals the UFO's turreted form. Edge enhancement (below) brings out the odd shape (and scratches in the negative); color contouring (bottom) confirms the three-dimensional nature.

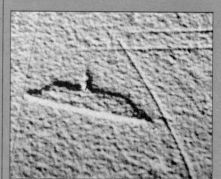

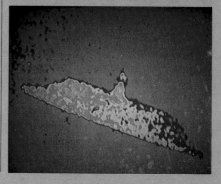

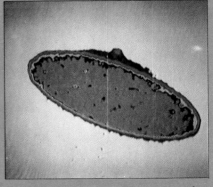

The second Trent photo (above) contains the classic disklike shape of a UFO but yields few details. Computerized edge enhancement (right) shows that the object had no supporting wires, and color contouring (far right) highlights its flat, evenly lit bottom.

haps most useful is the computer's ability to stretch color values, brightening or darkening individual pixels to bring out details.

Among the many tests investigators applied to the Trent photos were two kinds of stretching procedures. The first was edge enhancement, which sharpens subtle details in pictures by increasing contrast in adjoining pixels. This technique often brings out supporting wires and other hidden devices in faked UFO pictures: For example, the computer can detect a string with a diameter of .009 inch at a distance of up to ten feet.

The second procedure, called color contouring, involves assigning thirty discrete colors to the shades of gray in the original photo. An object's indis-

tinct patterns of highlights and shadows, vividly transformed by the process, can tell investigators much about its actual shape, material, and density. A cloud can thus be distinguished from a solid craft, and a flat cutout from a three-dimensional shape.

The Trent photos passed Spaulding's test with high marks. Edge enhancement showed the UFO was not suspended by a string from overhead wires, as some skeptics had suggested. Color contouring indicated a three-dimensional shape with a flat, evenly

lit underside. Further comparisons of the UFO with objects in the foreground seemed also to confirm that it was at least one kilometer away and about twenty to thirty meters in diameter. Although some questions still stand about the time of day (the shadows seem to indicate morning rather than evening sun) and the general veracity of the witnesses (who had claimed UFO sightings before), Spaulding and his associates believe that the Trents' snapshots may in fact be that rarity—genuine UFO photographs.

A Fakery Exposed

Paul Villa's handsome saucer photographs, long suspected of being fakes *(page 89)*, may have received their deathblow at the hands of William Spaulding and his Ground Saucer Watch technology. Villa claimed to have seen a seventy-foot-wide spacecraft many times near Albuquerque, New Mexico, and to have spoken to its attractive, seven-foot-tall inhabitants. They told him they had come on a peaceful mission from the constellation of Coma Berenices; earth people had not discovered them because their spaceships possessed antiradar devices. By 1963, Villa says, he was on such friendly terms with the aliens that they posed their ship for his camera.

Computer analysis, however, told a different story. In at least one of the photos, the spacecraft proved to be held aloft by a supporting wire or string. The sharpness of the image also suggested that the ship was close to the camera and no more than twenty inches wide. The Villa photos are typical of those examined by Ground Saucer Watch. Of the more than 1,000 supposed UFO photographs analyzed by the group's computers, 605 proved to be hoaxes, and most of the others seemed to be misinterpretations of phenomena such as balloons. Only forty withstood the computer's scrutiny to remain, for the time being, bona fide unexplained objects.

Relatively convincing in its original state, Paul Villa's UFO photo (below) takes on another look when subjected to edge enhancement (left): The ship appears to be held up by wire stretched between trees.

tionally brilliant meteor had blazed over southern England.

Others, conceding that perhaps a UFO did not land in the forest but unwilling to accept Ridpath's explanation, have suggested that the air force may have leaked accounts of a UFO to cover up the crash of an airplane carrying nuclear bombs. MUFON investigator Boeche wondered whether the incident was an accident involving some new kind of weapon, or the recovery of some fallen space-probe debris. In any event, there is no official explanation to date.

The Rendlesham Forest episode was followed by numerous other UFO events. A wave of sightings occurred in Pennsylvania in 1982. In 1983, thousands of people in New York's Westchester and Putnam counties reported a night-flying craft the size of a football field and the shape of a boomerang, with multiple running lights, flying overhead; traffic halted on the Taconic State Parkway as people goggled at the UFO. Police switchboards were jammed with calls.

In general, the police tried to explain this sighting as a flight of ultralight aircraft (basically hang gliders with engines) or as military flights, which the military denied. Among the thousands of witnesses were scientists and engineers. Later, however, other similar sightings of a V-shaped flying object turned out to be the result of a hoax; some local private pilots admitted that they had set out to fly in formation at night to stimulate more UFO reports.

Nor were UFO sightings restricted to the United States. In May 1986, for example, Brazil's air force minister went on television to explain that the country's defense system had gone on alert a few days earlier when twenty-one "uncorrelated targets" had shown up on radar. Jets went aloft and located and chased a number of mysterious objects with flashing lights, and in some instances were chased in turn. The pilots gave their own accounts in a televised press conference, and the air force minister summarized the incident: "The sky was entirely clear, and there were no aircraft in the sky when the lights were detected. Technically speaking, there is no explanation."

UFOs continued through the 1980s to surprise pilots and citizens, zooming overhead, evading jet pursuit. The Center for UFO Studies continued to receive between 800 and 1,200 reports a year. But, to the dismay of many ufologists, a certain kind of close encounter was increasingly prevalent—and increasingly well publicized.

In his 1972 book, J. Allen Hynek had hinted that, deep down, he wished all encounters of the third kind would go away because their frequently lurid details strained the credulity of even committed believers in UFOs. But, almost reluctantly, he later came to admit that some such accounts were plausible and otherwise inexplicable. Pascagoula was such a case. There had been, in the Pascagoula incident, features similar to the Barney and Betty Hill abduction *(pages 79-84)*. The victims claimed that they had been rendered powerless, taken aboard a strange craft, and subjected to physical examination. In other incidents, like Travis Walton's in Arizona, people found that after seeing a UFO they were missing time—usually hours but sometimes days—out of their lives. In most instances the allegedly missing time seemed to be concealed behind a veil of apparent amnesia that could be penetrated only by careful hypnosis. More often than not in these cases, people recalled having been taken into a large, brightly lit room, laid out on some sort of table, and examined carefully by short humanoids with large dark eyes. This examination was invariably a painful experience. Many of the subjects were subsequently found to exhibit the shame and guilt found among victims of rape; most would discuss their experiences only reluctantly. In this they are quite the opposite of the garrulous contactees, who seem to revel in publicity about their adventures. Nonetheless, abduction cases do embarrass many UFO researchers, because such stories—even more than other UFO reports—are so frequently greeted by ridicule, precisely as the victims fear.

The chief chronicler of abduction cases is a renowned New York artist named Budd Hopkins, who, believing he had sighted a UFO over Cape Cod in 1974, began looking into the Hill case anew. As a result of his research, he began to hear from many people who claimed similar experiences. He published a book in 1981 called *Missing Time,* in which he described a number of abduction experiences. Perhaps inspired by reading the travails of others, still more people came forward to tell similar stories. Among them was Kathie Davis (a pseudonym chosen by Hopkins to protect her privacy), a young woman from the state of Indiana. Her case became the subject of Hopkins's second book, titled *Intruders,* which sold briskly when it was published in 1987.

 athie Davis lived in an Indianapolis suburb called Copley Woods. In 1983, when the woman was 24, Copley Woods had evidently been visited by a UFO. Household electrical systems behaved strangely, and one morning the Davis family found a large, circular, scorched area in their backyard, a place where subsequently nothing would grow. It was then that Kathie began corresponding with Hopkins. In time, she told him of a dream she had had five years earlier in which she was visited by two small "men" with "dingy white, almost gray" skin and eyes that were "pitch black in color, liquidlike." They gave her a dark box with a glistening red light on top and then departed, telling her they would return.

Hopkins found Kathie's dream—and several other elements of her family's experiences, including mysterious scars found on the legs of three of them—to be similar to experiences related by other abductees. During the next few years, with the aid of psychiatrists, psychologists, and hypnotists, he obtained complex and frightening stories from Kathie Davis, all of which fit the general pattern of abduction cases.

It seems that early in her childhood, Kathie had first been visited by small alien creatures who examined her carefully. During the most recent visit, which Kathie recalled had taken place on the night her backyard was scorched, they had thrust a needle into her ear until she felt great pain. Hopkins suggested they were implanting some tiny device by which the alien beings could track her. The scar on her leg and those found on other members of her family, Hopkins thought, were incisions made to take cell samples. Hopkins reported that these scars were often found on people claiming to have had such experiences, and added, "of the fifty-eight people I've worked with who have recalled nearly complete abduction experiences, eleven have reported the insertion of what seem to be tiny implants into their bodies."

Kathie reported that she had become pregnant in her teens but in her first trimester had found that the pregnancy had ended without any sign. Her doctor was sure from early blood and urine tests that it was not a false pregnancy. Under hypnosis, Kathie related that the aliens had visited her and performed an uncomfortable gynecological procedure, after which she became pregnant. A few months later, they returned and removed the developing fetus, Kathie recalled, as she screamed at them not to take away her baby.

Subsequently, Kathie married and gave birth without complications to two boys. Then, she said, the aliens returned and displayed to her a female creature that looked like a more human version of themselves. Later, they returned and thrust another tiny, wrinkled, gray-skinned infant at her. This appeared to be an especially "wise" baby, and she held him instinctively to her breast while the aliens observed her intently. To Hopkins, this suggested that the aliens were seeking to learn how humans nurture a child.

From Kathie's reported experiences and many other people's tales of alien abduction accompanied by genital probing, Hopkins concluded that the aliens are researching certain bloodlines. Perhaps, he wrote, they are performing crossbreeding experiments, possibly to regain for themselves some lost genetic strength or variability.

To be sure, Kathie's stories may resemble the ravings of the mentally disturbed. But Hopkins subjected Kathie and many other informants to a sophisticated series of psychological tests. The results, he claimed, showed that none were paranoid, schizophrenic, or otherwise emotionally crippled. There was a pattern, however: All suffered from lack of self-esteem, and none seemed fully at ease with themselves physically. Said one psychologist: "They're just more vigilant, more hesitant to trust, than the average person."

Hopkins has set up networks for these people so that

they can discuss their experiences with others who have had them and, in the manner of group therapy sessions for rape victims, come to grips with the emotional aftermath. One such person was a novelist, Whitley Strieber, whose claimed experiences paralleled the others' and were described in great detail in his best-selling book, *Communion,* published almost simultaneously with Hopkins's *Intruders.*

Not surprisingly, the avid UFO debunker Philip Klass dismisses the abductees' tales as nonsense of the first order. "Why has not a single one of them," he asks, "ever reported the abduction to the FBI?" Where, he wants to know, is the hard evidence, the souvenirs? No alleged abductee, Klass has observed wryly, has ever returned from his or her travels bearing the alien equivalent of an ashtray or matchbook. Ufologist Bruce Maccabee is also concerned, worrying that the wave of abduction reports will bring "all sorts of nuts and kooks out of the woodwork."

But if the stories of abductions are in fact coming from people who are not, as Hopkins has indicated, mentally disturbed, who generally have little to gain from telling of their experiences, and who are geographically separate, then the stories may not constitute a mere case of hysterical contagion. And if, as UFO historian and abduction researcher David Jacobs has commented, it is some wholly new psychological phenomenon, then that in itself would seem to merit research and explanation.

When the U.S. government formally withdrew from the investigation of UFO sightings in 1969, declaring them unworthy of serious consideration, many people hoped that the controversy over such events would fade away. Instead, it has grown and taken unexpected twists and turns. There are still vociferous believers and nonbelievers alike, as well as a handful of peo-

ple who simply plead for honest scientific study of what is quite obviously a real phenomenon of some kind.

And whatever may lie behind it, public interest in UFOs remains inexhaustible. To the organization's dismay, the National Science Foundation learned in 1986 that 43 percent of American adults surveyed believed that "it is likely that some of the unidentified flying objects that have been reported are really space vehicles from other civilizations."

Enthusiasts continue to embrace alleged evidence of earthly visitations by these vehicles. In mid-1987, for example, there was a major stirring in ufology circles when a trio of investigators released copies of what they claimed was a top-secret document relating to the classic Roswell, New Mexico, incident of 1947. The document,

Author of Missing Time and Intruders, Budd Hopkins is also an award-winning painter and sculptor. He has investigated UFOs since 1975, specializing in alleged abductions of humans.

A purported UFO landing site in Kathie Davis's backyard forms a persistent scorched pattern: bare of grass in summer (top) and snow in winter (center), and devoid of vegetation and insects a full two years later.

which had arrived on microfilm in a plain brown wrapper at the Los Angeles home of one of the researchers, seemed to be a briefing paper prepared in November 1952 for President-elect Dwight D. Eisenhower. It states that spacecraft wreckage and small humanoid bodies were recovered and studied after the crash of a UFO near Roswell. Supposedly, a team of federal scientists had determined that the dead creatures were biologically dissimilar to human beings; investigators had been unable to determine the power source used by the unidentified object or to decipher examples of writing that was retrieved from the debris.

Most observers, including many who devoutly hope that tangible, irrefutable evidence for UFOs will someday appear, describe the Roswell briefing paper as a probable hoax. Even so, it is likely to remain the centerpiece of a hot debate. Among some ufologists, for example, news of the document revived a mild paranoia about the government's role in the UFO phenomenon. Such diehards are likely to continue their insistence that the government surely has collected crashed UFOs at one time or another, and even the bodies of aliens. But others, among them UFO historian David Jacobs, point out that if any branch of the government had indeed collected physical evidence of UFOs—a piece of a craft or the craft itself or its inhabitants—there would be no way that the secret

could be confined to the enormous number of scientists who would have to be involved in studying the material over the decades.

The pressures to dismiss UFO reports—competition for research funds, concern for individual reputations, unremitting derision by the debunkers—continue to prevail. They are fostered to an extent by scientific "realism," but they may be spawned, too, by what J. Allen Hynek called a "certain smugness," a universal tendency toward "a complacent unawareness of the scope of things not yet known."

One of the most objective thinkers ever to get embroiled in the UFO controversy, Hynek voiced a plea throughout most of four decades, until his death in 1986, that seems likely to remain unanswered for years to come. He urged that researchers accept the UFO phenomenon as worthy of study, avoid getting tangled in unverifiable preconceptions about what UFOs are, study the data as thoroughly as possible, and above all remain aware of their own ignorance.

Whatever accounts for this long-lived, irrepressible phenomenon, Hynek wrote, will be "as incredible to us as television would have been to Plato." Summing up, he came to a tantalizing conclusion. The explanation for UFOs, when it is at length discovered, "will prove to be not merely the next small step in the march of science but a mighty and totally unexpected quantum jump."

A Universe of Possibilities

Do we have neighbors in the cosmos? Or is their existence no more than a mirror of our fantasies? Perhaps in the infancy of our species we are like children in the dark. We peer into the blackness, fearing it yet seeking within it some reassurance that we are not alone. We cling to the notion that somewhere in the void are beings not unlike us, but maybe wiser, better — creatures who can tell us secrets that will save us from ourselves. We need to believe.

Some scientists argue that we *are* alone, that human intelligence is the product of a process so subtle and intricate that it could not be replicated elsewhere. Others say the universe must abound with intelligent forms of life. Earth is but a speck in a stellar vastness so great our minds cannot begin to encompass it; to think ourselves unique is absurd, a cosmic egocentricity.

But if our neighbors do exist, how could we hope ever to meet them? Who are they, where are they, and how could they possibly traverse the interstellar immensities to make themselves known? At the leading edge of today's mathematics and physics are theories that offer not answers but intriguing riddles for new imaginings. For believers, rightly or wrongly, the theories are things to conjure with.

A black hole is a gravitational field so dense it swallows light itself. Where black holes are, the very fabric of space-time is warped. In such a place, do the known laws of physics still govern? Some astronomers think not. Some even theorize that black holes might be portals to other universes or other dimensions—passageways where the familiar rules of time and space, cause and effect, have no purview. The believer wonders: Could beings enter and survive to find themselves instantly in some other place, some other time? Are black holes shortcuts through the universe, detours where there is no celestial speed limit?

Suppose our cosmic neighbors need not get here. Suppose they already *are* here.

Mathematicians seeking equations to encompass all cosmic mass propose a theory of whimsical elegance: What if a shadow universe parallels our own? It is omnipresent but in-visible; light passes through it. It shares with our universe only gravity. Its veiled and whirling spheres might attract the solid orbs of our cosmos into inex-plicable orbits and, in turn, make their own phantom revo-lutions in our heavens. Could intelligent beings actually exist in this shadow realm, beings who see us as the shadows? Could they have found a way to penetrate the dimensional threshhold between us?

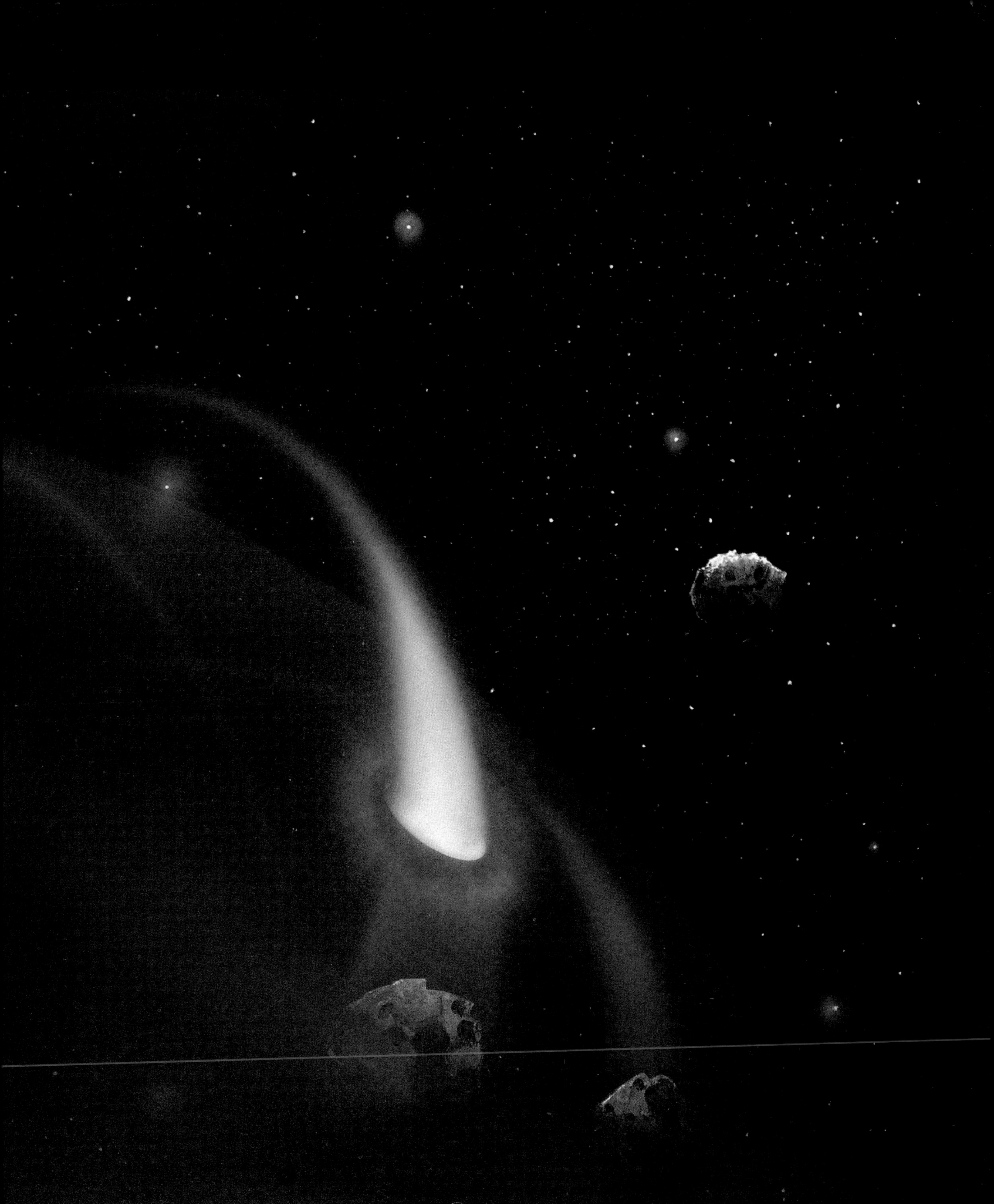

Some scientists suggest that our universe is of no more consequence than a single atom in a solar system. Innumerable universes might exist, and conceivably, each could have its own intelligent life, multiplying prodigiously the chances that we are not alone. Conceivably, too, each could have its own template of reality. Consider, for instance, the possibility of a universe with only two dimensions, or twenty; or a cosmos in which past, present, and future all exist at once, and where travel between worlds is instantaneous. Such are the speculations on the frontiers of science. And—who knows?—there may be truths far stranger than anything a human mathematician or astrophysicist has yet come to dream.

ACKNOWLEDGMENTS

The index was prepared by Lynne R. Hobbs. The editors wish to express their appreciation to the following individuals and organizations:

Walter Andrus, International Director of the Mutual UFO Network, Seguin, Tex.; Anny Baguhn, Hamburg, West Germany; Tom Benson, Trenton, N.J.; Countess Maria Fede Caproni, Museo Aeronautico Caproni di Taliedo, Rome, Italy; Mario Cingolani, President, Centro Ufologico Nazionale, Florence, Italy; Jerome Clark, Editor, *Fate* magazine, Highland Park, Ill.; Hilary Evans, London; Prof. B. Roy Frieden, University of Arizona, Tucson, Ariz.; Barry Greenwood, Stoneham, Mass.; Budd Hopkins, Wellfleet, Mass.; James Karales, New York; Greg Long, Kennewick, Wash.; Ilo Brand von Ludwiger, Feldkirchen, West Germany; Hiroshi Motoyama, Institute for Religious Psychology, Tokyo, Japan; Roberto Pinotti, Secretary, Centro Ufologico Nazionale, Florence, Italy; *Yamagata Shimbun*, Yamagata, Japan; William Spaulding, Phoenix, Ariz.; Ronald Story, St. Petersburg, Fla.; Erling Strand, Project Hessdalen, Eidsvoll, Norway; Rolf Streichardt, Institut für Grenzgebiete der Psychologie und Psychohygiene, Freiburg, West Germany.

PICTURE CREDITS

The sources for the pictures in this book are listed below. Credits for pictures shown from left to right are separated by semicolons; credits from top to bottom are separated by dashes.

Cover: Art by Lloyd K. Townsend. 6, 7: Art by Giraffics, Inc. 9: William Warren/Backgrounds from Woodfin Camp & Associates, UFO art by Alfred T. Kamajian. 10, 11: Art by Alfred T. Kamajian. 13: Catalog No. 148148, Department of Anthropology, Smithsonian Institution; BPCC/Aldus Archive, London—Department of Archeology, Faculty of Arts and Letters, Tohoku University, Sendai, Japan. 14: Mary Evans Picture Library, London. 15: Courtesy Josef Blumrich. 17: Painting by Ghirlandaio, Loeser Collection, Palazzo Vecchio, Florence, photo courtesy Scala, Florence—Momčilo Djordjević, Belgrade/Dečani Monastery, Yugoslavia; Jean-Pierre Muzard/Collegiale Notre Dame, Beaune, France. 18: "Vädersolstavlan" by Urban Målare, photo by Francis Bruun, courtesy Stockholms Stadsmuseum. 19: American Numismatic Association Photographic Services. 20: Betty and Dennis Milon; Herman Hoerlin courtesy *Sunsets, Twilights and Evening Skies,* Aden and Marjorie Meinel, Cambridge University Press, 1983—Dick Ruhl/APRO—June M. Gilby. 21: B. T. Matthias and S. J. Buchsbaum-AT&T Bell Laboratories; Jerome Wyckoff (2). 22: Courtesy Tom Benson; courtesy Walter Andrus, Mutual UFO Network. 23: Courtesy Tom Benson; Mary Evans Picture Library, London. 24: Fotokhronika TASS, Moscow. 26: Fortean Picture Library, Wales. 27: Erik Reuterswärd, Uppsala, Sweden. 29: © by Universal Pictures Division of Universal City Studios, courtesy MCA Publishing Rights, a Division of MCA, Inc. 30, 31: © by Universal Pictures Division of Universal City Studios, courtesy MCA Publishing Rights, a Division of MCA, Inc.; *War of the Worlds* © 1953 by Paramount Pictures Corporation, all rights reserved, photo courtesy the Kobal Collection Ltd., New York. 32, 33: © 1977 by Columbia Pictures Industries, Inc.; © 1977 by Columbia Pictures Industries, Inc. 34, 35: © by Universal Pictures Division of Universal City Studios, courtesy MCA Publishing Rights, a Division of MCA, Inc., photo courtesy the Kobal Collection Ltd., London. 37: Craig Arness/Backgrounds from Woodfin Camp & Associates, UFO art by Alfred T. Kamajian. 39: Reprinted by permission of *Fate* magazine, photo courtesy Mary Evans Picture Library, London; Fortean Picture Library, Wales. 40: UPI/Bettmann Newsphotos. 42, 43: UPI/Bettmann Newsphotos—Associated Press/Wide World Photos; Associated Press, courtesy Martin Luther King Memorial Library, Washington, D.C. 45: Associated Press, courtesy the *Washington Star* Collection, Martin Luther King Memorial Library, Washington, D.C. 47: Fortean Picture Library, Wales. 48: Juan Guzman, Mexico/*Time.* 50, 51: National Archives Record Group 341, Project Blue Book Case No. 978, except bottom right: James F. Coyne/*Time.* 52: Wilhelm Reich Museum. 53: Leni Iselin/Nancy Palmer Agency, courtesy Encyclopaedia Britannica. 54: National Archives Record Group 341, Project Blue Book Case No. 3088. 55: Albert Fenn for *Life.* 56: Reprinted from *Popular Science* with permission, © 1952 Times Mirror Magazines, Inc., photo courtesy Library of Congress. 57: Art by Wendy Popp, detail from pages 60-61. 58-63: Art by Wendy Popp. 65: © Steve Vidler/After Image 1987, UFO art by Alfred T. Kamajian. 67: From *UFOs: A Pictorial History from Antiquity to the Present,* by David C. Knight, McGraw-Hill Book Company, 1979, New York. 68: Mary Evans Picture Library, London, except left: Leonard Stringfield, courtesy Mutual UFO Network. 69: Fortean Picture Library, Wales; Mary Evans Picture Library, London; Fortean Picture Library, Wales—drawing by Gene Duplantier and Jennings H. Frederick, from *Gray Barker's Newsletter.* 71: © 1939 Loew's Incorporated, copyright renewed 1965 Metro-Goldwyn-Mayer, Inc., photo courtesy the Kobal Collection Ltd., London. 72: UFOIN-Rome, Ohio. 73: Reprinted from the *Saturday Evening Post,* © 1956 by Curtis Publishing Co., photo courtesy Library of Congress. 74, 75: © GAF International, Vista, California, photos courtesy Mary Evans Picture Library, London, except bottom left: Fortean Picture Library, Wales. 77: Art by Bryan Leister. 78: Unarius Education Foundation. 79: Amalgamated Flying Saucer Clubs of America/Gabriel Green. 80, 81: Colin Maher, London. 82: UPI/Bettmann Newsphotos. 83: Drawing by David C. Baker from *Visitors from Outer Space* by Roy Stemman, © 1976 by Aldus Books Limited, London. 84, 85: Fortean Picture Library, Wales. 87: National Archives Record Group 341, Project Blue Book Case No. 1501, detail from photo page 97. 88: National

Archives Record Group 341, Project Blue Book Case No. 9654. 89: National Archives Record Group 341, Project Blue Book Case No. 8398. 90: National Archives Record Group 341, Project Blue Book Case No. 9318. 91: National Archives Record Group, Project Blue Book Case No. 7027. 92: National Archives Record Group 341, Project Blue Book Case No. 6311. 93: National Archives Record Group 341, Project Blue Book Case No. 9816. 94: National Archives Record Group 341, Project Blue Book Case No. 10913. 95: National Archives Record Group 341, Project Blue Book Case No. 11263. 96: National Archives Record Group 341, Project Blue Book Case No. 7824. 97: National Archives Record Group 341, Project Blue Book Case No. 1501. 99: Jack Elness/ Comstock, Inc., UFO art by Alfred T. Kamajian. 100, 101: Art by Jack Pardue. 102, 103: James H. Karales. 105: Courtesy Philip J. Klass. 106, 107: From *Flying Saucers, a Look* Special, by the editors of Cowles and UPI, © 1967, headline © 1966 by the *New York Times* Company, reprinted by permission. 108: UPI/Bettmann Newsphotos. 110, 111: Courtesy NICAP/ CUFOS (National Investigations Committee on Aerial Phenomena/Center for UFO Studies), except bottom drawings: Fortean Picture Library, Wales (2). 112, 113: UPI/Bettmann Newsphotos. 114, 115: UPI, courtesy *Washington Star* Collection, Martin Luther King Memorial Library, Washington D.C., except sketch by Deputy Spaur, from *The UFO Investigator*, Vol. 3, No. 7, March/April 1966, photo courtesy Library of Congress. 116: Carl Iwasaki/ *Time*. 117: OLIPHANT, by Pat Oliphant, © 1967 by Universal Press Syndicate, reprinted with permission, all rights reserved. 118: Stan Wayman for *Life*. 119: Courtesy Don Berliner. 121: Richard Laird/FPG, UFO art by Alfred T. Kamajian. 122: UPI/Bettmann Newsphotos. 123: Rob Stapleton/*People*. 125: Bob Skinner/Fortean Picture Library, Wales—courtesy J. Allen Hynek Center for UFO Studies and Tom Benson (2)—Shinichiro Namiki, Tokyo. 126: NASA photo. 127: Arecibo Observatory, a part of the National Astronomy and Ionosphere Center, Cornell University/National Science Foundation. 128: UPI/Bettmann Newsphotos. 130: NASA photo. 131: Westlands plc, Yeovil, Somerset. 133: Project Hessdalen/ Mary Evans Picture Library, London. 134: Leif Havik/Project Hessdalen. 135: Greg Long—Harley Rutledge. 137: Eduard (Billy) Meier—Eduard (Billy) Meier, © Genesis III Publishing, Inc. 138, 139: GSW, Inc., Phoenix, Arizona. 140: GSW, Inc., Phoenix, Arizona—Paul Villa, courtesy GSW, Inc., Phoenix, Arizona. 143: Jack Vartoogian/*People*. 144: Courtesy Budd Hopkins. 145: Art by Giraffics, Inc., detail from pages 148-149. 146-151: Art by Giraffics, Inc.

BIBLIOGRAPHY

Abell, George O., and Barry Singer, eds., *Science and the Paranormal.* New York: Charles Scribner's Sons, 1983.

Allman, William F., "Cosmic Inflation." *Science 82,* December 1982.

Anderson, Craig W., *Science Fiction Films of the Seventies.* Jefferson, N.C.: McFarland & Company, 1985.

Apfel, Necia H., and J. Allen Hynek, *Architecture of the Universe.* Menlo Park, Calif.: Benjamin/Cummings, 1979.

Arnold, Kenneth, "I Did See the Flying Disks!" *Fate,* spring 1948.

Arnold, Kenneth, and Ray Palmer, *The Coming of the Saucers.* Boise, Idaho: Ray Palmer and Kenneth Arnold, 1952 (privately published).

Barrow, John D., and Joseph Silk, *The Left Hand of Creation: The Origin and Evolution of the Expanding Universe.* New York: Basic Books, 1983.

Bartusiak, Marcia F., *Thursday's Universe.* New York: Random House, 1986.

Berlitz, Charles, and William L. Moore, *The Ros-well Incident.* New York: Grossett & Dunlap, 1980.

Bloecher, Ted, *Report on the UFO Wave of 1947.* Tucson, Ariz.: Institute of Atmospheric Physics, University of Arizona, 1967.

Blumrich, Josef F., *The Spaceships of Ezekiel.* New York: Bantam, 1974.

Boeche, Raymond W., "Bentwaters—What Do We Know Now?" *Mutual UFO Network 1986 UFO Symposium Proceedings,* East Lansing, Mich., June 1986.

Boslough, John, *Stephen Hawkins's Universe.* New York: William Morrow, 1985.

Brookesmith, Peter, ed.:
The Alien World. London: Orbis, 1984.
The UFO Casebook. London: Orbis, 1984.

Brosnan, John, *Future Tense: The Cinema of Science Fiction.* New York: St. Martin's Press, 1978.

Browne, Malcolm W., "Physicist Aims to Create a Universe, Literally." *The New York Times,* April 14, 1987.

Butler, Brenda, Jenny Randles, and Dot Street, *Sky Crash.* Suffolk, Great Britain: Neville Spearman, 1984.

Cadogan, Peter H., *From Quark to Quasar: Notes on the Scale of the Universe.* New York: Cambridge University Press, 1985.

Calkins, Carroll C., ed., *Mysteries of the Unexplained.* Pleasantville, N.Y.: Reader's Digest Association, 1982.

"Carl Jung." *The New Encyclopaedia Britannica.* Vol. 6, 1985.

Christian, James L., ed., *Extra-Terrestrial Intelligence: The First Encounter.* Buffalo: Prometheus Books, 1976.

Cohen, Daniel, *The Great Airship Mystery.* New York: Dodd, Mead, 1981.

Condon, Edward U., *Final Report of the Scientific Study of Unidentified Flying Objects.* Ed. by Daniel S. Gillmor. New York: Bantam Books, 1969.

"Crashed Discs—Maybe." *International UFO Reporter,* July-August 1985.

Crease, Robert P., and Charles C. Mann, "Physics: The Gospel of String." *The Atlantic,* April 1986.

de Camp, L. Sprague, *The Ragged Edge of Science.* Philadelphia: Owlswick Press, 1980.

Downing, Barry H., *The Bible and Flying Saucers.* New York: Avon Books, 1970.

Evans, Hilary:

"What Happened at Roswell?" *The Unexplained* (London), Vol. 9, Issue 102.

"A Night to Remember." *The Unexplained* (London), Vol. 12, Issue 136.

"Making Up for Lost Time." *The Unexplained* (London), Vol. 12, Issue 138.

"The Unended Journey." *The Unexplained* (London), Vol. 12, Issue 139.

"Have UFOs Crashed on Earth?" *The Unexplained* (London), Vol. 9, Issue 100.

Fawcett, Lawrence, and Barry J. Greenwood, *Clear Intent.* Englewood Cliffs, N.J.: Prentice-Hall, 1984.

Flammonde, Paris, *UFO Exist!* New York: G. P. Putnam's Sons, 1976.

Fowler, Raymond E.:

The Andreasson Affair. Englewood Cliffs, N.J.: Prentice-Hall, 1979.

Casebook of a UFO Investigator. Englewood Cliffs, N.J.: Prentice-Hall, 1981.

Frank, Alan: *The Science Fiction and Fantasy Film Handbook.* Totowa, N.J.: Barnes & Noble, 1982.

Fuller, Curtis:

"Fate's Report on the Saucers." *Fate,* May 1954.

"Let's Get Straight about the Saucers." *Fate,* December 1952.

Fuller, John G., *Incident at Exeter.* New York: G.P. Putnam's Sons, 1966.

Green, Michael B., "Superstrings." *Scientific American,* September 1986.

Green, Michelle, "Making Communion with Another World." *People,* May 11, 1987.

Greenfield, Jerome, *Wilhelm Reich vs. the USA.* New York: W. W. Norton, 1974.

Greenstein, George, *Frozen Star.* New York: Freundlich Books, 1984.

Gribbin, John, *In Search of the Big Bang: Quantum Physics and Cosmology.* New York: Bantam Books, 1986.

Guth, Alan H., "Astrophysics." *Physics Today,* January 1985.

Guth, Alan H., and Paul J. Steinhardt, "The Inflationary Universe." *Scientific American,* May 1984.

Hardy, Phil, *The Aurum Film Encyclopedia of Science Fiction.* London: Aurum Press, 1984.

Henize, Karl G., "J. Allen Hynek: 1910-86." *Sky & Telescope,* August 1986.

Higgins, Mary, and Dr. Chester M. Raphael, eds., *Reich Speaks of Freud.* New York: Farrar, Straus and Giroux, 1967.

Hopkins, Budd:

Intruders. New York: Random House, 1987.

Missing Time. New York: Richard Marek, 1981.

Hynek, J. Allen:

The UFO Experience. Chicago: Henry Regnery, 1972.

"UFO Update." *Omni,* April 1984.

"Interview: J. Allen Hynek." *Omni,* February 1985.

Jacobs, David M.:

"J. Allen Hynek and the UFO Phenomenon." *The UFO Controversy in America.* Bloomington, Ind.: Indiana University Press, 1975.

"Abductions: The Consequence of Nonexistence." *Mutual UFO Network 1986 UFO Symposium Proceedings.* East Lansing, Mich., June 1986.

Keyhoe, Donald E., *Flying Saucers from Outer Space.* New York: Henry Holt, 1953.

Keyhoe, Donald E., and Gordon I. R. Lore, Jr., eds., *UFOs: A New Look.* Washington, D.C.: National Investigations Committee on Aerial Phenomena, 1969.

Kinder, Gary, *Light Years.* New York: Atlantic Monthly Press, 1987.

Klass, Philip J.:

"Crash of the Crashed-Saucer Claim." *The Skeptical Inquirer,* summer 1987.

"FAA Data Sheds New Light on JAL Pilot's UFO Report." *The Skeptical Inquirer,* summer 1987.

"Radar UFOs: Where Have They Gone?" *The Skeptical Inquirer,* spring 1985.

UFOs Explained. New York: Random House, 1974.

UFOs: The Public Deceived. Buffalo: Prometheus Books, 1983.

Knight, David C., *UFOs: A Pictorial History from Antiquity to the Present.* New York: McGraw-Hill, 1979.

Lawson, Alvin, "The Aliens Within." *The Unexplained* (London), Vol. 9, Issue 105.

Lemonick, Michael D., "A Theory of Everything." *Science Digest,* February 1986.

Leslie, Desmond, and George Adamski, *Flying Saucers Have Landed.* New York: British Book Centre, 1956.

McLaughlin, Robert B., "How Scientists Tracked a Flying Saucer." *True,* March 1950.

Menzel, Donald H.:

Flying Saucers. Cambridge, Mass.: Harvard University Press, 1953.

"The Truth about Flying Saucers." *Look,* June 17, 1952.

Menzel, Donald H., and Lyle G. Boyd, *The World of Flying Saucers.* Garden City, N.Y.: Doubleday, 1963.

Menzel, Donald H., and Ernest H. Taves, *The UFO Enigma.* Garden City, N.Y.: Doubleday, 1977.

Michel, Aimé, *The Truth about Flying Saucers.* New York: Criterion Books, 1956.

The New Layman's Parallel Bible. Grand Rapids, Mich.: Zondervan Bible Publishers, 1981.

Oberg, James, "Tunguska Echoes." *The Skeptical Inquirer,* winter 1978.

Olson, Edward C., "Intelligent Life in Space." *Astronomy,* July 1985.

Pagels, Heinz R., *Perfect Symmetry: The Search for the Beginning of Time.* New York: Simon and Schuster, 1985.

Persinger, Michael A., "The Earthquake-UFO Connection." *Fate,* July 1986.

Persinger, Michael A., and Gyslaine F. Lafrenière, *Space-Time Transients and Unusual Events.* Chicago: Nelson-Hall, 1977.

Pickard, Roy, *Science Fiction in the Movies.* London: Frederick Muller Limited, 1978.

Randles, Jenny:

"Impact—and After." *The Unexplained* (London), Vol. 9, Issue 106.

"The Rendlesham Forest Mystery." *Flying Saucer Review,* June 1982.

UFO Reality. London: Robert Hale, 1983.

Randles, Jenny, and Peter Warrington, *Science and the UFOs.* New York: Basil Blackwell, 1985.

Reich, Ilse Ollendorff, *Willhelm Reich.* New York: St. Martin's Press, 1969.

Ridpath, Ian, "The Woodbridge UFO Incident." *The Skeptical Enquirer,* fall 1986.

Rimmer, John, *The Evidence for Alien Abductions.* Wellingborough, Northamptonshire, Great Britain: Aquarian Press, 1984.

Rodeghier, Mark, "Editorial." *International UFO Re-*

porter, September-October 1984.

Ruppelt, Edward J., *The Report on Unidentified Flying Objects*. Garden City, N.Y.: Doubleday, 1956.

Sachs, Margaret, *The UFO Encyclopedia*. New York: Perigee Books, 1980.

Sagan, Carl, *Cosmos*. New York: Ballantine Books, 1980.

Sagan, Carl, et al., *Murmurs of Earth*. New York: Random House, 1978.

Sagan, Carl, and Thornton Page, eds., *UFO's—A Scientific Debate*. Ithaca, N.Y.: Cornell University Press, 1972.

Saleh, Dennis, *Science Fiction Gold: Film Classics of the 50's*. New York: McGraw-Hill, 1979.

Sanderson, Ivan T., *Uninvited Visitors*. New York: Cowles Education Corporation, 1967.

Saunders, David R., and R. Roger Harkins, *UFOs? Yes!* New York: World, 1968.

Schuessler, John:
"Anguish of the UFO Victims." *The Unexplained* (London), Vol. 9, Issue 108.
"Blind Terror in Texas." *The Unexplained* (London), Vol. 9, Issue 107.
"Cash-Landrum Case." *Mufon UFO Journal*, September 1983.
"Five Easy Pieces." *The Unexplained* (London), Vol. 10, Issue 110.
"Cash-Landrum UFO Case File: The Issue of Government Responsibility." *Mutual UFO Network 1986 UFO Symposium Proceedings*. East Lansing, Mich., June 1986.

Schwarz, John H., "Completing Einstein." *Science 85*, November 1985.

Shalett, Sidney:
"What You Can Believe about Flying Saucers: Part One." *Saturday Evening Post*, April 30, 1949.
"What You Can Believe about Flying Saucers: Conclusion." *Saturday Evening Post*, May 7, 1949.

Sharaf, Myron, *Fury on Earth: A Biography of Wilhelm Reich*. New York: St. Martin's Press, 1983.

Smith, Marcia S., and George D. Havas, *The UFO Enigma*. Washington, D.C.: Congressional Research Service, Library of Congress, 1983.

Sobchack, Vivian, *Screening Space*. New York: Ungar, 1987.

Stemman, Roy:
Mysteries of the Universe. London: Aldus Books, 1980.
Visitors from Outer Space. Garden City, N.Y.: Doubleday, 1976.

Story, Ronald D., *The Encyclopedia of UFOs*. Garden City, N.Y.: Doubleday, 1980.

Story, Ronald D., with J. Richard Greenwell, *UFOs and the Limits of Science*. New York: William Morrow, 1981.

Strieber, Whitley, *Communion*. New York: William Morrow, 1987.

Suarès, Jean-Claude, and Richard Siegel, *Alien Creatures*. Los Angeles: Reed Books, 1978.

Suplee, Curt, "Return of UFOria!." *The Washington Post*, March 9, l987.

Symposium on Unidentified Flying Objects: Hearings before the Committee on Science and Astronautics, U.S. House of Representatives. Washington, D.C.: Government Printing Office, July 29, 1968.

Taubes, Gary, "Everything's Now Tied to Strings." *Discover*, November 1986.

Trench, Brinsley le Poer (Lord Clancarty), ed., *The House of Lords UFO Debate*. London: Pentacle Books, 1979.

Trimble, V., and I. Woltier, "Quasars at 25." *Science*, October 10, 1986.

"Unidentified Flying Object." *Naval Aviation News*, June 1973.

Unidentified Flying Objects: Hearing by Committee on Armed Services of the House of Representatives. Washington, D.C.: Government Printing Office, April 5, 1966.

Vallee, Jacques:
Anatomy of a Phenomenon. Chicago: Henry Regnery, 1965.
Messengers of Deception. Berkeley, Calif.: And/Or Press, 1979.
Passport to Magonia: From Folklore to Flying Saucers. Chicago: Henry Regnery, 1969.

Von Gunden, Kenneth, and Stuart H. Stock, *Twenty All-Time Great Science Fiction Films*. New York: Arlington House, 1982.

"What the Air Force Believes about the Flying Saucers." *Fate*, November 1949.

Williams, Gurney, III, "The Fourth Dimension and Beyond." *Omni*, May 1987.

INDEX

Numerals in italics indicate an illustration of the subject mentioned

A

Abduction by aliens, 57, *58-63*, 79-86, 129, 141-143, *144*

Adamski, George, and encounters with aliens, *74*, 76

Aerial Phenomena Research Organization (APRO), and investigations of UFOs, 53, 69

Aerospace Defense Command, and investigation of UFOs, 119

Aetherius Society, and cosmic batteries, 78, *80-81*

Agobard (Archbishop of Lyons; quoted), and UFO sightings, 14-15

Air Materiel Command (Wright Field, Ohio), and investigations of UFOs, 38. *See also* Project Sign

Airships: in fiction, 19; sightings of, 19, 22

Akers, David, and Yakima Indian Reservation UFO window site, 133-134

Aldrin, Edwin (Buzz), and first moon landing, 120

Aliens: ancient-astronaut theory, 13; and the Bible, 12 *14, 15, 17*; encounters with, 64-86, *68, 69, 72*; faked accounts of, 16; in legend, 12-18, *13, 14*; motivation of, 28, *29-35*

Alpert, Shell, and alleged UFO photograph, *97*

Alvarez, Jose, and Levelland UFO

sighting, 68

Alvarez, Luis, and Robertson report, 55

Amalgamated Flying Saucer Clubs of America, Inc., and Gabriel Green, 79

American Association for the Advancement of Science (*UFO's—Scientific Debate*), and UFO symposium, 122

Ancient-astronaut theory, *13*

Andreasson, Betty, and abduction by aliens, 62, 84-86

Andrews Air Force Base (Maryland), and UFO sightings, 53, 55

Ann Arbor (Michigan), and UFO sightings, 106-110

Antimatter, 24

APRO. *See* Aerial Phenomena Research Organization

Arecibo (Puerto Rico), and radio telescope, 124, *127. See also* Search for extraterrestrial intelligence

Armstrong, Neil, and first moon landing, 120

Arnold, Kenneth, and Cascade Mountains UFO sighting, 36-37, 38, *39*, 56, 69, 74, 131

Aura Rhanes (alleged alien), and Truman Bethurum, 76, 78

Aurora borealis, mistaken for UFOs, 14

Avis family, and abduction by aliens, 84

B

Baker, Russell (quoted), and UFO possibilities, 109

Ballen, Lloyd, and Levelland UFO sighting, 69

Ball lightning, as possible explanation for UFOs, 26-27, 69, 104, 105

Barnes, Harry G. (quoted), and Washington, D.C., UFO sighting, 53, *55*

Barnett, Grady Landon (Barney),

and Roswell UFO crash, 74-75

Bentwaters Royal Air Force Base (England), and Rendlesham Forest UFO sighting, 132, 136-141

Berlitz, Charles, and Roswell UFO crash, 74-75

Bertrand, Eugene, and Exeter UFO sighting, 99-*102*, 104

Bethurum, Truman (*Aboard a Flying Saucer*), and encounters with aliens, 76, 78

Bible: and alleged alien visitations, *15, 17;* alleged UFO sightings in, *12-14*

Black holes, 24, *146-147*

Blavatsky, Helena Petrovna (*The Secret Doctrine*), and alien visitors, 16

Blumrich, Josef F. (*The Spaceships of Ezekiel;* quoted), and alleged biblical UFO sightings, 14, *15*

Boeche, Raymond, and investigation of Rendlesham Forest UFO sighting, 136, 141

Book of Dyzan, and alien visitors, 16

Brazel, Mac, and Roswell UFO sighting, 39

Brown, Harold (quoted), and investigations of UFOs, 110-111

Brown, T. Townsend, and National Investigations Committee on Aerial Phenomena, 69

Byland Abbey (Yorkshire, England), and alien visitors, 16

C

Caldwell, Jonathan E., and pseudo UFOs, *45*

Carter, Jimmy, and UFO sighting, *128*

Cascade Mountains (Washington), and UFO sighting, 36-37. *See also* Arnold, Kenneth

Cash, Betty, and UFO sighting, 8-9, *10-11*

Cash-Landrum incident, 8-9, *10-11*, 132

Center for UFO Studies (CUFOS), 121

Chavez, M. S., and Socorro encounter with aliens, 73

Chiles, C. S., and Montgomery UFO sighting, 42

Christian Science Monitor (newspaper; quoted), and UFO possibilities, 109

Civilian Saucer Investigation (CSI), and investigations of UFOs, 69

Clarion (alleged planet), and Truman Bethurum, 76, 78

Clark, Jerome, and investigations of UFOs, 23

Clem, Weir, and Levelland UFO sighting, 68-69

Close encounters: three kinds of, 121-122; third-kind encounters with aliens, 65, 68-69, 70-73

Close Encounters of the Third Kind (film), and alien visitors, 28, *32-33*

Clouds, mistaken for UFOs, *20*

Comets, mistaken for UFOs, *20*

Condon committee: and Edward U. Condon, 115-*116;* and Condon report, *116, 117,* 118-119, 120, 121, 126, 138; formation of, 115-116; and McMinnville UFO sighting, 48

Coyne, Lawrence J., and encounter with UFO, 126-127

CSI. *See* Civilian Saucer Investigation

CUFOS. *See* Center for UFO Studies

D

Davis, Kathie, and visitation and probing by aliens, 142, *144*

Desert Center (California), and encounters with aliens, 76, 78

Downing, Barry H., and alleged biblical UFO sightings, 12, 14

Drake, Frank, and search for extraterrestrial intelligence, 124

Drona Parva (quoted), and UFO sighting, 12

E

Edwards, Frank, and National Investigations Committee on Aerial Phenomena, 69

E.T. (film), and alien visitors, *34-35*

Exeter (New Hampshire), and UFO sighting, *99-106, 100-101*

Exon, J. James, and investigation of Rendlesham Forest UFO sighting, 136

Ezekiel's wheel, and alleged biblical UFO sightings, *12-14, 15*

F

Fahrney, Delmer S., and National Investigations Committee on Aerial Phenomena, 69

Fargo (North Dakota), and UFO sighting, 44

Fate (magazine), and Kenneth Arnold's UFO sighting, *39*

Fawcett, Lawrence, and investigations of UFOs, 128-129

Fireballs, 46; mistaken for UFOs, *26*

Fish, Marjorie, and Hill abduction story, 84

Fontes, Olavo T., and Villas Boas abduction story, 85

Foo fighters. *See* Fireballs

Forbes Air Force Base (Kansas), and UFO sighting, 66

Ford, Gerald (quoted), and UFO possibilities, 109, 110

Fortenberry, William, and Norfolk UFO sighting, 52

Fort Knox (Kentucky), and UFO sighting, 41

Fowler, A. J., and Levelland UFO sighting, 68

Fowler, Raymond E., and Exeter UFO sighting, 103

Fry, Daniel W., and encounter with aliens, *73*

Fuller, John (*Incident at Exeter*), and Exeter UFO sighting, 102-104

Fund for UFO Research, 131

Futch, Max, and Project Blue Book, 56

G

Gander (Newfoundland), and UFO sighting, 48-49

Geophysical theory of UFOs, 134

Ghost rockets, *27*

Giant Rock Space Conventions, 78

Gill, Reverend William Booth (quoted), and encounter with aliens, 70-73

Godman Air Force Base (Kentucky), and UFO sighting, 41

Goldwater, Barry, and National Investigations Committee on Aerial Phenomena, 69

Gorman, George, and Fargo UFO sighting, 44

Goudsmit, Samuel, and Robertson report, 55-56

Gray, Glen, and encounter with aliens, 129

Gray Goose Corporation, and pseudo UFOs, *45*

Green, Gabriel, and encounters with aliens, *79*

Greenwood, Barry, and investigations of UFOs, 128-129

Ground lights, mistaken for UFOs, 51

Ground Saucer Watch Inc.: and Trent UFO photographs, *138-139;* and Villa UFO photographs, *140*

H

Hale, Virginia, and UFO sighting, *103*

Hall, Robert L., and hysterical contagion theory, 123

Halley, Edmond (quoted), and UFO sighting, 15

Halt, Charles I. (quoted), and Rendlesham Forest UFO sighting, 132, 136

Hamilton, Alexander (quoted), and UFO sighting, 23

Harder, James A. (quoted), and investigation of UFOs, 117-118

Hart, Carl, Jr., and Lubbock UFO sighting, *50-51*

Haught, Warren (quoted), and Roswell UFO sighting, 39

Heflin, Rex, and alleged UFO photograph, *88*

Hessdalen Valley (Norway), and UFO window site investigation, *133-134*

Hickson, Charles E., and abduction by aliens, 60, 62

Hill, Barney and Betty (quoted), and abduction by aliens, *58-59*, 60, 62, 79, *82-84*

Hillenkoetter, R. H., and National Investigations Committee on Aerial Phenomena, 69

Hillsdale College (Michigan), and UFO sightings, *106-107*

Holloman Air Force Base (New Mexico), and fireball sightings, 46

Hollow earth theory of UFOs, 131

Hopkins, Budd *(Intruders, Missing Time),* and investigations of abduction by aliens, 141-*143*

Hopkins, Herbert, and alien visitor, 77

Hopkinsville (Kentucky), and alien visitors, 64-65

Hunt, David, and Exeter UFO sighting, *102,* 104

Huston, Wayne, and Ravenna UFO sighting, 111, 113

Hynek, J. Allen *(The UFO Experience),* 121, 126, 141; (quoted) and Ann Arbor UFO investigation, 107-109, *108;* categories of UFOs, 121-122; (quoted) and congressional symposium, 117; and Papua (New Guinea) UFO investigation, 72; and Project Grudge, 49; and Project Sign, 41-42; and Ravenna UFO investigation, 115; (quoted) research recommendations of, 144; (quoted) and Socorro encounter with aliens, 73; strangeness-probability chart, 122; and swamp gas phenomenon, 108-109; and Yakima Indian Reservation UFO window site, 133-134

Hyperspace theory of UFOs, 131

Hysterical contagion theory, 123

I

Ice crystals, mistaken for UFOs, *18, 21,* 26-27

Integratron, and George Van Tassel, 78

It Came From Outer Space (film), and alien visitors, 28, *29,* 30

J

Jacobs, David (quoted), 9; and investigation of abduction by aliens, 143; and investigation of UFOs, 144

Jaroslaw, Dan and Grant, and faked UFO photograph, *95*

Joint Army-Navy-Air Force Publication (JANAP), and UFO secrecy, 70

Journal of Natural History and Philosophy and Chemistry, and report of UFO sighting, 16

Jung, Carl, and UFO mandala theory, *53*

K

Kelly-Hopkinsville event, and encounter with aliens, 64-65, *68*

Keyhoe, Donald E. *(Flying Saucers from Outer Space),* 56; (quoted) and Condon committee, 116; (quoted) and National Investigations Committee on Aerial Phenomena, 69, 70; and investigations of UFOs, 46, *47*

Kilburn, Steven, abduction by aliens, 58, 60-61

King, George, and Aetherius Society, 78-79

Klass, Philip J., 127, 143; debunking UFOs at Exeter, 104-106, *105*

L

Landrum, Vickie, and UFO sighting, 8-9, *10-11*

Reservation UFO window site, 133-134

Levelland (Texas), and UFO sighting, *67-69*

Lewis, Danny, and Loring UFO sighting, 127-129

Life (magazine; quoted), and UFO possibilities, 51, 109

Lightning, mistaken for UFOs, *20, 21*

Look (magazine): and Donald E. Keyhoe's UFO investigations, 56; and Donald H. Menzel's UFO theories, 51

Lorenzen, Coral and Jim, and Aerial Phenomena Research Organization, 53

Loring Air Force Base (Maine), and UFO sighting, 127-129

Low, Robert (quoted), and Condon committee, 116

Lubbock (Texas), and UFO sighting, 49-50, 51

Lusk, Charles, and 1896 airship sighting, 18

M

Maccabee, Bruce (quoted): investigation of abduction by aliens, 143; investigation of UFOs, 130-131

McCulloch, Pat, and Levelland UFO sighting, 68-69

McDonald, James E. (quoted), investigation of UFOs, 115-117

McLaughlin, Robert B., and White Sands UFO sighting, 46-47

McMinnville (Oregon), and UFO sighting, 47-48, 138

Malmstrom Air Force Base (Montana), and UFO sighting, 129-130

Mandala theory, *53*

Mannor, Frank, and Ann Arbor UFO sighting, 106, 109

Mantell, Thomas, and UFO chase, 41

Meier, Eduard, and UFO photographs, *137*

Men in Black (MIB), *77*

Menzel, Donald H. *(Flying Saucers;* quoted), 56; and alleged biblical UFO sightings, 14; debunking UFOs, 118, 122, 123, 131; and Lubbock UFO sighting, 50-51; and Norfolk UFO sighting, 52-53; and temperature inversion, 53, 55

MIB. *See* Men in Black

Military aircraft, mistaken for UFOs, 141

Milne, Robert Duncan, airship stories of, 19

Mirage, mistaken for UFOs, 14

Moi, Stephen, and encounter with aliens, 70

Montgomery (Alabama), and UFO sighting, 42

Moore, William, and Roswell UFO crash, 74-75

MUFON. *See* Mutual UFO Network

Mulholland, John (illusionist), *56*

Multiple universe theory, *150-151*

Muscarello, Norman J., and Exeter UFO sighting, 99-102, *103*

Mutual UFO Network (MUFON), and investigation of Rendlesham Forest UFO sighting, 136, 141

N

Nash, William B., and Norfolk UFO sighting, 52, 53

National Academy of Sciences, and Condon report, 118

National Investigations Committee on Aerial Phenomena (NICAP): and Condon committee, 116; and Exeter UFO sighting, 103, 105

Natural phenomena, mistaken for UFOs, *18, 20, 21. See also individual phenomena*

Naval Aviation News (magazine), and UFO sightings, 48-49

Nebel, Long John, and alien spacecraft, *74*

Neff, Wilbur L. (quoted), and Ravenna UFO sighting, 111-115

NICAP. *See* National Investigations Committee on Aerial Phenomena

Nicolai, Renato, and UFO sighting in France, 121-122

Norfolk (Virginia), and UFO sighting, 52

Norman, Ruth (pseud. Uriel), and Unarius Foundation, *78, 79*

O

Oliphant, Pat (cartoon by), and Condon report, *117*

Orgone, 52

Orthon (alleged alien), and George Adamski, 76

Oz factor, and feeling of displacement, 71

P

Page, Thornton, and American Association for the Advancement of Science symposium, 122

Panzenella, Frank, and Ravenna UFO sighting, 113

Papua (New Guinea), and UFO sighting, 70, 72-73

Parallel universe theory, 148-149

Parhelion, mistaken for UFOs, 14

Pascagoula (Mississippi), and alien visitors, *69,* 141

Pease Air Force Base (New Hampshire), and Exeter UFO sighting, 102

Persinger, Michael A., and geophysical theory of UFOs, 134

Phoenix (Arizona), and UFO sighting, 40-41

Piedmont (Missouri), and UFO window site investigation, 134, *135*

Piezoelectricity, 134

Pioneer 10, 126; message to alien civilizations, 124

Pioneer 11, message to alien civilizations, 124

Planets, mistaken for UFOs, *20*

Plasmas, 104-105

Poe, Edgar Allan, and transatlantic balloon flight, story of, 22-23

Professor Tulli, and alien visitors in Egypt, 16

Project Blue Book, 87, *88-97,* 98, 110, 111, 115, 118, 120; activation of, 49; and Ann Arbor UFO sighting, 107; disbanding of, 119; and Lubbock UFO sighting, 51; and Norfolk UFO sighting, 52; and Ravenna UFO sighting, 113-115

Project Cyclops, and search for extraterrestrial intelligence, *126*

Project Grudge, 44, 47, 87; disbanding of, 46; reactivation of, 49

Project Hessdalen, and Hessdalen Valley (Norway) UFO window site investigation, *133-134*

Project Identification, and Piedmont UFO window site investigation, 134, *135*

Project Sign, 38, 87; disbanding of, 44; and Fargo UFO sighting, 44; and Fort Knox UFO sighting, 41; and Montgomery UFO sighting, 42; and Phoenix UFO investigation, 41

Project Skyhook, 41; and White Sands UFO sighting, 47

Project Twinkle, and fireballs, 46

Q

Quazgaa (alleged alien), and Betty Andreasson, 86

Quintanilla, Hector, Jr., and Project Blue Book, 110, 111, 114

R

Radar, use in UFO investigations, 54

Radio transmissions, and search for extraterrestrial intelligence, 124, *127*

Ramey, Roger, and Roswell UFO sighting, 39

Randles, Jenny (quoted): and Oz factor, 71; and radar evidence of UFOs, 54

Ravenna (Ohio), and UFO sightings, 111-115

Reich, Wilhelm, and orgone, *52*

Reidel, Walter, and UFO possibilities, 52

Rendlesham Forest (England), and UFO sighting, 132-141

Rhodes, William A., and Phoenix UFO sighting, 40-41

Ridpath, Ian, and investigation of Rendlesham Forest UFO sighting, 136, 141

Rivers, L. Mendel (quoted), and UFO investigations, 109, 110

Robertson report (quoted), and H. P. Robertson, 55-56

Rosenberg, Samuel, and legends of alien visitors, 16

Roswell (New Mexico): briefing paper on UFOs, 144; and UFO crash, 74-75; and UFO sighting, 38-*40*

Royal Australian Air Force (quoted), and Papua (New Guinea) UFO sighting, 72

Ruppelt, Edward J.: and Project Blue Book, 49, 51, 52, 87; and Project Grudge, 49

Rutledge, Harley D., and Project Identification, 134, *135*

S

Sagan, Carl: and American Association for the Advancement of Science symposium, 122-123; and congressional symposium, 117; and message to alien civilizations, with Linda Sagan, 124; and Sagan's paradox, 123

Saint Elmo's fire, mistaken for UFOs, 69

Samford, John A., and Washington, D.C., UFO sightings, 55

Saunders, David R. *(UFOs? YES! Where the Condon Committee Went Wrong),* and the Condon report, 119

Search for extraterrestrial intelligence (SETI), 124-126, *127*

Senareus, Philip, airship stories of, 19

SETI. *See* Search for extraterrestrial intelligence

Shalett, Sydney (quoted), and debunking of UFOs, 44

Simon, Benjamin, and Hill abduction story, 82-84

Socorro (New Mexico), and encounter with aliens, 73

Space People (alleged alien group), and George Van Tassel, 78

Spaulding, William H., and Ground Saucer Watch Inc., computerized analysis of UFO photographs by, *138-140*

Spaur, Dale (sketch by), *115;* and UFO sighting, 111, *113-115*

Spook bombs, 27

Stanton, William (quoted), and investigations of UFOs, 114

Stars, mistaken for UFOs, *20*

Static electricity, mistaken for UFOs, 26-27

Stephens, David (quoted), and encounter with aliens, 129

Strangeness-probability chart, and J. Allen Hynek's UFO investigations, 122

Strieber, Whitley *(Communion),* and abduction by aliens, 62, 143

Sullivan, Walter (quoted), and Condon report, 118

Sutton, Lucky, and encounter with aliens, 64-65

Swamp gas phenomenon, mistaken for UFOs, 108-109

T

Taylor, Billy Ray, and encounter with aliens, 64-65

Temperature inversion, possible explanation for UFOs, 53, *55*

Terauchi, Kenju, and Japan Air Lines UFO sighting, *123*

Thirteenth Annual Spacecraft Convention, *112*

Tillighast, Wallace E., flying machine of, 25

Toland, Reginald (quoted), and Exeter UFO sighting, 99, 102

Trent, Mr. and Mrs. Paul, and UFO sighting, 47-48, *138-139*

True (magazine), and Donald E. Keyhoe's UFO investigations, 46

Tunguska explosion, 23-25, *24*

U

UFO sightings: categories of, 121-122; landing sites, 125; pseudo UFOs, 16, *42, 45, 89, 95, 97, 118, 130, 131*

Ultralight aircraft, mistaken for UFOs, 141

Unarius Foundation, 78-79

Undersea civilization theory of UFOs, 131

Uriel. *See* Norman, Ruth

U.S. Air Force, and investigations of UFOs, 38, 87, *88-97;* Regulation 200-2, and UFO secrecy, 70. *See also* Project Blue Book; Project Grudge; Project Sign

V

Vallee, Jacques, and investigation of UFOs, 131-132

Vandenberg, Hoyt S., and Montgomery UFO sighting, 42

Van Tassel, George, and Integratron, 78

Verne, Jules *(Robur the Conqueror),* airship stories of, 19

Villa, Paul, and alleged UFO photographs, *89, 140*

Villas Boas, Antonio, abduction by aliens, *84, 85, 86*

von Däniken, Erich *(Chariots of the Gods?):* and ancient-astronaut theory, *13;* and Ezekiel's wheel, 14

W

Walton, Travis, and abduction by aliens, 129, 141

War of the Worlds (film), and alien visitors, 28, *30-31*

Washington, D.C., and UFO sightings, 53, 55

Westover Air Force Base (Massachusetts), and Exeter UFO sighting, 104

Wheeler, Jim, and Levelland UFO sighting, 68

White Sands (New Mexico), and UFO sighting, 47

Whitted, J. B., and Montgomery UFO sighting, 42

Wilson, Jesse, and alleged UFO photograph, *92*

Window sites, *133-135*

Wizard of Oz (film), and feeling of displacement, *71*

Woodbridge Royal Air Force Base (England), and Rendlesham Forest UFO sighting, 132-141

Wright, Newell (quoted), and Levelland UFO sighting, 68

Wright-Patterson Air Force Base (Ohio), and Project Blue Book, 98

Wurtsmith Air Force Base (Michigan), and UFO sighting, 129

Y

Yakima Indian Reservation (Washington), and UFO window site investigation, 133-134, *135*

Z

Zamora, Lonnie (quoted), and Socorro UFO sighting, 73

Zeppelin, mistaken for UFO, 25

Zeta Reticuli star system, and Hill abduction story, 84

Time-Life Books Inc.
is a wholly owned subsidiary of
TIME INCORPORATED

FOUNDER: Henry R. Luce 1898-1967

Editor-in-Chief: Jason McManus
Chairman and Chief Executive Officer: J. Richard Munro
President and Chief Operating Officer: N. J. Nicholas, Jr.
Editorial Director: Ray Cave
Executive Vice President, Books: Kelso F. Sutton
Vice President, Books: George Artandi

TIME-LIFE BOOKS INC.

EDITOR: George Constable
Executive Editor: Ellen Phillips
Director of Design: Louis Klein
Director of Editorial Resources: Phyllis K. Wise
Editorial Board: Russell B. Adams, Jr., Dale M. Brown,
Roberta Conlan, Thomas H. Flaherty, Lee Hassig, Donia
Ann Steele, Rosalind Stubenberg, Kit van Tulleken,
Henry Woodhead
Director of Photography and Research:
John Conrad Weiser

PRESIDENT: Christopher T. Linen
Chief Operating Officer: John M. Fahey, Jr.
Senior Vice President: James L. Mercer
Vice Presidents: Stephen L. Bair, Ralph J. Cuomo, Neal
Goff, Stephen L. Goldstein, Juanita T. James, Hallett
Johnson III, Carol Kaplan, Susan J. Maruyama, Robert H.
Smith, Paul R. Stewart, Joseph J. Ward
Director of Production Services: Robert J. Passantino

Editorial Operations
Copy Chief: Diane Ullius
Production: Celia Beattie
Quality Control: James J. Cox (director)
Library: Louise D. Forstall

MYSTERIES OF THE UNKNOWN

SERIES DIRECTOR: Russell B. Adams, Jr.
Series Administrator: Elise Ritter Gibson
Designer: Herbert H. Quarmby

Editorial Staff for The UFO Phenomenon
Associate Editors: Sara Schneidman (pictures); Pat Daniels
(text)
Writers: Janet P. Cave, Laura Foreman
Assistant Designer: Lorraine D. Rivard
Design Assistant: William Alan Pitts
Copy Coordinator: Darcie Conner Johnston
Picture Coordinators: Bradley Hower, Betty H. Weatherley
Editorial Assistant: Donna Fountain

Special Contributors: Christine Hinze (London, picture
research); George Daniels, Thomas A. Lewis (editing);
Douglas McCreary Greenwood, Herbert M. Mason, Jr.,
John I. Merritt, Jake Page, John Tompkins (text); Eleanor
Barrett (design)

Correspondents: Elisabeth Kraemer-Singh (Bonn); Maria
Vincenza Aloisi (Paris); Ann Natanson (Rome).
Valuable assistance was also provided by Pavle Svabic
(Belgrade), Judy Aspinall (London), Liz Brown, Christina
Lieberman (New York), Dag Christensen (Oslo), Ann Wise
(Rome), Mary Johnson (Stockholm), Dick Berry (Tokyo).

The research for *The UFO Phenomenon* was prepared un-
der the supervision of Time-Life Books by:
Bibliographics Inc.
President: David L. Harrison
Researchers: Richard A. Davis, Jill M. Denney, Denise Der-
sin, Mary Dreesen, Martha L. Johnson, Sydney Johnson,
Christian D. Kinney, Mary Mayberry, Jared Rosenfeld, Co-
rinne Szabo, Elizabeth D. Ward, David W. Wooddell
Editorial Assistant: Lona E. Tavernise

The Consultants:
Marcello Truzzi, professor of sociology at Eastern Michigan University, is also director of the Center for Scientific
Anomalies Research (CSAR) and editor of its journal, the
Zetetic Scholar. Dr. Truzzi, who considers himself a "con-
structive skeptic" with regard to claims of the
paranormal, works through the CSAR to produce
dialogues between critics and proponents of unusual scientific claims.

David Michael Jacobs, author of *The UFO Controversy in
America* and *UFOs and the Search for Scientific Legitimacy*
and an expert on abduction phenomena, is a professor of
twentieth-century United States history at Temple University. He is a member of the Society for Scientific Exploration, an academic organization devoted to the study of
anomalies, as well as the Center for UFO Studies
(CUFOS) and the Mutual UFO Network (MUFON).

Other Publications:

TIME FRAME
FIX IT YOURSELF
FITNESS, HEALTH & NUTRITION
SUCCESSFUL PARENTING
HEALTHY HOME COOKING
UNDERSTANDING COMPUTERS
LIBRARY OF NATIONS
THE ENCHANTED WORLD
THE KODAK LIBRARY OF CREATIVE PHOTOGRAPHY
GREAT MEALS IN MINUTES
THE CIVIL WAR
PLANET EARTH
COLLECTOR'S LIBRARY OF THE CIVIL WAR
THE EPIC OF FLIGHT
THE GOOD COOK
WORLD WAR II
HOME REPAIR AND IMPROVEMENT
THE OLD WEST

*For information on and a full description of any of the Time-
Life Books series listed above, please write:*
  Reader Information
  Time-Life Customer Service
  P.O. Box C-32068
  Richmond, Virginia 23261-2068
Or call: 1-800-621-7026

This volume is one of a series that examines the history
and nature of seemingly paranormal phenomena. Other
books in the series include:
Mystic Places
Psychic Powers

Library of Congress Cataloging in Publication Data
The UFO phenomenon.
   (Mysteries of the unknown).
   Bibliography: p.
   Includes index.
   1. Unidentified flying objects.
   I. Time-Life Books.   II. Series.
TL789.U195 1987 001.9'42 87-17969
ISBN 0-8094-6324-5
ISBN 0-8094-6325-3 (lib. bdg.)